THE WORLD'S MY UNIVERSITY

Poverty, loneliness, an unhappy home life, defective eyesight, and a crippled hip certainly load the scales against a boy's prospects. But Jim Ingram never allowed these handicaps to stand in the way of his ambitions, which included a university education, travel and archaeology. True, the struggle was long and hard, but today he is happily married, holds a Bachelor of Science degree in Economics and can look back on many adventures and considerable archaeological experience.

JIM INGRAM

THE WORLD'S MY UNIVERSITY

Complete and Unabridged

ULVERSCROFT
Leicester

First published in Great Britain in 1965 by
George G. Harrap & Co. Ltd.
London

First Large Print Edition
Published September 1977
SBN 0 7089 0050 X

Published by
F. A. Thorpe (Publishing) Ltd.
Anstey, Leicestershire
Printed in England

This book is dedicated to
the Nursing and Medical Staffs
who looked after me while I was in hospital
and in particular to
two Surgeons
the late MR. MILNES-BRIDE, FRCS
of the Royal Eye Hospital, Manchester
and MISS PEARSON, FRCS
of Pinderfields Hospital, Wakefield
and to
two bootmakers who put me on to
my feet, and helped to keep me there
MR. POOLE, *of Leeds*
and MR. DUPLEDGE, *of Manchester*

PREFACE

Why do we read biography or auto-biography? Because we all have problems to face and difficulties to overcome. To read how people like ourselves faced similar problems helps us to realise that we are not the only persons to encounter such difficulties. If they could overcome *their* problems, then maybe we can overcome *ours*. Most of us spend years overcoming personal difficulties, and while doing this we are learning how to live our lives. Learning how to get on with other people is a difficult problem, but learning to live with ourselves can be even more difficult. It may take most of a lifetime to learn to do that.

This book is a record of some problems I had to overcome in order to live my life. In a narrative spanning thirty-five years of a man's life and depending very often upon memory for details of people and events in days gone by it is hardly likely that I have escaped committing some errors of fact, but I have done my best to reduce these to a minimum.

Thanks are due to a number of persons and organisations for their assistance: to the Editor of *The Sunday Times* for permission to use the chapter-title "The Midnight-oil University" and the facts about correspondence-course students which appear on pages 407–417; to the Senate of the University of London for permission to reproduce the examination questions which appear on pages 419–420; and to John Long, Ltd., for permission to quote on pages 127 and 155–156 material which appeared in two previous books of mine, *I Found Adventure* and *The Land of Mud Castles*, both of which have been out of print for a number of years. The chapter-title "Give God a Chance" is unashamedly cribbed from the book of that title by Dr. W. E. Sangster, and I recommend that stimulating little volume to readers in search of straightforward answers to some of their religious problems. I should like to thank Canon Wilfrid Garlick of St. George's Vicarage, Stockport, for permission to quote his letter on pages 427–429, and the Wardens of Fircroft College, Bournville, past and present, for information about the college.

J.I.

1

A WEEK TO LIVE

BLIND, with both eyes bandaged, with my crippled leg twisted under me, I lay on the bed in the hospital ward and prayed. The darkness was frightening, the outside world was remote, my future grim, so — I prayed. I prayed for a sight of the sunlight, to be able to walk among the hills again, to know life and love and laughter. Lying there alone in the dark, on that black December day, all these ambitions of mine seemed impossible of attainment. They were — just dreams.

Of what use to anyone was a life such as mine? The thought came to me then, as it was to come to me so many times. Poor, friendless, helpless, often in pain. Alone. Useless. Unwanted, unless there was a God who cared for us, as some people alleged.

Surely a child was better dead?

What sort of life could one make of such unpromising beginnings?

Now, more than thirty-five years later, I can look about me and observe that everything I prayed for has been granted. I can see and I can walk. My wife and daughter sit facing me across the table in our cosy home ten miles south of Manchester, in England. About us are objects which evoke memories of experiences we have shared. Books, maps, pictures, souvenirs from Lapland, Italy, Morocco, and Palestine. An empty wine-bottle, straw-covered, to hint of cruising colourful seas to Greece. Memories of climbing mountain ranges through groves of orange- and lemon-trees.

Life has been good to me after all.

Among letters which the postman has just delivered are some from readers of books of mine, thanking me for having written them. Other letters are addressed to me as deputy headmaster of the school for physically handicapped children where I earn my living. For I have found a place in life and the job I like doing best of all.

One large envelope fills me with especial pride. It is from the University of London and contains an imposing document stating: "Mr. J. H. Ingram having passed the prescribed examinations has this day been admitted by the Senate to the degree of Bachelor of Science (Economics) as an external student." Soon, as a newly-fledged graduate, I must go to London to be presented to the Queen Mother, who is Chancellor of the University. It will be the proudest moment of my life. That university degree has cost me thirty-five years of studying and struggling.

It would seem then that my ambitions were not so impossible after all. Here were tangible answers to my prayers. The struggle to find my place in life had taken more than a quarter of a century. The way had been long and hard, heart-breaking at times. Many times I felt I had come to the end of things. For much of the time I seemed quite alone. But now I could believe that there is some meaning in life after all; I know that God does exist and He cares. Life can be worth living in spite of everything.

Many persons have ambitions — to achieve fame, riches, power, success — and in one way or another, many people achieve these. The assumption fostered by films and novels is that all persons are equally endowed to achieve their ambitions, if they wish to do so, all that is required being hard work and determination. It seems to be taken for granted that all people are born fit and healthy. But all persons are *not* born fit and healthy. Some begin life with physical handicaps. What of them?

Before the physically handicapped can attempt to achieve their ambitions — the same ambitions as those of fit people — they must first struggle for objectives which fit people take for granted. Imagine having to spend years of your life before you can walk, or see, or move your limbs! The fit can plunge straight to their goal, indifferent to anything else, but the disabled must first learn to live with their disability. Only when this is accomplished can they consider their ambitions. By then maybe the struggle will have proved too much for them.

One can spend a lifetime in just trying to keep alive.

Always conscious of their dependence upon the world about them, the disabled must seek faith and courage from some source outside of, and greater than, themselves. Such faith and courage can come from only one source, a belief in the power and guidance of God and Christ. This helps when all else fails.

So forgive me if some things written in this book sound like boasting. They are not meant to be. I have written of the things which happened to me, personally, merely to show what can be accomplished by one man, alone, with God's help and guidance. There are many others whose struggle to survive and make something of their lives has been greater than mine. This is just an essay to show what can be done even with the most unpromising start in life.

For my beginnings were very, very lacking in promise.

It was when I was a boy in southern Ontario, in Canada, in the 1920's, that the idea first came to me that it would be a fine thing to go to university and study to be an explorer or an archaeologist. I was not a Canadian by birth, for I had been born in Manchester, England, and brought to Canada by my parents when a child.

This ambition of mine was born, one might say, the day I discovered the grave of an Indian warrior in the gravelly bank of the river which flowed through our town. Much of my time out of school was spent exploring the woods and fields which stretched away on either side of that swift-flowing, winding stream, the Askenissippi or "River of the Forked Antler", as the Indians had called it in days gone by. Across the span of years that river is inseparably associated with the sunlit land of my boyhood, a landscape of curving yellow beaches and tall, dark woods, of foam-flecked rapids and misty, green marshes where snapping-turtles lurked and black snakes sunned themselves on the rocks.

During the long summer vacations we boys spent days at a time living in improvised camps located among the tall reed-beds along the riverbanks, emulating the lives of trappers and backwoodsmen. There were fish to catch and rabbits to trap and neighbouring orchards to rob, and when these sources of sustenance failed us and the pangs of hunger became too great we could always hasten back home to raid the larder for freshly baked bread and cookies or mouth-watering blueberry pie. Aboard clumsily constructed rafts we poled up and down the river, holding powwows on reedy islands, where we feasted on stolen provender.

This day I had been prowling about a steep bluff which rose for several yards above the swirling waters, when I observed that a recent rainstorm had torn a wide gash in the bank. The discovery encouraged me to probe into the gravel with my trowel, in the hope of finding something exciting. Each year a Hobby Fair was organised by the Rotary Club of London (our own town), where school-children exhibited things which they had made or collected. It was my ambition to win a first prize for my collection of arrow-heads and other Indian relics.

A large roundish object which at first I took to be a boulder proved, to my great astonishment to be a human skull. Then, before my startled gaze, the crumbling bones of a human skeleton appeared. Excitedly I cleared away the gravel with my trowel, until the burial was completely

7

exposed. There was not a great deal left — the skull, somewhat battered, with gaping eye-sockets, some longish bones, the remains of the legs probably, and some shorter curved bones which I took to be ribs. Glistening among the gravel were two or three triangular arrow-points, the remains of the dead man's weapons.

There he lay, this Indian warrior, where the men of his tribe had placed him perhaps three hundred years before I was born. One could imagine him as the chieftain of some stockaded prehistoric Indian village, a powerful leader, feared and respected. It seemed likely.

As I looked down upon those crumbling bones I experienced something of the fascination of the past, and the desire came upon me to learn more about the people who had lived long ago. What sort of people had they been, and how had they lived? What had this countryside looked like then? Instead of the cornfields and pastures and wood-lots which stretched away from the green embankments which enclosed the river now, then there would be only forest, primeval forest, with great trees in their thousands towering skyward on either side of the winding, rushing river. Instead of our bustling, modern city of London, with its wide, tree-lined roads and tall office buildings and apartment houses, then there would be only a solitary Indian settlement, a cluster of bark-walled huts surrounded by a log palisade, crowning the flat summit of a low hill. The wolf-packs had hunted then where we played at exploring now.

It was then that the idea came to me that it would be a fine thing if one day I could start off to explore lands untouched by modern civilisation and discover the remains of bygone peoples. Tales of exploration and discovery were always my favourite reading. That I might one day emulate the exploits of my favourite explorers — Mungo Park and DuChaillu in Africa, Lawrence in Arabia, Stefansson in the Arctic — was an idea which had not occurred to me before. My parents were ordinary working people, and I should have to earn my living as best I could when my schooldays were ended. Also, I was crippled, having begun life with a deformed hip, and I was engaged in a relentless struggle against approaching

9

blindness. Such handicaps were enough to daunt even the most ambitious youth.

As I stood there beside the long-dead Indian's grave, pondering over these questions, rain started to fall, and water began flooding in the hole I had made. If I did not move quickly no trace would be left of my discovery. Anxious to salvage the skull, if nothing else, I pulled off my woollen sweater and packed the skull inside, then placed the bundle carefully in my haversack. The rain was pouring down now, wetting me through, but I lingered for a few minutes longer, probing the gravel with my trowel to locate any other arrow-heads. When the hole was a foot deep in water and all traces of the grave had vanished, I was compelled to retreat to the shelter of some trees.

As soon as the rain slackened a bit I limped along the embankment towards my home, clutching my precious burden to my chest. The sun came out again, and I could feel my clothing drying on me as I walked. Tramping along, I looked across the reed-beds bordering the river to the blue hills beyond, and imagined myself an explorer penetrating into Unknown Africa or the Arctic. Why not?

My home appeared in sight. It was a single-storeyed, wooden house, standing in a garden walled round by hedges of tall, yellow-headed sunflowers. There was a long, green lawn at the front of the house, and past this ran the gravel road which ended at the river. Beyond, but some distance away, could be seen the factories and office buildings which formed London's skyline. From our front door one could see the tall, wooden fence surrounding London's baseball ground. During vacation some of us boys used to earn money by minding motor-cars outside the baseball ground. Our street was a cul-de-sac, so when a motorist slowed down seeking a place to park one of us would jump on the running-board and indicate an empty space where the vehicle could be left. For this service we might receive a tip ranging from five to twenty-five cents.

Anxious to show my find to my paernts, I dashed into the summer kitchen, shouting, "Hey, Mum! Hey, Dad!" but there was no response. My parents were out. I began to unpack the skull, changed my mind, and looked in the ice-box for something to eat. There were some sausages and a pumpkin pie, and by the time I had eaten most of these my plans were made. I would go into town and call at the office of the *London Free Press*, the local paper, and show my find to a reporter there. Boys who discovered anything unusual were in the habit of calling round at the local newspaper offices, in the hopes that it was worth a paragraph or two. The newspapermen were a good-natured lot, and had been known to give boys as much as fifty cents upon occasion for items of local news.

This London in which I lived was known as "The Forest City", for there were trees everywhere, maples mostly, along the streets and around the buildings; the town seemed embowered in greenery. Though the buildings and streets bore familiar English names — Blackfriars, Piccadilly, St. Paul's Cathedral, Covent Garden Market — and the river flowing through it was known as the Thames, there was little resemblance to London in England. It was old as cities go in Canada, having been established nearly a hundred years ago, and there was still enough of the small-town atmosphere about it for curiosity-smitten boys such as myself to wander into the offices of the *London Free Press* and seek the help of the staff in identifying natural history specimens or Indian relics.

The skull was looking the worse for wear by the time I reached the office, and threatening to disintegrate into a pile of dust, but the reporter to whom I showed it said it was worth a couple of paragraphs. Some days later I had the satisfaction of seeing a brief account of my discovery in print: "Young Archaeologist's Exciting Discovery. . . . Was this the grave of the prehistoric ruler of London?" Later I was told that a Mr. Jury, an archaeologist attached to the University of Western Ontario, wanted to see me, so that I could show him where I had discovered the grave, but though I waited expectantly each day to talk to a real live archaeologist, we did not meet.

"You ought to go to university to study ancient history, young fellow," the reporter told me encouragingly. "Maybe some day you'd make a big discovery — like Howard Carter, the archaeologist who discovered the lost tomb of King Tut in Egypt."

To go to university, to study archaeology; these were new ideas to me.

"How do you get to university?" I asked. "My folks are poor. And I've got a bad leg, though it does not stop me from doing things."

He looked embarrassed, as though he had not intended his remark to be taken seriously.

"You'd better ask your school-teacher about it, sonny," he advised. "You've got to go to high school first."

The matter was forgotten until, some time later, at the end of a history lesson, Miss Slater, our teacher, mentioned my discovery.

"Please, miss," I began hastily, "I'd like to go to university when I'm older, and learn more about how the Indians lived in olden times."

Miss Slater considered this remark thoughtfully before replying. "It is not easy for a person who is physically handicapped to go to university," she said. "You would find the work much harder than at this school."

Looking about our big sunlit classroom, with its dozen or so desks, its light and space, its bookshelves and workbench, I understood very well what she meant. Our class was a special one for partially sighted children. I suffered from failing eyesight as well as lameness, and much of my education during the past few years had been acquired in this room. My classmates were all afflicted by defective eyesight. Schooldays in that classroom were happy ones, for we were allowed to progress at our own speed, undisturbed by the pressure of examinations. Miss Slater was a gifted, patient teacher, prepared to go to any trouble to get the special books or equipment which we needed. What would it be like in the world outside, in an ordinary school, in competition with fit, normal children? I sensed that getting an education under such conditions would be much more difficult.

"You will be leaving us to go to high school one of these days," Miss Slater continued. "We will talk about your future then. How is your lame leg feeling today?"

Actually, my lameness did not bother me much in those days. Sometimes my "bad leg" hurt, and sometimes it did not.

Also it was a nuisance when I tried to climb over walls and fences. But at least I could walk with it — after a fashion. There *had* been a time when it had not been possible for me to walk at all, so that I could progress only by shuffling along the ground on my backside. Then had come a long time in hospital, and surgical operations, and now I could hobble about fairly happily.

Not until years later did Mother tell me I had been born with a diseased hip; she had fallen downstairs just before I was born, and I had been given only a week to live by the surgeon.

2

INDIANS AND SKYSCRAPERS

MY interest in the past dated from a very early age. I was about ten or twelve years old when I was taken for a ride in somebody's car to a farm a few miles from London. We left the car by a gravel road and walked across some fields until we came to a low hill covered with trees. We climbed the hill by a muddy path and came upon several men standing by a hole dug in the ground.

My father told me the men were a party of archaeologists who were excavating the site of an ancient Indian village. Through the trees I could see a green earthwork which formed part of the defences of the settlement. Then I saw, lying on the ground by the hole, a human skeleton. This was exciting enough; then one of the men thrust an arm-bone under my nose and said, "Look, laddie, this poor fellow was eaten! The people who lived in this village were cannibals."

17

It puzzled me that he could tell how the person to whom the bone had belonged had met his death in a cooking-pot. At school we had been learning Longfellow's poem *Hiawatha*, and it was hard to reconcile the "noble savage" with Indians who burnt their prisoners at the stake or cooked and ate them. Somehow I had never thought of Indians as possessing such nasty habits. Yet there was no logical reason for attributing nice behaviour to people living in the Stone Age. Why shouldn't they eat human beings?

The grown-ups went on talking, and I got bored, so I wandered off by myself to find what there was to be discovered. The old, green earthwork running along the edge of the hill appealed to me. How exciting to think that I was standing on the rampart of a real Indian fort! Standing there looking down upon Snake Creek winding its way through the fields below, one could imagine the scene as it might have looked three centuries earlier. There would be the rampart, with a log stockade on top, and behind it the houses of the settlement. The village would consist of two or three dozen "long-houses". Long-houses were communal dwellings built of log frameworks covered with walls of birch-bark. Each house would measure about thirty feet wide and a hundred feet long. One such building would shelter a number of families. These people would live by hunting and fishing, and by cultivating fields of corn, pumpkins, beans, and sunflowers, outside the ramparts of the fort.

I heard one of the archaeologists say that the inhabitants of this ancient village had been members of the race called the Neutral Indians. Father Daillon, the missionary who wintered among them in 1626, described them as a cruel, warlike people, capable of mustering four thousand warriors. They lived in fortified towns and villages in what is now south Ontario, and were still in the New Stone Age when the first white men reached this part of Canada. Nearly three hundred years before our time the Neutral Indians had been practically exterminated by their foemen, the savage Iroquois, and the ruins of their settlements had been left to moulder in the forests until all knowledge of them was lost.

As I stood there on the old earthwork, my foot dislodged something which glinted dully in the sunlight. It was an arrow-head, a triangular-shaped piece of stone of the type I discovered later was known as a "war-point". It gave me a thrill to hold in my hand an Indian arrow-head lifted straight from the gravel where it had lain for centuries. How exciting to feel the cool, damp touch of it, and to know that no other hand but mine had touched it since it had been placed there, perhaps by some dead warrior's side! Here was something personal to appeal to the imagination.

My first impulse was to run back to the others and show them what I had found. Then I thought again about the curious ways of grown-ups, and their warped sense of morality; probably they would compel me to give my find to the archaeologists. Thinking it best to keep quiet about my discovery, I thrust the arrow-head into my jacket pocket and started to grub about in the gravel, hoping to find more. The Neutrals, I had learned at school, had manufactured practically all the artifacts used by the Indian tribes living in this part of Canada, obtaining their supplies of raw materials from the shores of Lake Huron.

My father's voice made itself heard, calling for me, and declaring that he was in a hurry to get back to town. He seemed annoyed. Reluctantly, I abandoned the exciting quest for arrow-heads and hurried back. Two of the archaeologists were walking about thrusting long metal rods into the ground, probing the soil for the remains of the wooden posts which had formed the framework of one of the "long-houses". Then the outlines of the building could be drawn on a plan of the settlement. We walked back across the fields to the car, and a short time later were speeding along the highway to London.

The sequel you can guess: I spent the next few days digging holes in the back garden in the hope of uncovering an old Indian settlement, or at least discovering some arrow-heards. I found nothing, and Father, taking a short cut across the garden one dark night, fell headlong into my excavation and expressed his opinion of my activities in no uncertain terms. I was ordered to fill in the hole next morning before going to school, and was warned that if the hole was still there when he returned home from work that evening, then the tortures which Indians inflicted upon their prisoners would be as nothing compared with what would happen to me.

It must have been about a year later that I went with him on another trip into the country. Father was a typewriter mechanic by trade, and made calls on customers living in the district around London. At one place, as the grown-ups were talking, I heard the farmer remark, "Have you heard about the prehistoric elephant they're digging up over at the Jones's place?" Prehistoric elephants meant only one thing to me — mammoths, those huge, hairy beasts which lived in Canada at the end of the Ice Age, so I begged my father to stop at the scene of the excavations on the way back.

Presently we found ourselves in a marshy piece of country — Komoka Swamp, it was called — where several men were digging a ditch. Or, rather, what had begun as ditch-digging had now become an archaeological excavation. Embedded in the dark, peaty soils were some huge, discoloured bones which were evidently part of the

22

skeleton of some vast creature. William Jones, the farmer, had set his men to work to uncover the skeleton, under the supervision of two archaeologists from the University of Western Ontario.

I gazed at these two men with awe, and guessed that they were professors, no less, though they looked young and neither sported a beard. One of them called out to the workmen to get a rope round the creature's head, so that it could be hauled out into the open air. Slowly part of a huge skull appeared out of the swamp, and in my eagerness to obtain a better view I nearly slipped over the edge of the excavation to join the bones down below. My father saved me by grabbing at my coat-collar and hauling me back, at the same time remarking that it was wonderful how kids could find so many different ways of breaking their necks.

Meanwhile a team of horses was hauling at the other end of the rope, and then suddenly, with a lovely squelching sound, first the big skull and then some equally massive leg-bones were hauled out of the swamp. The bones were not those of a mammoth, though; the skeleton was that of a mastodon, a much earlier type of elephant, which had lived in America ages before mankind. Later, in a museum, I was to see a reconstruction of one of these great beasts, and to realise that it stood nearly twelve feet high and seventeen feet long. How exciting it was to see the great bones being removed from the swamp where they had been buried for centuries!

"Say, son, I remember when I was your age watching Injuns ride by with scalps hanging from their saddles — white men's scalps!"

If the grey-haired old fellow standing beside me in the doorway of the log block-house on Bois Blanc Island, in the Detroit river, had wanted to startle me he could hardly have done it more dramatically. His words made me stare at him hypnotised. Indians in war-paint, carrying scalps, seemed a fitting background to this century-old building, whose wooden walls — slitted for riflemen to shoot through — made one's imagination hark back to the days when the Detroit river was the frontier between red men and white.

British redcoats had held this outpost

when great Indian war-chiefs such as Tecumseh and Pontiac were leading their tribesmen with rifle and tomahawk through the forested wilderness of Ontario and Michigan. Later, runaway slaves, making a perilous escape from bondage in the United States to Freedom in Canada, had sheltered within these log walls. Many other exciting events had happened here.

Yet that had been a long time ago — in history — and it was the 1920's we were living in now. The old fellow must be joking.

"How come you did not lose your own scalp?" I asked sceptically, eyeing his grey thatch.

"Let me tell you," he replied. "Out West it was — moren't forty years ago — after the Battle of the Little Big Horn River. Custer — he was an American general — and a bunch of United States cavalry, well, they rode into an ambush. They were surrounded by a Sioux war-party led by Chief Sitting Bull. Custer and his men died to a man, and Sitting Bull led his braves north to the Canadian border."

"Go on," I said, fascinated.

"The Injuns were met at the border by a patrol of Canadian North West Mounted Police," my companion went on. "That's how I came to see them, when I was a kid of your age. My Pop had taken me west with him on a prospecting trip, and we were camped near the border when Sitting Bull and his braves rode by."

"What happened then?" I asked.

"The Mounties told Sitting Bull and his men that they'd have to behave themselves or they'd be in trouble with the Canadian Government. The Sioux drifted around that part of Canada for a while and then went back home. I guess it must have been the last time Injuns and white men fought. I tell you, boy, the sight of Sitting Bull and his braves in their war-paint and feathers was enough to give anyone the creeps."

That must have been the last time Indians had taken scalps on the war-path, I reflected. How odd to think of a Stone Age people fighting against the white race within the lifetime of the man standing by my side! It made history seem much closer, almost in my own time, confirming what our teacher told us at school.

"History is not merely something which happened a long time ago. History is being made all the time. What happens to you now, in your own lifetime, is history."

As a boy in Canada I loved to read books and look at pictures about strange, far-away lands and peoples. Lost cities, unknown tribes, ruined palaces, inscribed stones, tombs filled with treasures — such things fascinated me. The world was full of exciting things to do and wonderful places to visit; I was determined that one day I should see some of these wonders for myself. *To find out* — that was what made life exciting and worthwhile.

The Indians, for example, which the old fellow had told me about. What were they like nowadays? Were they what Wild West films and stories made them out to be? Asking myself the question — how had Stone Age people adapted themselves to modern civilisation? — I obtained an answer in a very unexpected manner.

The trip to Bois Blanc Island had been made in a river steamer from Detroit, where I was spending the summer vacation at the home of my aunt. Detroit appeared too much of a great, modern industrial centre in which to discover remains of the past, yet I spent days wandering about its streets, fascinated by what I saw. One way led me to the river, where ships docked from all parts of the Great Lakes, and another route took me into mean streets lined with cheap lodging-houses and eating-places. In some parts of Detroit the people's skins ranged in colour from African ebony to Chinese yellow, and one could hear almost every language spoken except English.

Exciting though all this was, it seemed no place to look for representatives of Stone Age man, until one day I was attracted by the sight of a spidery network of steel girders rising against the sky. A new skyscraper was being built — forty storeys high, I was told by a passer-by — so, boylike, I stopped to watch the men of the construction crew walking catlike along girders high above my head. A whistle sounded for the midday meal, and the men quickly descended to the pavement. As one of them came towards me, carrying his meal in the traditional lard-pail, I stared at him in surprise. He was no white man, for his coppery-red skin and hooked nose and high cheek-bones proclaimed him to be of the race which inhabited America before the white men came.

"Say, are you an Indian?" I blurted out.

"Sure, boy," he replied.

"And are all those fellows building that skyscraper Indians?"

"Sure they are, boy." He saw the look of bewilderment on my face. "Us Indians have gotta earn our keep same as white folks."

"But — working on a skyscraper," I protested, "that's an engineer's job."

"You mean, you expected to find us Indians running round with feathers in our hair," he remarked. "Maybe doing a bit of trapping or portaging for hunters?"

I nodded.

"My tribe used to do that once," he went on. "They used to help portage freight round the rapids of the St. Lawrence river. 'Course, that was a long time ago. When canals and steamships were built my people gave up portage work and tackled jobs which needed plenty of wits and skill. They were good at climbing — they had good heads for heights — so when New York started growing upward it was us

Indians who helped to build the first sky-scrapers. As the buildings got higher and higher Indians got used to working high. Now my people are known all over Canada and the States as specialists in high-level construction work."

Here was a paradox. Skyscrapers, symbols of the modern industrial civilisation, were being erected around skeletons of steel girders built by sure-footed Indian construction crews. The Stone Age had turned modern with a vengeance!

"Just you watch us, boy," my informant continued. "We are called the 'spider-men'. Wherever there are skyscrapers to be built — in New York, Chicago, Montreal, or 'Frisco — you will find us on the job. It takes a fellow who is as sure-footed as a cat to work on a high-level job. You only fall once."

I stared upward, fascinated. Skyscrapers and Indians! It still seemed odd.

By such chance encounters, and by the reading of many books and maps, was the ambition to make something of my life enabled to develop — that ambition to do the kind of things experienced by the heroes of the books I read — to write, to explore, to uncover the past. I was resolved that when I left school I *must* go to university and study to be an explorer and an archaeologist. Crippled and half-blind, well, so I was; I do not recall ever thinking that these handicaps might prevent me doing what I wanted. I had no brothers or sisters, no relations or family friends to influence me, so I could, in my own secretive way, plan for the future without being discouraged by other people's criticisms. Young men took it for granted that they would go to college, even if it meant working one's way as janitor, salesman, or waiter. *Everybody* went to college.

Lameness and blindness can be fought, or endured, but emotional difficulties eat into one's soul like acid. My mother and father did not get on well together. They quarrelled frequently, each appealing to me to side with them. Sometimes for days at a time they would not speak to each other, and I had to carry messages from one to the other. Their violent rages made me so frightened that I used to hide kitchen-knives and other sharp implements for fear one of them would do the other an injury. Then I would hide in my own room, venturing out only when the storm had subsided. As the years passed, these quarrels grew less, and, instead, they treated each other with icy contempt. My crippled condition must have been a great disappointment to my father, for he had been a sergeant in the Army and a professional footballer, and in neither of these spheres could I follow in his footsteps. Gradually he drew apart from us, and lived a self-contained life of his own.

Subconsciously I acquired a philosophy of life, based perhaps upon the attitude of my father and of the people among whom we lived. Learn to stand on your own feet and expect no help from anybody. Expect no sympathy because you are disabled, but fight or go under. Trust nobody, and always have your fist ready to ward off a blow. In this life it is kill or be killed, and there is no place for weaklings. If you were too poor or disabled to fight, then the poor-house was the place for you. Fear of the poor-house was to haunt my dreams for years.

Adolescence was a time of utter misery, for there was no one to whom I could confide my troubles. My leg and hip hurt, and my eyes were foggy. Those persons who declare that suffering ennobles are guilty of sophistry; there is nothing noble about pain or agony. Pain is hell. It embitters the disabled, and takes away the joy of living. At times I thought I was going out of my mind, that it was better to be dead, and not till later did I discover that such thoughts are common to many adolescents.

Sometimes I walked along the riverbank and looked at the buildings of the University of Western Ontario and the students strolling about the grounds. Oh, you lucky young people, I thought, who are fit enough to study there! I would have given half of any years of life remaining to me to be able to see and learn about the subjects which fascinated me — history, geography, archaeology, the study of mankind. Would I never have the chance?

I was attending high school now, struggling to keep up with a boisterous crowd of healthy, high-spirited, normal young people. "Struggling" is the correct verb, for life was a continual fight against failing eyesight. A greyness was obscuring everything, making it difficult for me to distinguish objects more than a yard or two away. I could not see what was written on the blackboards, and only by developing my memory was I able to make anything of the lessons. There was to be no going to university for me.

Life was full of hatreds. I hated wearing glasses because they made me feel inferior. I hated high school, for everything conspired to make me conscious of my own inferiority. I hated the teachers, hated my fellow-students, hated life itself. I hated everything which kept me apart from other young people. I knew I possessed courage and ability, if only my wretched body would not keep failing me. Worst of all was the loneliness, for I was without friends or companionship.

Yet even as lameness and failing eyesight were making life more and more impossible, the urge to do something towards the achievement of my ambition drove me on. In one way and another I explored much of southern Ontario, getting lifts in cars driven by travelling salesmen employed by the typewriter firm for which my father worked. Other places were reached by means of an old bicycle purchased for five dollars. A terrific urge to find out what the world was like gripped me; I wanted to go everywhere, see everything. It was as if I belonged to the breed of whom a poet has written:

We were dreamers, dreaming grandly,
In the man-stifled town,
And we yearned beyond the sky-line,
Where the strange roads go down.

Unaided, I made my first field-geography notebook, drawing crude maps and sketches. Stockaded Indian settlements, linked by winding trails, had once occupied clearings in the primeval forests of Ontario, and though a modern agricultural landscape had now replaced that earlier one, evidence of earlier days remained hidden in the ground if one cared to look. The war-trails of the Indian tribes — Hurons, Neutrals, Iroquois, even the shadowy race known as the Woodlanders — had followed the morainic ridges, and where their walled villages had stood were now thriving modern cities. As I travelled about the countryside, awheel or afoot, the feeling came to me that history and geography were not rigidly separated subjects, but one — the study of Man in Time and Place. Some of these ideas I put down in writing, my first attempt at producing a book, but this had to wait twenty-five years for publication.

Knowledge was not acquired without various misadventures. Twice I was bitten by snakes, through treading on them with my bare feet. The doctor had no anaesthetic, so the subsequent operation had to be performed with two men holding me down. A roof-fall while cave exploring and a fall into a twelve-foot-deep pool taught me not to be careless. Another time, scaling the ice-covered cliffs bordering the river, I slipped and shot downward towards the swirling black waters. A drifting ice-floe lodged at the base of the cliff stopped my fall and provided a temporary refuge. The cliff was too icy for me to climb up, so I spent an unpleasant half-hour squatting on the ice-floe, till a man arrived with a rope and hauled me to the top. Looking downward, I saw the ice-floe split across the middle and slide away into the black swirl of the rapids.

Though in such ways I proved to my own satisfaction that I was as capable as any other boy, these were individual efforts; the praises of society were reserved only for those who excelled in team activities. Only if you could knock a ball about were you considered of any value at school, or out of it for that matter. Now at knocking balls about I was absolutely hopeless, and considered it the most boring occupation imaginable. This is understandable, for if you cannot see a ball until it is within a yard or so of you, you have little chance of catching it or hitting it accurately, and if you are no good at games you cannot be expected to be interested in them.

Much of my spare time was spent reading books. London's public library was a large, rectangular red-brick building, with projecting red towers at the corners. These towers provided convenient retreats for readers seeking privacy. Many were the happy hours I spent alone in one of those towers, reading books dealing with all sorts of subjects; it was a cosy, friendly place. Most of the works of Mark Twain were read there, and many books by Jules Verne, and many more by Charles Dickens and Sir Walter Scott, and a great many works of travel and exploration. Books were my only companions.

Short-sighted children can read for hours on end without effort, and so tend to live in a world of books and fantasy, in which they wander dreamily about, getting a reputation for standoffishness. They are likely to pass their friends — if they have any! — in the street without seeing them, and miss many of the experiences which help in the development of normal children in a long-sighted world. So the handicapped child acquires a reputation for being peculiar, and is unpopular.

At high school I got into trouble because I copied inaccurately from the blackboard; teachers scolded me for mistakes it was not possible for me to see. It was a convention that the girls sat in the seats nearest the windows, and the boys in the seats nearest the inner wall. Since it was necessary for me to sit by the windows where the light was best, I had to ask permission to do this. Some women teachers refused to believe my explanation, and made me sit on the darker side of the room. So for all the good their lessons did me, I might as well have gone fishing.

As my eyesight gradually faded I became increasingly aware of how many fascinating branches of knowledge there were to be explored — anthropology, social history, geology, economics, politics, woodcraft, natural history — oh, ever so many! It was as if a new world was opening about me. Even as the fascination of learning gripped me, so fate, it seemed, was determined that I should not have the opportunity to learn anything.

Our local doctor could not tell what was causing my sight to fail, and fees paid to a quack for so-called electrical treatment were money wasted. If we remained where we were, in London, it seemed I was doomed to lifelong blindness. But across the sea, in my home town of Manchester, in England, there was an eye hospital which had a world-wide reputation for curing eye diseases. My parents decided to leave Canada and return to England, to try and find a doctor who could restore my eyesight. Mother's health had also suffered during the severe Canadian winters, and it was thought that the English climate would suit her better. We had been told that economic conditions were much better in England now, and that my father would have no difficulty in getting a job.

One of my last expeditions in Ontario, before my sight failed me, was a trip to the shore of Lake Erie, thirty miles south of London. My heart craved wildness and distance, and a sense of discovery. Away from the little fishing village of Port Stanley, with its hot-dog stands and dance-hall, the lakeshore curved away into illimitable distances. I tramped westward as far as I could, past tawny cliffs scarred by steep-walled gullies and bizarre earth pinnacles. And there was the great lake itself, stretching away from the pale-yellow beach like a vast, blue bowl under a hot, cloudless sky. For a crippled boy confronted by blindness there was something restful and soothing in just watching the waves lapping against the sand and feeling, with eyes closed, the hot beat of the sun against one's cheeks.

Almost the last words I wrote, before my vision finally failed, were some lines copied from a poem by a Canadian poet, for they epitomised the appearance of the lake as I remembered it:

A dash of yellow sand,
Wind-scattered and sun-tanned,
Some waves that curl and crawl along
    the margin of the strand;
And, creeping close to these,
Long shores that lounge at ease,
Old Erie rocks and ripples to a fresh,
    south-western breeze.

A few days later, from the deck of the
liner *Montcalm* as she steamed down the
St. Lawrence river towards the open
Atlantic, I took my last look at Canada.
That night we passed Cape Diamond, and
I looked upward at the cannon-guarded
ramparts of Quebec and the twinkling
lights of the old French-Canadian city. In
my diary I scrawled:

So this is the mighty St. Lawrence river.
Miles of forest, little stone mills, churches,
narrow strips of fields, the purple-topped
Laurentian Mountains in the distance.
And a river which gets wider and wider
as the hours passed. What is happening in
those hills back of the forest? I should
like to step off the ship and live there for
a while.

A day or so later, when I went on deck, there was only a vast expanse of heaving, grey water about the ship. Canada had vanished.

The year was 1928, and I was nearly sixteen years old.

3

BOY ALONE

NOW another city was to play an important part in my life:

"Manchester, a city in Lancashire, 187 miles north-west of London. The city covers about thirty-four square miles, and has a population of 766,333. It is the centre of the cotton-manufacturing industry, and has many other industries. The city has two famous Association football clubs."

Manchester, my birthplace.

Among my earliest memories are of being a small boy in Manchester, and of spending hours in queues outside shops, ration cards clutched tightly in my hand, waiting my turn to be served. There was a war on somewhere, and my father was away at some vague place always referred to as "the front". My mother went out to work each day and did not get back till nightfall, so I had to help with the shopping. Our home was a small room in a dilapidated house in a dingy back street in Greenheys, near Manchester University.

At an early age I had to learn to take care of myself, for I had no brothers or sisters, and grown-ups were too occupied with their own affairs to bother with the troubles of small boys. Sometimes I was at school, sometimes not. With my twisted leg stuck out stiffly in front of me, I spent a lot of my childhood sitting on the pavement, watching the soldiers marching by or the big convoys of lorries rumbling along the cobbled streets.

Discomfort is something a small boy learns to accept. Hunger is another matter. I was always hungry. I remember one day being in a house with nothing to eat and watching a cat being given its dinner of hot meat and vegetables. How I wished I was that cat! Fear of being hungry was to stay with me until I was grown-up. Being hungry and homeless and helpless — these were my three private nightmares.

Standing in a queue outside the doorway of a butcher's shop one day, reading a comic, I was startled by an argument which broke out suddenly between the shopkeeper and some customers. The women wanted to buy meat. The butcher refused to sell it to them. He wanted to keep it for his regular customers, he said. (This happened before rationing began.) At once the shop became filled with a mob of shouting, screaming women, and the the butcher disappeared from sight in their midst.

"You fat old bastard, you should be out in the trenches where my husband is," one burly housewife shouted. "At him girls!"

Several brawny women grabbed the butcher and flung him down on the chopping-block. Another woman grabbed a carving-knife. What she intended to do I do not know, but the butcher anticipated having his throat cut, and screamed with terror. A woman standing beside me cried out, "Get the kid out of this," and at that moment a policeman came running towards the shop. Two women seized me and hustled me outside, the crowd of women parted, and the butcher was left lying on the floor, sobbing. When I passed the shop again the windows were boarded up, and there was a policeman walking up and down along the pavement.

A number of times we left Manchester and went to live with my grandmother, a grey-haired old lady who lived in a thatched cottage in a small village in Suffolk. Her home was an old, old place beside the river Stour, and all about it were wide cornfields and lines of tall Lombardy poplars, whose branches made an odd moaning sound when the wind blew through them on dark nights. When anything went wrong with crops or cattle the old people would say, "Ah, that's old Mother So-and-So's doing. The witch is up to her tricks again." Then my grandfather would tell me solemnly how he had been bewitched when he was a boy. Certainly, the little old woman dressed in rusty-black clothing who was pointed out to me as the "witch-woman" fulfilled a small child's idea of what a witch should look like, and appeared quite capable of flying past the cottage on a broomstick on dark nights. But nothing exciting like this ever happened.

Every night at sundown the German prisoners would come marching past our cottage door, followed by an English soldier carrying a rifle with fixed bayonet.

At sundown, also, a deep, booming sound reverberated across the Suffolk plain, and they told me it was the roaring of the guns over in Flanders. Sometimes we walked across the fields to the village of Kedington, where my mother had been born, and there in the churchyard outside the grey-walled old church I was shown the graves where my ancestors had been laid to rest.

One night there came the roar of aircraft engines far above us in the dark, and a violent knocking on the cottage door, and the sound of a voice exclaiming, "Open up, boy, open up; they bombers be a-comin'!" We scrambled out of our beds and hurriedly dressed ourselves and rushed out into the starlit night. As we rushed for the shelter of the nearest ditch there came the roar of an exploding bomb, and looking back across the fields we saw the glow of burning buildings. As we sheltered in the ditch we saw an old couple from a neighbouring cottage come staggering along the road, bent double under the weight of a heavy iron trunk. They would drag it a few yards, rest, drag it a few yards farther, rest again, making for the ditch where we were sheltering. When they were still a few yards away the next bomb came down, and we were flung in all directions. Next morning there was no sign of the old couple, but the iron trunk was still there — empty.

But always we came back to Manchester.

Sometimes a cloud descends upon our lives, and when it lifts we find that a complete break has been made with our past life. We find ourselves living a new life, without any connection with our old one; it is as if all the threads which bound us to our old life have been severed.

So it was with me.

At sixteen I had been living the life of a high-school student in London, Ontario, hoping to go to university to study geography and history. At the age of seventeen I was a patient in the Royal Eye Hospital in Manchester, in England, engaged in a struggle against blindness which was to last four years. There was to be no going to university for me; instead I was to be constantly in and out of hospital. When I was not in hospital, in order to earn some money I took the only job available and worked as errand-boy in a greengrocer's shop. The contrast between my two lives could hardly have been greater. But I did not realise this at the time.

Each one of us, I imagine, feels that there are certain times in our lives when we have just about reached the limit of human endurance: life can hardly be grimmer or more difficult. The future seems to hold no hope of improvement. We can only endure. We live from day to day, hoping that our troubles will soon be over.

This feeling was mine many times during the four years after we returned to England. The surgeon in the Royal Eye Hospital in Manchester quickly diagnosed the cause of my failing eyesight as cataract. "Most unusual to find this trouble in one so young," he remarked, and informed my parents that the necessary operations to remove the trouble could not be performed until the cataracts were sufficiently "ripe". It would be necessary for me to be almost completely blind before a cure could be attempted. I must wait until I was sent for.

Several months passed before the surgeon considered that my eyes were ready for the first operation to be performed. By then the grey cloud which had been gradually cutting me off from the world about me was almost impenetrable. A person with complete cataract has perception of light only. That period of waiting was one of the loneliest and most heart-breaking of my whole life. My friends, my ambitions, my hobbies, my happiness, had all been left behind in Canada; in their place I had — nothing.

My home now was an attic high up under the eaves of a dingy old house in Greenheys, in one of the mean streets near the university. There I spent many hours, sitting, thinking. No one was friendly, no one spoke to me, contact with the outside world became less and less. It was as if I was dead. Like a dumb animal one could only endure patiently.

It was with relief rather than foreboding that I made my way one day to the big red-brick building in Oxford Road which houses the eye hospital, and on the day following stretched myself out on the operating-table and watched the white-clad surgeon stand beside me holding something shiny in his hand. Anything was better than this half-a-life which I had lived during the past year.

"Never mind, old fellow," I heard the surgeon say. "We will get your sight back, though it may take some time."

On and off it was to take four years.

The operation for cataract was painless, but the aftermath was very unpleasant. With both eyes tightly bandaged, you were laid out on a bed and told not to move. You might have to lie there four or five days till your eyes had recovered from the operation. Several days without any movement at all can become sheer agony. The urge to sit up, to turn over, becomes almost overwhelming.

Even when the bandages have been removed, and you can see the world about you — grey and blurred — there are still weeks to be spent in bed, and after that weeks, months perhaps, of waiting to learn if the "op" has been a success. For the danger following cataract operations, I was told, was of the retina becoming detached, and this meant complete and instant blindness, with no hope of recovery. So one spent weeks shuffling about hospital corridors, or sitting dispiritedly in the day-room.

All this applied if the operation had gone right, but if it had not gone right, if something went wrong with the eye — as it did with mine — then your stay in hospital would be so much longer, months maybe, or a year.

When I first went into hospital I thought it was only a matter of having an operation and getting my eyesight back. It was months later when I realised it would take a whole series of operations before I could see fairly well again, and these operations would extend over several years. After my first operation I spent some time in hospital and was then sent home. Several months passed before the surgeon sent for me again. The second operation kept me inside hospital for four months, and I had hardly been discharged and got back home when something went wrong with my eye and I had to go back to hospital again for a like period. After that I had a year or so of peace, before having to go back to hospital for more operations. Altogether, it took seven or eight "ops" to restore my sight.

During those years between the ages of sixteen and twenty my life was a curious one. There were the weeks and months spent in the eye hospital. This was mere existence, to be endured with what courage one might command. Home, after a long stay in hospital appeared unreal, and my parents seemed strangers. Then there were the periods in between when I was well enough to work. And there were times when I was neither in hospital nor fit enough to work, but free to tramp the roads of England, though often with little or no money in my pocket.

Hospital became a sort of second home to me, more real than my own home. Doctors and nurses were friendly, and their kindnesses brightened up the dullness of life.

Even in hospital life can have its brighter moments. Nurses new to the hospital were often the victims of practical jokes. Once somebody had the idea of putting Sammy, the hospital skeleton, into an empty bed and then asking one of the new nurses to see if he needed anything. A temperature chart was drawn up and placed at the bottom of Sammy's bed, in the accustomed position. The ward was in partial darkness when the new nurse approached the bed, took up the chart and studied it, and then drew back the bedclothes. We watched, chuckling, as she stared horror-struck at Sammy's bony countenance. Then she let out a wild yell and ran screaming from the ward.

Another new nurse upon whom this trick was played was made of sterner stuff. She regarded Sammy without a qualm and called out, "Nurse, the doctor must be sent for at once. This patient appears to be suffering from a most peculiar complaint."

A similar trick was played upon me when I was able to walk about the ward. Asked to carry some vases of flowers from the ward and put them in a storeroom for the night, I burdened myself with as many vases as I could carry, and hurried along to the room indicated. My arms were so full that I could not reach the electric-light switch, so I simply kicked the door open and strode inside. The room was almost in darkness, and I nearly dropped my burden on to the floor when I observed hundreds of human eyes staring at me in the gloom. As I stepped back in dismay, a bony hand came out and touched my arm, and I spun round and found a skeleton leering at me. I left that room with extreme rapidity, learning later that the eyes were specimens kept for students to examine.

Smoking in the wards was forbidden, so cigarettes had to be indulged in in secrecy. To me fell the task of giving warning of Matron's approach. But once, while I dallied with one of the younger nurses, Matron approached unexpectedly. Captain Rooney, poor fellow, had time only to thrust his cigarette under the bedclothes, unscrew the stopper of his hot-water bottle, and thrust the cigarette inside. Unfortunately in his haste he failed to screw the stopper back into place again, before Matron had reached his bedside. A tell-tale trickle of water descended from the bed to the floor. Matron eyed it grimly and in a voice which penetrated the length of the ward called out, "Nurse, bring a bottle. You have a patient here who cannot control his bladder."

There was a patient named Nobby who became friendly with a ward-maid, and the pair of them would disappear into a convenient broom cupboard when the opportunity arose. One day Paddy, who was an inveterate practical joker, locked the pair of them in. But when he went along to unlock the door, there was Matron approaching the cupboard, followed by her little poodle. Something had to be done to save the situation, so, as she turned a corner, I grabbed the poodle, stifled its yaps with my hand, and with the creature tucked under my arm sought refuge in the men's toilet. Matron paused in her mission in order to investigate the disappearance of her faithful hound, which just gave Paddy long enough to unlock the cupboard door and let the scared couple out. A couple of minutes later came Matron's disgusted snort, proclaiming her chagrin at finding the cupboard empty.

Matron was a martinet, and I was in her bad books a number of times. When I had an eye to see with I helped the nurses in the ward; I emptied bottles and bed-pans, polished taps, dusted lockers. My reward was fruit and jellies intended for paying patients. Patients not confined to bed had to eat dinner in the big hospital dining-hall, under Matron's hostile gaze. One day I arrived late, having spent too long polishing taps, and Matron promptly pounced.

"What do you mean by coming here half dressed?" she demanded.

I looked about to discover which article of my clothing was missing, but the only fault I could discover was the button of one shirt-cuff unfastened.

"Do you mean this?" I asked stupidly.

"Of course!" she snapped. "Don't you dare come in here again with your buttons undone."

"I won't do it again," I promised, "for I won't be coming in here again at all. I'll eat my dinner in the ward in future."

I turned on my heel and walked quickly out of the dining-hall, with her staring after me, and the last thing I heard was her loud voice crying out, "Come back, you, come back!"

As a soldier in the Army remembers the sergeants of by-gone days, so some of us remember hospital Matrons.

In Canada, if you remember, I had looked across the river Thames at the buildings of the University of Western Ontario, and watched with envy the comings and goings of the young people who were fortunate enough to spend several years of their lives studying within its walls.

Now this same pattern of events was to repeat itself in England. This time it was the buildings of Manchester University and the students passing in and out at which I gazed enviously. What a fine thing it would be, I thought, when my sight had been restored, to study at the university! Sometimes, when attending free lectures there on Saturday afternoons, I tried to imagine what it must feel like to be a real student, studying for a degree in geography or history. Only later was I to realise how one's hope of future achievement could be blighted by lack of opportunity to study.

These were the 1930's we were living in now, with millions of men unemployed, and only the "dole" or dead-end jobs as errand-boys for many young people to look forward to. The newspapers recorded daily clashes between police and unemployed, hunger-marches to London to compel the Government to do something, the prospects of another war if this man Adolf Hitler had his way. Go to university — you want your head examining mate!

Our kind are beaten before we even begin. Geography or history, if you were mug enough to want to study such subjects, could be learned from books borrowed from the public library. But where did it get you?

The bitter spirit of the angry young men of the generation which wasn't wanted was hard to evade. What crazy ideas some of us had — that it was possible, without friends or relatives or anyone to help, to become whatever we wanted! University education wasn't intended for working-men. If they'd any sense they'd stay down where they belonged. Roll on next war, my merry lads, when jobs will be found for young people whose services are at present of no value to society. Maybe the Blackshirts marching along Oxford Road are right, and one should exclaim with them — "to hell with culture!"

And yet — how difficult to deny the insistent inward urge to acquire knowledge! Not for all of us the ranks of the teddy-boys and the beatniks arguing jazz and sport over cups of coffee, or the equally depressing ranks of the oldsters deploring juvenile delinquency. Twenty miles south-east of Manchester is some of the most magnificent hill country in all England — the Peak District, whose high, heathery moorlands are trenched by rocky valleys through which flow tumultuous streams. In that delectable countryside, astride a bicycle purchased for ten shillings, one could explore — if one had sight — gorges and cliffs and caves, castles, prehistoric camps and temples. All these objects appealed to my sense of wonder.

What was it Lionel McColvin, the librarian, had written in his stimulating little book *How to Find Out*: "In the grimmest material circumstances life can be made an enjoyable experience if we give our minds a chance. The universe with a myriad of exciting experiences lies open to us if we follow the call of what interests us." One must have faith in the future and never give up hope.

Begin right where you are, instead of crying for the moon. Manchester, which hitherto I had regarded merely as a drab, smoky, industrial city, assumed a new significance when I learned that it took its name from a Roman fort. To walk through the busy streets of Manchester and near a railway arch to come upon a piece of blackened walling, to touch it and to comprehend that this was the last remnant of a fortress from which Roman soldiers had once marched to conquer northern England — that was exciting. It gave two thousand years of history to the neighbouring streets and buildings.

Manchester Museum was another exciting discovery, for it was filled with fascinating things — Egyptian mummies and inscriptions, fossil trees and animals, Roman coins and pottery, and, best of all, Indian and Eskimo weapons and equipment. The museum was a short walk from the eye hospital, and after sitting on a hard wooden bench for hours waiting to see the specialist it was good to wander round the museum and look at the exhibits and let one's imagination wander. More practically, one could compare Indian arrow-points collected in Canada with English specimens dating back to the Bronze Age and earlier.

Searching for objects appealing to my sense of wonder, one morning I walked away from New Brighton, which faces Liverpool across the mouth of the river

Mersey, with the intention of following the coast of the Irish Sea as far as the mouth of the river Dee. For between these two rivers Cheshire thrusts a narrow projecting strip of land shaped somewhat like the spout of a teapot — the Wirral Peninsula, it is called — so that a walk of but ten miles or so will take you from one river to the other.

The skyline of Liverpool across the Mersey appealed to me less than the little fort with its round towers and old cannon which stands on Perch Rock at the mouth of the river. Dark caves showing in the Red Noses — red sandstone cliffs — were obviously old smugglers' haunts. Leasowe Castle among its trees was not, I discovered, a real old English castle, but a castellated mansion of red brick. But the high, windswept sandhills by the Irish Sea were real enough, and soon I found myself walking across flat, open countryside, with the sea on one side and open, marshy land on the other.

It was good to walk for mile after mile along the embankment built to keep the sea from flooding over the land, to breathe the salty tang of the sea and hear the gulls screaming overhead. Then came something really fascinating — the remains of a forest submerged by the sea. Once this Cheshire coastline stretched much farther out to sea than it does now, but as the land sank beneath the waves the forest became submerged. At low tide, so I had been told, the stumps and roots of the ancient trees were exposed along the foreshore. Presently I found myself wandering among an expanse of black mud out of which showed rotting oak-stumps and lengths of roots and blackened pieces of tree-trunks half exposed by the falling tide. Once there had been a Roman town here, but of this I saw nothing.

I went on, and came to a low red sandstone headland from which I could look across the Dee estuary to the mountains of Wales. Out in the wide expanse of wet sand showed the dark outlines of an island. It appeared possible to walk across the sand to the island, so I started out. I walked for some time, but the island did not seem to get any nearer. The thought came to me that if the tide started to come in, then my position would be awkward.

There might not be time to get back to the mainland before the water engulfed me. I hurried on.

The shores of the island drew nearer, so that low red rocky cliffs were visible, and greenery, and scattered buildings. The cliffs were almost reached when suddenly there appeared between me and them a channel curving through the sand, with a stream rushing seaward. Unable to find a better crossing-place, I splashed through the shallow water, and scrambled up on the shingle beach below the cliffs. A grassy road led me the length of the island to a lighthouse at the seaward end. The centre of the island was occupied by what appeared to be farm buildings, and by some wooden bungalows of the type frequented by holidaymakers.

The side of the island looking towards Wales dropped steeply down to the water in sheer cliffs of a brilliant red colour. The red of the rocks and the blue of the sea made one of the most striking pictures I had seen anywhere. From time to time a curious barking noise could be heard, but though I looked round me for signs of a dog, none was visible. Later a fisherman told me that it was the barking of seals I had heard, for these creatures congregate on the sands at the mouth of the Dee.

But where was I, and what was this island called? A man came towards me, so I called out to him, asking the island's name. He replied, "This is Hilbre Island, and if you want to get back to the mainland you had better start now before the tide turns. Otherwise you will have to wait here for several hours, and you won't get anything to eat."

I turned back, splashing through the channel, then walked across the sands as fast as possible, till I reached the mainland again. Some time later I looked back and saw that the island was really an island, for now a wide expanse of water stretched between me and it. Hilbre Island is really quite an exciting place, had I but known, for there was a monastery there in days gone by, and the old farm buildings had been a resort of smugglers a century or so ago.

Taken altogether, that walk from the Mersey to the Dee was as fruitful of "wonders" as many a journey several times as long.

The years went by. Now I was almost twenty-one. Life had given me so very little, and I seemed to have no future.

The question which had puzzled me for years continued to frustrate me. How could I learn something about foreign lands and their inhabitants? Borrowed books and bicycle trips and free lectures and reading newspapers given me by customers to wrap fish in; so one learned a little, but not nearly enough. They took one's mind away from the wilderness of council housing estates, but progress was so slow that one's life would be gone before anything was accomplished. There must be something more to life.

I grew desperate. My God, how I wanted to get away from it all, how I wanted to live a different kind of life, to see these foreign lands, to find out about the past, to talk about the things which interested me! To live one's life in a little box of a house in a prison of a street, often with no sun in the sky, that was not living. How unsatisfactory, too, were parents, who, if they no longer quarrelled violently as they had when I was a small child, now acted towards each other almost as if they were strangers! Dad's life was the local pub, football pools, and racing; Mother's was her home, her neighbours, and the local mission hall. As the years went by they lived their lives more and more apart.

Those were lonely years. Life consisted mainly of work. It seemed to me that people often failed to get what they wanted because they wanted too much. If you wanted something, then you must be prepared to give up something else to get it. If you wanted to be a traveller and a writer, then you must be prepared to give up smoking, cinemas, dancing, pleasant companionship. You must decide which things you wanted most, and give up the lesser things in order to secure that which you really wanted. You could not have both.

In the end I solved my problem without help from anyone. It was useless to be envious of those fortunate persons who were able to travel to far-off lands and write books and magazine articles about their experiences. Gradually the idea came to me: *You can do the same as they*. It is up to *you*. Start out now, from Manchester, with the few pounds you have saved up, and find out what the world is like for yourself. Go places, do things, meet people. You must help yourself. It is no use waiting for somebody to come along and give you a helping hand; that only happens in fiction.

Stephen Leacock, the Canadian writer, had said that if one could not get an education by going to university, then all that was needed was a good chair and plenty of books. One could try that method when one was older. Meanwhile, if it was not possible to study for a degree in geography at university, then might it not be possible to learn something about the subject by starting off with a rucksack on one's back and a few pounds in one's pocket, to seek experiences along the world's great roads? Surely by working one's way across different countries and looking at landscapes and asking questions it was possible to learn *something*? In that way the world could be one's university.

A newspaper cutting decided the goal of my first journey. The cutting was headed: "GOVERNMENT OF FINLAND COMPLETES ONLY MOTOR ROAD IN WORLD LEADING TO

ARCTIC OCEAN". It described the completion of the "Great Arctic Highway", the most northerly motor road in the world. This highway had been constructed across the forest-covered wilderness of Finnish Lapland, and it ended at a mysterious port on the Arctic Ocean, three hundred and fifty miles north of the Arctic Circle. To follow that road to its very end, to learn something about the Lapps and their reindeer herds, seemed to me to be an instructive exercise in field-geography.

Should I go northward then — to the Polar Sea?

4

TO THE POLAR SEA AND BACK

I WAS walking along a road. It was a road with a surface of yellow gravel, and there were tall pine-trees on either side. Ahead of me the road curved upward towards a range of bare, rocky hills whose splintered summits rose above the forest. A few miles back those hills had appeared smoky purple in colour, but closer examination showed them as grey granite crags with patches of snow on their summits. Against their greyness the trees showed dark green. The ground on either side of the road was green also, but a much lighter shade, the pale green of the moss upon which the reindeer feed. Yellow sunlight blazed down out of a cloudless blue sky. It was early summer in the Arctic, and the year was 1934.

I was walking along this road with a rucksack on my back and a stick in my hand. My lame leg was giving me a bit of trouble, but what did that matter? It was fine to be alive and free and twenty-one years old. How good it was to breathe fresh air and feel the warm sunlight, and stride along through the forest for mile after mile!

A deep, tree-filled valley appeared beside the road. There was a river flowing through it, a swift, tempestuous stream, dropping in white-flecked falls and rapids. I knew that I was nearing my destination, for this was the Ivalo river whose waters would eventually reach the Arctic Ocean, far to the north. Not far away was Laanila Goldfield, named after a solitary farm near the river. There was a prospect of making money by finding gold at Laanila, and for that reason I was tramping north-ward. Also, somewhere out on the fells beyond the river the last remaining nomad Lapps in Finnish Lapland lived and moved about with their reindeer herds. How these age-old Arctic people were managing to survive in the modern world was an investigation worth recording in a geography field-book.

A narrow track led me away from the road, and following this for a mile or two

I reached a group of log cabins, clustered about a grass-grown road. The camp was surrounded by tall trees, and prowling about among these I came upon more abandoned buildings, piles of rusty machinery, and deep shafts whose mouths were covered by rotting boards. Gold had first been discovered in this district in 1868, and there had been several minor gold-rushes. In 1920 a company had tried gold-mining on a large scale, but the project had been abandoned. The truth is that though the auriferous area is fairly extensive, the deposits are not particularly rich.

One of the cabins in the abandoned camp would serve to shelter me for a few days while I looked around, I decided, and after that I would go westward across the river in search of the Lapps.

It had been a long journey from that council-house in Manchester to this camp beside the Ivalo river. A fish-lorry had taken me to Hull, and £5 had paid my steamship fare from there to Helsinki, the capital city of Finland. A nine-hundred-mile journey by train, bus, lorry, canoe, and my own flat feet had brought me to the town of Rovaniemi, almost on the Arctic Circle. On the way there I had undergone many unusual experiences; I had stayed at a Russian monastery on an island in Lake Ladoga, and lived for a while in a village on the Finnish-Russian frontier, where I had been arrested for wearing a red shirt. I had experienced most of the usual discomforts and misadventures of a traveller journeying across a strange land "on the cheap", with little knowledge of the language. But I had reached Lapland, and the beginning of the road known as the Great Arctic Highway.

One morning, looking out of a railway-carriage window, with a map on my knee, I saw that there were no more railway tracks. This was the "end of steel", to use a railwayman's expression, the end of the line. Beyond was only Arctic wilderness. With what delight, a little while later, I walked away from the scattered wooden buildings which comprised Rovaniemi, and started tramping northward along the Great Arctic Highway. An hour later, by the side of the road, there appeared a signpost, and on it were the words

ARCTIC CIRCLE

This was the Arctic at last. The Polar Sea lay only 330 miles to the north.

With the help of lifts on lorries proceeding northward to the polar port of Petsamo, I had reached the track leading to Laanila goldfield in two days. In those two days I had revised many of my conceptions about the Arctic. First there was the landscape; the thick forest with the pine- and spruce-trees stretching away in every direction as far as the eye could see. Then there were the people and the buildings seen at intervals alongside the road. The buildings — houses, inns, schools, churches, military posts, post-offices — were sturdy structures constructed of timber or concrete. They were equipped with electric lights, telephones, radio-sets, sometimes with central heating. People were dressed very much as the people hundreds of miles farther south — the men in lumberjackets or woollen shirts with checkered patterns, heavy blue or brown trousers, and cloth caps. The women wore cotton dresses of various colours, pink, blue, or green, and had coloured handkerchiefs knotted about their heads. All wore knee-length leather boots with curled-up toes.

And the weather — no snow or ice, except on the mountain-tops, no blizzards, no darkness — for in summer the sun shines the whole twenty-four hours. The brilliance of the sunshine was astonishing, not only its heat, but the wonderful clarity it gave to the landscape, so that everything was as clear and colourful as a picture postcard.

Why Bill (or Vilho, in the Finnish language) had forsaken his ship at the port of Kemi, to come northward in search of gold, was the sort of question one doesn't ask a chance acquaintance. I only know that he came striding out of the forest to where I stood on the riverbank studying the deserted mine-workings with a speculative eye. He was a tall, lean man with a face the colour of old saddle leather and a pair of startling blue eyes. He was dressed in the oldest of clothes — blue dungaree trousers, brown jacket, with an old felt hat pulled low over his eyes. He had a rucksack on his back, and carried over one shoulder a long wooden sluice-box; from the other were suspended a pick and shovel and round metal bowl. A gold-prospector if ever I saw one, was my first thought, and just the sort of person I needed to meet.

"Hello," I said, in my best Finnish. "Let me carry some of those things for you. It is a hot day."

He looked at me, surprised, with those blue eyes of his and said, "Hallo, English — yes," and I nodded, and took hold of the pick, shovel, and metal pan, and we walked off down the valley together.

"It is good to have some person to talk to in this country," Bill said, in precise English. "You look for the gold, hey?"

Down by the rushing waters of the Ivalo I was initiated into the mysteries of prospecting for gold. The layer of gold-bearing gravel lay two feet below the surface, and we took it in turns to break this up with the pickaxe. Then the gravel was emptied, a shovelful at a time, into a long wooden sluice-box, through which water flowed from the river. The sandy residue which remained was collected in the round metal bowl. Then one had to squat on one's haunches by the riverside, and swirl the bowl round and round, until it was empty save for a few flakes of yellow metal.

"Gold," Bill explained, briefly, and took a glass tube out of his pocket and dropped the yellow flakes inside.

All that long, hot day Bill taught me how to prospect for gold, how to know the right places to look for it, in narrow gullies and on ledges which acted as catchments. A second washing produced a tiny nugget, and we got a little more gold before Bill decided to finish for the day. We were both hungry, so we cut a couple of saplings for fishing-rods and went down the river to catch some fish for our evening meal. Later, on a camp fire outside the old miners' bunk-house, we grilled trout and made coffee. Supper over, we stretched ourselves out on mattresses of fir-boughs covered with reindeer-skins, and discussed plans for the future.

"I go west to the country of the Lapp-men," Bill said. "You come too, hey? Maybe we have more luck at finding gold there."

The following morning, packs strapped

on our backs, we started off. We forded the river, and within five minutes the forest had closed about us on every side and we were in an absolute wilderness, with no trace at all of man or his activities. From a hilltop we saw the forest, stretching wave upon wave towards the far horizon, ridge beyond ridge. Ever so far off were mountains, remote, snow-covered. This was the wild country which my heart craved — hundreds of square miles without a road or a house, hardly a path even, where one travelled by making a straight traverse from one point to another, across ridge and bog and forest. This sort of travel was thrilling enough for any amateur explorer.

We marched all day, and that evening camped on the summit of a pine-clad ridge near a spring of clear water. We marched all the next day across the same kind of country. Forest and yet more forest. The timber-line was eight hundred feet, and above the forest the rounded fell summits were clothed with grey-green reindeer moss. The high, rolling fells rose out of wide, green valleys through which flowed swift-running streams. Now and again the forests gave way to wide open spaces covered with purple willow-herb or pale-green moss. Still we saw no signs of life.

One evening we reached a black conical tent pitched on a hillside, and in reply to our shouts several Lapps came out to greet us — small men, dark-faced, slant-eyed, like Mongol tribesmen from far-off Asia. Their appearance was colourful enough — dark-blue tunics reaching almost to the knees, narrow blue trousers, and brown boots with turned-up toes, made of reindeer-hide. Each man's tunic was decorated at the shoulders, collar, and cuffs with coloured stripes, yellow, blue, or red. Each had a long knife in a curved leather sheath suspended from his belt, and carried a lasso over one shoulder. Grass stuffed into their boots took the place of stockings. In reply to our greeting an old Lapp with a wrinkled face, who appeared to be the head-man, called out something in an unintelligible language.

"He is inviting us to join them," Bill explained. "Remember to shake hands with each man in the tent as you enter."

The tent was a circular affair of pine-poles covered with dark-coloured blanket cloth. Entering, we found several Lapps sitting round a fire in the centre. I gravely shook hands with each man in turn, pulled my rucksack off my shoulders, and sat down on the floor. The floor was covered with birch-twigs, with a few reindeer-skins scattered about to serve as seats. There were no tables, chairs, or bedsteads, only some boxes made of birch-bark, used for storing personal possessions, and a few pots and pans made of metal. Afterwards we stretched out on the skins and slept. There were no partitions. The family lay on one side of the fire and we on the other.

The following morning, exploring the camp, I discovered other tents pitched not far away. Big, black Samoyed-like dogs came charging out at me, as I watched the little Lapp children in their colourful costumes playing at being reindeer-herders. Their parents showed no surprise at our arrival, for in a country where inns were non-existent, hospitality to casual wanderers is general. Bill told me that these people were part of a Lapp *sida*, or tribal division. In Lapland the term "village" does not mean a fixed collection of buildings. It refers to the whole district and the group of Lapp families living there. The unit of life is the clan, not the family, for only by working together as a community can the people survive the many hardships of life in the Arctic; life is too precarious for a man and his wife and family to survive alone. A *sida*, therefore, consists of two or three families who travel together with their herds of reindeer, along with any servants and camp-followers who may choose to join them. They wander together year after year, always following the same route.

Bill and I remained at the camp for several days, exploring the neighbourhood. On the first day he said he was going prospecting along the fell streams near the camp, but after we had worked for several hours without finding any gold to repay our efforts I decided it would be more profitable to watch the Lapps engage in their various activities. Though there were quite a number of reindeer in the neighbourhood of the camp, I had come too late to watch the yearly round-up and migration of the herds. These Forest Lapps of Finnish Lapland, unlike their kinsmen, the Mountain Lapps who live over to the west, stay in the woodlands the whole year round, looking after their herds.

The life of the Lapps revolves round their reindeer, although it would be untrue to say that nowadays the Lapps do not use anything except reindeer products, as their forefathers did. Alive, the reindeer provides them with milk and a means of transportation; dead, it furnishes them with meat, skins (used for making tents, clothing, and blankets), and sinews for thread and string. Without the deer the Lapps' way of life would come to an end. A rich Lapp family may own as many as a thousand deer, but a family can live comfortably with three hundred. Lapps therefore are not poor folk, as many people imagine.

Leading a pack-reindeer seems simple enough, but when I asked Per, the headman, to let me try it I could not get the animal to move. I tugged and pushed and coaxed and swore, but the obstinate beast refused to budge. The Lapps stood around and stared at me solemnly. Then, when I paused for breath, the deer lowered its head and hit me such a blow on the bottom that I toppled over backward into the river with a loud splash. The Lapps laughed; evidently they *did* possess a sense of humour.

Although reindeer are supposed to be tame they are much wilder than domestic animals such as cows or sheep. They have to be lassoed before they can be milked or loaded with packs, and the Lapps are as expert with their lassos as the Western cowboy; the only difference, indeed, is that the Lapp works on foot. A reindeer cannot carry a man, but can carry about 130 pounds on its back, or nearly twice as much when pulling a light, boat-shaped sledge in winter.

One day in August I stood on the banks of a wide, swift-flowing river, waiting for the Lapp postman. With an Austrian ornithologist named Rauenhofer for companion, I proposed going overland to the isolated Lapp settlement of Karasjok, on the Tana river. The postman was prepared to act as guide part of the way, and after that it was up to us to manage as best we could. The sight of those glittering snow-peaks seen to the west, remote and seemingly inaccessible, was luring me even farther into the western wilderness. I could take care of myself.

The Lapps arrived, little Mongol-like men in colourful costumes of blue and red. We started off immediately. A narrow reindeer trail led away into the heart of the forest, for this was part of the great wilderness which stretches for hundreds of miles between Finland, Norway, and Sweden. It was rough going, for the country consisted of a seemingly endless series of steep ironstone ridges with swamps in the hollows between. We would scramble up a steep ridge, slither down the other side, cross the bog at the bottom by means of logs placed end to end, climb another ridge, slither down, and then repeat the performance again and again. The Lapps marched with a short, quick step, so that I could hardly keep pace with them, and if they had not stopped to rest for a few minutes in every hour I should have been left behind.

We passed occasional Lapp homesteads — rough log dwellings consisting of one or two rooms. Nowadays wealthy Forest Lapps who own large herds have settled down and live in houses, leaving their servants to tend the deer. When somebody told me, "There are many rich people in this neighbourhood," I naïvely wondered why anyone should choose to live in this desolate region, forgetting that in this part of the world wealth is measured not in money but in deer.

Presently we came to another river, flowing between wooded hills, the watershed of the Tana river. The Lapps boarded boats and went upstream. My companion and I hired a boat and a Lapp guide and followed them. Eventually we reached a Lapp camp on a bluff above the river. Three canoes were drawn up on the beach, and their crews sat around a fire, drinking coffee. Rauenhofer proposed that we cross the watershed on foot, build a raft, and float down the Tana river to Karasjok. It sounded like a great adventure, but I was feeling feverish and doubted if I could manage the journey. For weeks I had not had enough to eat, and now hunger and tiredness were beginning to take their toll. This wilderness was no place for a sick man.

He went on, and I turned back alone. I spent the night at a Lapp house, and next day tried to follow a compass-course across country to Inari, but the ground was filled with iron-ore and the needle of the compass spun round uselessly. After losing my way in a bog I reached the river again in time to get a lift in a canoe going downstream. The Lapp boatman left me at a cabin in the woods, where I slept for some hours and then started off again. Whether it was night or day I have no recollection, for by now I was desperately ill. There was no darkness at night, only the red glow of the sun on the horizon.

As the hours passed, the heat seemed to become greater. I felt so tired I could have lain down on the track and slept. It seemed a long time since I had seen a human being or a house. My eyes were giving me trouble, and at times I suffered from the hallucination that somebody was marching by my side, but each time I looked there was nobody there. The river flowed out into a big lake, and on the farther shore I could see the red-walled buildings of a Lapp settlement. I lit two fires, and was feebly trying to send up a smoke-signal when sharp eyes on the farther shore observed my predicament, and presently a boat came across with two Lapps in it, and so I was rescued.

The Lapp settlement was an orphanage and boarding-school run by the Finnish YWCA, where children who were orphans or whose fathers were away tending their herds could live and be educated. The kindly Matron promptly took charge of me, put me to bed, and nursed me for a couple of days. Then, since I got no better, she announced that I must go to the hospital at the village of Ivalo, forty miles away; at the same time a message was sent to the doctor at Sodankyla, over a hundred miles to the south. These figures convey some idea of the distances and difficulties of maintaining a civilised standard of life in the Far North.

The Matron sent me by motor-boat to a place where a road was being cut through the forest, and here a car was waiting to take me to hospital. Of the appearance of that hospital, or the village of Ivalo, I have little recollection, for events happened as if in a dream. I lay in bed coughing and feeling sorry for myself, and was not surprised to be informed by the doctor, when he arrived three days later, that I had bronchitis and various complications. I could only lie there helplessly in bed, staring through the mosquito-netting at the hot, green forest outside.

After a week or so in bed I was allowed to get up and sit on the veranda, and practise speaking Finnish with the nurses. The hospital was staffed wholly by women, who spoke only Finnish. When I wanted to explain what was wrong with me I had to resort to sign language, for Finnish is a most complicated language with no Latin or Germanic affinities. The most I ever learned of it were a few simple phrases such as *Hyvää paivää* ("Good-day"), *Puhutteko englantia* ("Do you speak English?") or *Kuinka paljon* "(How much?"), but I was baffled when confronted by such words as *yhdeksänkymentäyhdeksan* or *yks-suuntainemkatu*, or even a simple word like *syyskuu*.

The day came when I was discharged from hospital, and, with only a few shillings in my purse, started northward again along the Great Arctic Highway. It might have been sensible, perhaps, to have turned southward to some port on the Gulf of Bothnia, where a job on a ship going to England was a possibility, but I was determined to finish my journey first and reach the Polar Sea — or die in the attempt.

Travelling north along the highway, sometimes getting lifts on lorries, sometimes on the big yellow buses of the Finnish Postal Service, I realised how Lapland was indeed Europe's Arctic frontier. Everywhere people were hard at work, building houses, workshops, garages, constructing new roads, bridges, settlements. Twentieth-century civilisation was being pushed northward towards the Arctic shore with all possible speed. It was good to have witnessed such exciting developments.

For the last hundred miles of its course the Great Arctic Highway northward curved in a gigantic letter S before ending at the Polar Sea, where the new ice-free port of Liinahamari was in process of construction. The forbidding granite heights known as the Petsamo Mountains were the reason for the road behaving in this fashion, for their bare, rocky bastions thrust northward almost to the ocean's edge. The highway curved round through the dark pine forests by Salmi Lake, where the mountains showed as dark purple shapes to the east, then started to climb up above the tree-line, seeking the lowest crossing. As the road climbed higher the trees thinned out, then disappeared, and all about one was an undulating, wind-swept countryside, miles and miles in extent. This was the tundra, the region of treeless plains, a vast expanse of bare rock, tussocks of coarse grass, and innumerable pools of water, above which the mosquitoes hovered in their millions.

One afternoon towards the beginning of September I trudged across this forbidding landscape, and saw before me a great valley opening out and stretching northward to where a vast sheet of water blocked the horizon. It was the valley of the Petsamo river, and that far-off sheet of water was the Arctic Ocean. Thick forest filled the valley, buildings showed here and there, and blue smoke curling above them indicated human activity. After the stark solitude of the tundra it was good to see signs of life again. The mouth of the Petsamo river forms a natural, ice-free harbour, invaluable in peace or war, so here in latitude almost seventy degrees north one finds modern civilised communities, their activities based on lumbering, fishing, and mining.

The tolling of a bell greeted me as I walked down the mountain-side into the forest. Above the tree-tops I saw the sunlight glinting on a gilded dome, and presently in a clearing in the forest there appeared before me a group of wooden buildings, the sight of which took my thoughts back to pictures of the holy Russia of Tsarist days. There was a church with bulbous Byzantine domes, a pilgrims' hostel, chanters' huts, workshops, and other buildings, grouped round an expanse of grass where horses were grazing. It was St. Trifon's Monastery, founded in 1533, the most northerly monastic establishment in the world.

The main building of the monastery was a big structure built of squared logs, painted red and brown, and here I was greeted by an old man wearing a black robe and tall black hat. He was the Abbot, so I asked him for a night's lodging, and he called a lay-brother, who escorted me to the pilgrims' hostel. This was another large wooden structure, full of little rooms where visitors could sleep on iron bedsteads, with the musty smell of antiquity about them. When I had flung my rucksack on a bed in one of the rooms the lay-brother — whose name I discovered was Alexis — took me to the kitchen. Soon I was seated on a bench by a warm, white brick stove, sipping a glass of hot tea with slices of lemon in it. On the table in front of me a big copper samovar bubbled away merrily.

When it was time for the evening meal Alexis escorted me to the refectory, where I was seated at the long wooden table facing the Abbot. Only the Abbot and I had plates to ourselves; the other diners shared plates, one to every four men. After a short prayer serving-men came in with bowls of hot soup, which they placed before us, and when this had been disposed of, they brought in plates of boiled fish and potatoes. At the end of each course the Abbot would pick up a big bell and ring it vigorously, and as soon as he did so the serving-men would rush in and seize our plates, whether we had finished eating or not. I soon discovered why the monks ate as though they all had trains to catch.

After the meal the lay-brother showed me round the monastery church, a tall, wooden building, surmounted by the typical gilded, onion-shaped domes of Russian churches. Inside were strange and colourful objects, holy lamps and ikons from far-off Novgorod and Kiev, ecclesiastical vestments stiff with gold brocade, sent from Moscow via Archangel and Murmansk. My guide slid back a panel in the wall to reveal the altar, and gazing at its vivid colouring and decoration, I had a feeling of having stepped back into the past, into medieval Russia. Only the fact that this monastery stood on land ceded to Finland after the First World War had saved it from the fate which had overtaken the other monasteries in the USSR. Now the monks devoted themselves to farming and fishing, and ministering to the wants of the local Greek Catholics, mostly Lapp fishermen, who lived in this district.

Next morning I walked along the Petsamo Valley to the end of the Great Arctic Highway, where the seaport of Liinahamari was being built. Fish docks, warehouses, a military post, a bank, a school, a hotel, settlers' homes — the nucleus of the new Arctic settlement was there. Waiting for me in the post-office was a letter from my parents in Manchester, and I read it as I rested by the roadside.

A track leading over the granite hills brought me to the tiny settlement of Nurmensätti. It consisted of a few log cabins and a turf hut used as a chapel, where a priest came once during the fishing season to celebrate Mass. Among the sand-hills were the Lapp graves, low green mounds with the dead man's oars and axe placed on top. The Fishing Lapps belonged to the Russian Church, but I was told they still clung to some of their ancient pagan beliefs.

I climbed a grey granite ridge which rose behind the settlement and found myself looking down upon a vast, sombre sheet of water which seemed to stretch away to the world's end. There below me, crashing in great breakers against the granite cliffs, was the Arctic Ocean. My journey was ended. I had done what I set out to do, and now it was time to turn back. Far southward was Manchester and the eye hospital, and soon it would be time to go inside again for another "op". When I came out of hospital again, probably next spring, I would come back to Lapland again and make a second journey to the Polar Sea.

Southward then — to Manchester!*

* From Petsamo I hitch-hiked to Rovaniemi, went by train to the port of Oulu, on the Gulf of Bothnia, then worked my passage as assistant cook on a tramp steamer bound for Grimsby, and so hitch-hiked back to Manchester.

5

THE WINDJAMMER FLEET
RACES HOME

IT was the year following, June 1935.
The four-masted barque *Herzogin
Cecilie*, the biggest sailing-ship in the
world, was racing homeward across the
Baltic Sea to Finland. With her sails
bellowing out before the wind and carrying
every piece of canvas of which she was
capable, the *Herzogin Cecilie* presented a
striking picture of the almost vanished era
of wind-driven ships. From where we — a
group of amateur sailormen — stood on her
deck we could gaze admiringly upward at
the towering mass of canvas above our
heads. The ship was sweeping resolutely
along at a speed of nearly sixteen knots,
and the deck seemed to vibrate with the
surge of her passage through the water.
A great steel ship, acres of billowing
canvas, a strong wind and a rushing sea,
and there you have all the makings of an
epic, I thought.

The island of Gotland was somewhere to the north of us, and the shores of Denmark lay miles away to the south-west. But we had not got the Baltic entirely to ourselves, for against the skyline showed the topsails of other ships. They were also big sailing-ships, and they were also carrying all the sail they could, in an endeavour to catch up with us. We knew that behind them were other ships, and that there were more sailing-ships in the Sound between Denmark and Sweden, while back in the North Sea there were still more ships. The last of the world's great sailing-ship fleets were racing home, and our vessel was in the lead.

Many ships with famous names were strung out in a long, irregular line behind us, great towering ships with white-arched sails, a line of them a hundred miles long. The sound of their names was like the roll of drums — *Pamir, Ponape, Parma, Lawhill, L'Avenir, Killoran, Olivebank, Viking, Winterhude*, and the rest. I liked to imagine all these ships, the last of their kind, out there in the blue, somewhere behind us. Standing there on the *Herzogin Cecilie*'s heeling deck that blustery summer day, one sensed the excitement of it all, the urgency, the feeling that this was the last voyage home for many of the wind-jammers.* Soon they would all be gone, and gone also would be the chance to witness such a sight again.

Consider this ship, the Finnish four-masted barque *Herzogin Cecilie*, upon whose deck I was standing. She was big for a sailing-vessel, three hundred and fourteen feet long with a beam of forty-six feet, and was steel-hulled, with a cargo capacity of four thousand tons. Her main-mast was nearly one hundred and fifty feet high, and her total spread of canvas was 56,000 square feet. She had been built at Bremerhaven in 1902, as a training vessel for apprentices of the Norddeutscher-Lloyd Line. Not only was she the largest sailing-ship registered at Lloyd's, in London, but she also had the reputation of being the fastest. Under a former master, Captain de Cloux, she was said to

* This *was* to be the last voyage home of the *Herzogin Cecilie*, for the following year she was wrecked and totally destroyed off Bolt Head, on the Devonshire coast.

have attained a speed of twenty-one knots. She had been eight times winner of the "grain race".

The windjammer fleet of which the *Herzogin Cecilie* was the flagship might not have existed at all had it not been for the activities of a very remarkable man, Captain Gustaf Erikson, of Finland. This shipowner had been born on one of the Aland Islands, which lie between Sweden and Finland, and had begun life as a sea-cook. He had acquired his fleet when sailing-ships were being sold off cheaply, because other shipowners could not make them pay. His success was due to two facts: he concentrated upon the delivery of cargoes such as wheat, where the sailing-ship's slower speed was an asset rather than a handicap (for grain being conveyed in a ship's hold is not costing the owner warehouse charges), and he manned his vessels with young men anxious to learn seamanship. Many countries required their ship's officers to have had training on square-rigged vessels, and as such craft became less in number it was only in ships belonging to Captain Erikson that such training was obtainable.

Each year these big wind-ships brought grain from Australian ports to Britain — the so-called "grain race" — after which they returned to Finland. Each year the number of these ships grew less, for storms and shipwreck and the inability to secure cargoes reduced their number; some went to the scrapyards, some to the sea-bed, others rotted away on the mudbanks of the world's seaports. Presently they would all be gone and the world would not see their like again.

It was to try to recapture something of the spirit of the last great days of sail that I went over to Belfast to sign on as deck-hand for the voyage to Finland. Finland was the jumping-off place for my second trip across Arctic Lapland, and what better way of getting there than by making a voyage on one of the last of the old-time sailing-ships? What a grand sight it was, also, to see rising above the waters of Spenser's Basin, in Belfast, the four tall masts of the *Herzogin Cecilie*. I, for one, felt that romance would never leave the world while one of those grand old ships remained afloat.

It had been an exciting voyage from

Belfast to the Baltic. Just before the ship was due to sail the donkey-engine boiler blew up, killing two men and damaging the ship's mainmast. This seemed to confirm the truth of the old sea superstition that women aboard a windjammer are unlucky, for the *Herzogin Cecilie* carried five. But her master, Captain Sven Erikson (a relative of the owner), did not seem to be daunted by the fact, but greeted us — several would-be amateur sailormen — quite cheerfully when we boarded his ship. I often wondered what his private thoughts were concerning us; O'Toole and King were schoolteachers from Liverpool, Martin was a doctor, recently returned from service in northern Canada, Lord Bangor was Speaker in the Ulster Parliament, and I — well, what was I? One by one in the captain's spacious cabin we all signed the ship's articles, promising to perform such duties as might be required of us in our capacity of deckhands, for the agreed wage of one Finnish mark.

Then a tug towed the *Herzogin Cecilie* out to the open sea, and with all sails set and a strong wind blowing the voyage to

Finland began. The ship's course was to be round the northern tip of Scotland, then across the North Sea to the channel between Denmark and Sweden, and so across the Baltic Sea to Finland. For twenty-four hours the ship lay becalmed within sight of the lonely islands of St. Kilda, but Karlsson, the mate — a tall, rangy, energetic individual who seemed to have the faculty of being everywhere at once — saw to it that we did not suffer from boredom. We spent part of the time down in the hold, where we were initiated into the art of shifting ballast. A big pile of discarded road-material from Belfast's streets needed attention, so we toiled with shovels and bare hands at the job of levelling it.

To be honest, although we did do some work now and again, we were little more than passengers who were willing to pay £12 for the experience of making a voyage on one of the world's last sailing-ships, but we were all prepared to tackle any job going in order to learn. We learned to haul lustily — if not always intelligently — on seemingly interminable ropes, and we learned something about sails, so that we could speak familiarly of "royals" and "to'gants", and we quite distinguished ourselves at manning the capstans. Those of us who fancied ourselves as artists were given the job of painting the ship's metalwork with red-lead.

Some of us would have borrowed a boat and tried to make a landing on St. Kilda, but the Captain hoped to catch the wind at any moment and would not give us permission. Our closest rival in the race to Finland, the three-masted barque *Winterhude*, was reported to be somewhere ahead of us, and Captain Erikson was anxious to catch up with her and overtake her. People had lived on St. Kilda for generations, and gained a livelihood by fishing and crofting, but the present-day population had been evacuated to the Scottish mainland five years earlier, and their settlement left to fall into ruins. The prospect of investigating the deserted village appealed to my archaeologist's instincts, and it was with a feeling of regret that I watched St. Kilda disappear into the blueness of the sea as the ship sailed on.

It may be wondered how a crippled man can make himself useful on a big sailing-ship, but the truth is that it is possible to accomplish wonders if one tries. Adaptability is the secret, and, of course, youth is a great asset. So whatever the others did, I tried to do also. Was it painting, or scraping, or working in the galley, or making a hammock under Lord Bangor's watchful gaze, then I would try it.

I had a great envy of those persons who could climb up to the main-top, the railed-in platform situated more than halfway up the ship's mainmast, and though it was no part of a deckhand's duties to go aloft, I decided that if those others could do it, then I could do it also. Mind you, the sight of the mast swaying to and fro with the movement of the ship, a hundred feet and more above my head, made me feel distinctly unhappy. My chance came suddenly one day, when somebody (it was either Karlsson or the bosun), said with a twinkle in his eye, "Just nip aloft and get the brush I left there, will you?" A most curious request, for he could have been up the rope-ladder and down again while I was thinking about it. So there was more to the request than that. Maybe I had opened my big mouth too much about my adventures in the Arctic, and maybe this was a little stratagem of theirs to cut me down to size. All I had to do was to say, "I can't do that. Send somebody else."

I went up the rope-ladder hand over hand, and it wasn't so bad. The ladder got narrower the higher one ascended, and there seemed to be a lot of empty space around. Somebody had told me that you could get up on to the platform either by climbing outward along a rope-ladder, with nothing between you and the sea below but empty air, or by clambering through an opening known as the "lubber's hole"; to do the latter was to be subjected to the ridicule of your shipmates. Ridicule did not worry me, but climbing up an outward-sloping rope-ladder did; but when I got underneath the main-top there was no "lubber's hole" to crawl through, so I had to climb the sloping ladder after all. Within a week I was climbing up and down without a qualm.

While all this was happening the ship was sailing on. The wind got stronger, and with all sails set the *Herzogin Cecilie* rounded the northern headland of the Orkney Islands — with Fair Isle showing as a dark cloud in the distance — and then drove on across the North Sea to Denmark. Two days later she rounded the Skaw, and from the deck we looked across towards the long sandbank which is Denmark's most northerly point. This dropped astern, and in half a gale, with the ship's deck tilted at an angle of twenty-seven degrees, the *Herzogin Cecilie* plunged on into the sheet of water known as the Kattegat, between Denmark and Sweden. Through the darkening storm we saw the outlines of another windjammer ahead of us; it was the *Winterhude* battling her way against the gale.

Yard by yard the *Herzogin Cecilie* crept up on her rival, and then — when the two ships were nearly level — then, as we all stood anxiously watching by the rail, and the sky kept going black, then white, then black again, as squall after squall engulfed both ships — ever so slowly, a yard at a time, we saw our own vessel draw ahead. An hour or so later and there was no doubt about it: we *were* ahead, and the *Winterhude* was behind us. We watched our bosun walk to the stern and hold up a rope's end derisively to the crew of the

Winterhude as they lined her rail. He was offering them a tow, the worst insult one can offer a windjammer's crew, for it implies they cannot get enough speed out of their ship to keep her moving.

But soon the tables were turned. We lost the wind off Elsinore, on the coast of Denmark, so some of us borrowed a boat and went ashore. Those members of the crew who were interested in literature went off to explore the castle in which Shakespeare had set the luckless Hamlet; the rest, more concerned with the alleviation of thirst, went off in search of beer. In the midst of these interesting occupations, about midnight, a seaman came dashing ashore from a motor-boat with a sudden command from Captain Erikson that we all return to the ship at once. We had just clambered back on board, and felt the surge of the ship beneath our feet as she moved seaward, when a pale, ghostlike shape passed us in the gloom: the *Winterhude* had overtaken us and was now in the lead. This time it was the turn of a member of her crew to wave a rope's end derisively in our direction.

The day after that Captain Erikson, by

coaxing the ship along when there seemed only a breath of wind, managed to draw the *Herzogin Cecilie* once more level with the *Winterhude,* now becalmed. For a second time we passed our rival. Then the wind came up in half a gale, and with all her sails bellowing full out the *Herzogin Cecilie* plunged on alone into the Baltic. Would the *Winterhude* catch up with us again, or would our bigger vessel maintain her head until the end of the voyage?

We saw the dark, pine-clad shores of the island of Gotland show up on the horizon, and felt confident that we had as good as won the race. "I could write a sonnet about your Easter bonnet," gurgled a crooner's voice over the radio, but this was cut short abruptly by a weather report: GALE WARNING TO SHIPPING. Half an hour later the *Herzogin Cecilie* was in the thick of it. The barometer had been falling rapidly, and now we were about to encounter one of the worst storms of the century.

The sky went black as night, then white, then black again, and the roaring of the wind was something to marvel at. The last thing I heard before the whine of the wind blotted out all other sounds was Captain Erikson's voice ordering all sail to be got in as quickly as possible. Seamen swarmed up into the rigging, scrambled out along the yards, fighting to haul in that vast expanse of canvas and get it lashed down and under control. Flung into the scuppers by the tilting deck, I found myself clinging to the rail with one hand and to Pike, the captain's big Alsatian, with the other. Looking down, I could see great green seas poised below.

A staysail tore to ribbons and went hurtling off, and then the mainsail, big as a tennis-court, burst apart with a crash like thunder. Parts of it swept away into the gloom, leaving the remainder as ragged ribbons streaming from the yards. A wire cable, ripped from the mast, whirled along the deck like a striking snake, threatening to rip the head off the shoulders of any person unlucky enough to be in its path. The men got the rest of the canvas in, and with her masts bare of sails, and with three men clinging grimly to the steering-wheel, the *Herzogin Cecilie* plunged on into the darkness.

All that night, and the next day, and the

day after that, the windjammer's mad pace continued. The roaring of the wind seemed never-ending. All of us on board were jolted and battered and flung about, till we prayed for anything to happen if only the wind would stop. On the third day the wind did calm down, and ahead of us we saw the yellow shore-line of some unknown land: it was the coast of Lithuania, near Memel. The *Herzogin Cecilie* had been blown a long way off her course, and now had no hope of winning the race. The other vessels in the race had had time to overtake her.

We got back in sight of Gotland at last, but the remnants of the storm were waiting for us and drove the ship back again. The *Herzogin Cecilie* had to spend two more days fighting her way back to Gotland for the third time. At last the storms were gone, and now there were only blue skies and favourable winds for the rest of the voyage. Days passed swiftly and pleasantly, with scarcely any need to change sail. How grand it was to lie out on the bowsprit and look up at the great expanse of canvas towering above and feel the ship moving under you like a live thing, as she drove through the water! No longer were the clanking of the capstan or the creaking of the yards the principal sounds to be heard; instead the music of gramophones and radios, with people lying on the hatches in the warm sunlight, writing letters and diaries.

One night we smelled the fragrant scents from invisible pine forests, and knew that Finland was not far away. As a blood-red moon rose over the sea a Finnish gunboat came alongside, and her captain stopped to give us the news. Our rival the *Winterhude* had docked three days before, and we had lost the race. Several other ships of the windjammer fleet had overtaken us and were now nearing their journey's end.

Three weeks after leaving Belfast the *Herzogin Cecilie* sailed into Nystad, a port on the south-western coast of Finland. "Velcome to Finland," boomed a cheery voice, and I found myself shaking hands with a ruddy-faced, stocky man wearing a reefer and seaman's cap. It was Gustaf Erikson himself, owner of the windjammer fleet. To see this almost legendary figure appear in front of me in real life was something of a surprise. Behind him came a swarm of Erikson clan, flaxon-haired girls and tall, blond young men, and almost before we knew what was happening we had all been hustled ashore to join a party being held at the big wooden Erikson mansion.

Nystad, with its wharves and warehouses, its church towers and red-painted houses, appeared as colourful as a picture-postcard, but to me it was just a jumping-off place. For several months, when not in hospital, I had been working and saving money for another journey to the Far North. I planned this time to walk across Swedish Lapland to Norway, then go round North Cape by ship to Petsamo, the district in Arctic Finland I had reached the previous autumn. On remote Fisherman's Peninsula, jutting out into the Arctic Ocean where Russia and Finland joined, were some mysterious stone ruins; it seemed to me they were worth investigating.

All winter I had planned this journey, saving every penny. Only my mother encouraged me; my father thought me a fool. His attitude towards anything I planned was usually one of condemnation. Many times as a child I had been repelled by that deadly criticism he displayed towards anything I did. Often when I had hastened to show him some work I had done — writing, drawing, a map — he found some fault with it; if he could not criticise he remained silent. He never praised. Later I learned better than to expect him to show interest in anything I did.

It was two weeks later.

From where I stood by that rushing mountain river I could see the high peaks of the Lapland Alps rising up like a wall in front of me, range beyond range. Directly in front of me was Mount Kebnekaise, said to be more than seven thousand feet high, the highest peak in Europe north of the Arctic Circle. Two days previously, with a Lapp guide named Anta, I had climbed that mountain, and looked down upon the wilderness which lay beyond. The view of snowfields, valleys, and splintered peaks and ridges had challenged me to make the crossing to the far-off Atlantic Ocean.

Grouped around Mount Kebnekaise were other peaks, snow-covered, appearing almost as high. Between these peaks and the ridge where I stood stretched a wide, stony desert, trenched by rushing, milky-white rivers. There was little sign of life anywhere, save moss and lichens, for this spot was high above the tree-line. The only sound was the sighing of the wind among the rocks.

In the valley down below I could see the little settlement of Kebnekaise, just a few mountain huts; on the other side of the ranges, far away, was the tourist resort of Abisko. I proposed to walk over the mountains to Abisko, then follow the railway line to Narvik, the Norwegian port from where it was possible to get a passage on a ship to Petsamo, the jumping-off place for Fisherman's Peninsula. A roughly-marked trail linked Kebnekaise with Abisko, but how far it was from one place to another or how long it would take me to walk that distance were things I did not know. The only information I possessed about the route had been gained in conversation with an American student in a hotel in Helsinki a fortnight before.

Ah well, why worry?

It was time to go!

The slope leading upward towards that line of peaks in front of me was not too steep to trouble that lame leg of mine very much. I stamped my way over the loose gravel and boulders, conscious of the weight of the pack on my back. The trail was marked by cairns of stones, located a certain number of yards apart, the topmost stone of each pile having been painted a vivid red. One progressed as best one could from cairn to cairn, scrambling over the stony, moss-covered ground, with the ice-capped mountains always in front. It was like walking into a picture. The sky was blue and cloudless, the air was wonderful stuff to breathe, and one felt glad to be alive.

My pack was heavy because it contained enough food to last me for a week. There were tins of beans and corned beef, slabs of hard rye bread, chocolate, coffee, sugar, dried fruit. Also some bundles of birch-bark, rolled up tightly, to be used as fuel for cooking, since there was no wood for a camp-fire where I was going. I had been told that a party of travellers would be coming south from Abisko, and that I should meet them somewhere along the trail, and be able to buy more food if my own supply proved insufficient.

My journey had hardly begun when an incident happened which threatened to end it there and then, and unpleasantly. My way was barred by a rushing river, and I did not fancy wading across the ice-cold glacier stream, for if I got my feet wet it might prove difficult to get my boots and socks dried out again. It seemed more sensible to cross the stream at its narrowest point, jumping from rock to rock. So I argued, but the inevitable happened: I slipped and fell in, and the rushing stream grabbed hold of me and threatened to carry me over a waterfall. The weight of my pack pulled me down, and I could not reach the buckle to unfasten the strap, so had a horrid vision of drowning.

Scared out of my wits, I grabbed frantically at an Arctic willow growing out of the bank, and though the river tugged at me like a live thing, I was able to drag myself ashore. For a few minutes I could only lie there gasping for breath, and thinking of the narrow escape I had had. Not only had I got my feet wet, but now all the rest of me was wet as well; I had no choice but to continue the day's march as I was and trust that my clothing would dry out as I walked. After that I waded without hesitation through any river which flowed across my path, and though I was wet many times, I did not even catch a cold.

Some hours later I began to feel tired, so, coming to a rough wigwam of tree-trunks beside the trail, I camped there. I lit a fire and brewed some coffee and heated some beans and corned beef, and afterwards I curled myself up in my sleeping-bag and went to sleep. After sleeping for some hours I had another meal and then continued on my journey. Whether it was night or day I do not know, for the sun was still glowing redly in the sky and I had no watch. In Lapland, where in summer the sun shines the whole twenty-four hours, the terms night and day have no meaning.

Another day's walking followed, as I climbed steadily higher and higher into the mountains. The great, glittering, ice-covered peaks seemed to frown down upon me in a menacing semicircle. I estimated that now I must be near the pass over the ranges, and that from then on the going would be downhill. At the end of that day's march I reached another wigwam. Like my previous shelter, this also was a cone-shaped erection of birch-logs, covered with sods. A ring of stones in the centre served as a hearth, and the smoke escaped through a hole in the roof.

It was cold sleeping on the ground, even with a reindeer-skin under my sleeping-bag, and when I looked out again it was to find that newly-fallen snow had whitened the mountain-sides. Again I breakfasted on beans, beef, rye bread, and black coffee, but when the time came for me to move on, great clouds of mist swirled down from the mountains and blotted the landscape from sight. There would be no travelling for some time to come, so I got back into my sleeping-bag and spent the next few hours in drowsy contentment. I was not lonely, for there was much to think about, and when I had had my fill of sleeping there was a book of poems by Robert Service for me to memorise.

A chill wind was blowing off the ice-fields when I started out again. Mile-high peaks ringed me round on every side, glistening with glaciers. Still the guiding line of red-topped cairns stretched across the countryside, mile after mile, and day after day. By now I had lost all sense of time, and hardly cared whether it was day or night. It was a land without darkness, and one could go on and on like a man under a spell. To get to the other side of the mountains, that was all I asked, thankful for those two legs of mine which continued to propel me forward day after day, sometimes comfortably, sometimes not.

Time passed.

Time ceased to exist, for this was a land of utter timelessness. I marched until I felt tired, rested until I felt like marching again, ate when I was hungry. If I felt like it I sang. If I wanted to read I read. Sometimes I slept beside the track; sometimes I slept in draughty Lapp wigwams. Sometimes it occurred to me that it seemed a long time since I had seen anything alive. Only the lightening of my load as daily I ate up my food-supply told me that days were passing. But how long all this took me I do not know. I estimated that one day I covered five miles.

I wondered if I had strayed from the track sometimes?

There is a grandeur and a fascination about this Arctic land which it is difficult to put into words. The sun shines on the snow-fields and turns them pink and red, and there are the reds and golds and greens of the lichen-covered rocks. There are lakes of deepest blue. Even the wide expanses of grey splintered rock and the marshy pools and the tussocks of coarse grass have an elemental beauty about them. And everywhere there is falling water, plunging down the mountain-sides in white foaming cataracts. Such a landscape possesses appeal, in a grim and desolate sort of way.

One day, pausing to look back along the valley up which I had just toiled, I heard a far-off cry, like the howling of dogs. It was not dogs, I knew, but wolves. I was above the snowline now, and ahead of me was the pass over the mountains. Later I heard the wolf cry again, this time nearer. It was a frightening sound, and I tried to travel faster, but the roughness of the ground made this difficult. Somewhere ahead of me, though I did not know how far, was a mountain hut where I could take shelter from the pack — provided I reached it in time.

In my anxiety I plunged through a rushing, glacier-fed river which barred my path, heedless of wet clothing, and scrambled up the rocky bank on the other side. The soft, slushy snow made the going difficult, and my lame leg began troubling me, but I forced myself to keep going. I was very frightened, and hastened on until forced to stop by lack of breath. I leaned against a rock, panting.

The ground began to slope downward, and suddenly before me there opened out a view of a wide valley through which a milk-white river flowed, and beside the river I could see the red-painted walls of the hut which I was struggling to reach. Again I heard the long-drawn-out howling of the wolf pack. Moving on, more slowly now, I realised that the mountains were crossed at last. I forded the river and hurried up to the hut, calling out in the hope that the party of travellers coming down from the north might have arrived before me. There was no reply. The hut was deserted, and there was no sign of anyone having visited it for some time.

How eagerly I opened the door, scrambled inside the hut, shut the door, and bolted it! At least I was safe from the wolves within these strong log walls, and even if they had picked up my scent it was unlikely that they would remain in the vicinity once they realised their quarry had escaped. Tired, hungry, I explored my shelter. The hut was a strongly built structure of squared timbers, and contained wooden bunks, an iron stove, a supply of firewood, cooking equipment, and tools. In a more relaxed frame of mind I sat beside a warm fire, a thick blanket about me, and read some chapters of *Tom Sawyer*, a copy of which I found lying on a shelf.

I rested at the hut for a day, and then started off again. My food-supply was practically finished, and if I did not meet somebody soon from whom I could buy something to eat, then I was going to be very hungry. "Nobody travels through the mountains of Lapland without going hungry", runs the old Lapp proverb, but I had no desire to put it to the test. Two, or perhaps three, days' walking still separated me from the hotel at Abisko, and if I did not secure more food soon, then I might be too weak to get there.

It had rained while I slept, and the valley along which the trail led had been converted into a wide marsh. I seemed to wade endlessly through miles of water, but I was much too hungry to worry about getting wet now. Then from the summit of a low rise I looked down and saw the countryside spread out below me like a map. There was the forest, green and inviting, and a wide, winding river and a great lake, many miles in length. The lake was coloured the most wonderful shade of blue imaginable, and I guessed it must be Lake Tornea, by whose shores the tourist resort of Abisko was situated.

With what delight I reached the first trees, little, foot-high forests of birch and willow, which were gradually replaced by real forests, containing thick glades of spruce and pine! It was like coming home again. The trail-markers, stone cairns splashed with blobs of red paint, were now replaced by tree-trunks painted red. I was well down in the forest when I ate the last of my food — two small pieces of rye bread and jam — and with nothing but hunger to spur me on started out on the last lap of my journey.

That night was spent in a forestry hut, with a Dutch ornithologist for company — what a talkative person I must have appeared to him! — but he could spare me only two hard ship's biscuits from his own scanty store. The following day, when I went on again, my mind would dwell upon only one topic — food — food — FOOD. So great was my hunger that the beauty of the countryside was wasted upon me. Keep going, keep going, keep going. Would I last out until Abisko was reached?

Doggedly, like a man in a dream, I plodded along the seemingly endless trail. It seemed as though the forest would never end. Then through the trees came an oddly familiar sound — the soft *purr-purring* of an electric train. I hastened forward, stepped through a belt of trees, and found myself confronted by a railway-track. I had done it! The great barrier of the Lapland Alps was far behind, and the Atlantic was not very far ahead. And there, only a mile or so distant, were the buildings of Abisko, where a starving man might buy food to eat.

It was in the Arctic settlement of Vaitolahti, on the shore of the Polar Sea, that my most ambitious project first took place. It was the map of the world, hanging on the wall of the village schoolroom, which put the idea into my head.

A week or so previously I had gone by coasting steamer from Narvik on the Norwegian coast, round North Cape, to the port of Kirkenes, where I boarded another steamer bound for Petsamo. To view for a second time this Arctic outpost of Finland, which I had struggled so hard to reach by the overland route the year before, had been exciting. This time I was going farther north still. North of Petsamo oddly shaped Rybachi Peninsula thrusts itself out into the Polar Sea, and on its northern tip stood Vaitolahti, Finland's most northerly settlement. In a magazine I had read a report of some mysterious stone ruins which had been discovered out in the tundra, so in order to investigate these I travelled north to Vaitolahti on the little steamer which linked the settlement with the outside world.

The ship steamed into a wide inlet surrounded by low-lying, moss-covered plains.

At the head of the inlet one could see a wooden wharf and warehouses with walls painted red, where men in blue overalls sat gutting fish. A rough road led to the settlement, a cluster of neat-looking wooden houses painted yellow or red, and some older-looking cabins, built of logs, with roofs covered with turf. A large wooden structure, which combined the functions of military post, village hall, and schoolhouse, was the most important building in the village. Behind the houses were little hay-fields, and beyond tundra as far as one could see, flat, treeless, and windswept. The barbed-wire fence which served as the frontier separating Finland from the USSR divided the village into two parts; half was in one country, half in the other.

Accommodation was secured in a fisherman's home, and next morning I set off to find the ruins in the tundra. Under a dark sky which seemed filled with snow the wide-spreading, treeless countryside across which I tramped made me feel insignificant and unimportant. The only noise to be heard was the screaming of thousands of sea-birds. I came to a river, and after following it for some distance reached the place I was seeking. In my notebook I wrote:

The ruins lay half buried in the tundra, vague outlines of buildings, walls built of courses of flat slabs of stone, without mortar to bind them together; in places they still stood three or four feet high. With a trowel I scraped away the thin layer of soil at the base of a wall, seeking some evidence of the persons who had built the settlement, but I found nothing.*

Who had erected these buildings? The Norwegian Vikings had sailed this way, and after them the Finns and Russians. Sir Hugh Willoughby, seeking a North-west Passage to Asia in 1553, had been shipwrecked and died with all this men somewhere along this coast in the following year. Whalers and sealers, monks and hermits, had all visited Rybachi, and these crumbling ruins might be a memorial to any of them.

That evening, while I was having tea

* See *I Found Adventure*, by Jim Ingram (John Long, 1950).

with Helga Vurasmaa, the schoolmistress, in her cosy apartment, my great idea came to me. We were talking by the fire, and I was reflecting how pleasant it was — furniture of polished birchwood, tapestries and paintings on the walls, models of ships and a radio-set on the bookshelves. Through the doorway, in the schoolroom beyond, were desks for twenty pupils, blackboards, a printing-press, an organ. All this in seventy degrees north! I thought.

My gaze fell upon a big map of the world on the classroom wall. I got up and went to look at it. Tomorrow I would join the coastal steamer and return south to Petsamo, and go overland to Kirkenes, from where it ought to be possible for me to work my passage back to England on a ship. Soon this Arctic countryside would be buried deep under snow. Where then would I journey next?

"In Africa it will be warmer," Miss Vurasmaa suggested, tracing on the map with her finger a course from Vaitolahti to Africa.

And why not? I thought. Before leaving England I had copied out Manchester

University's syllabus of reading for a three-year geography course, and had made a start by reading a book dealing with the climatic regions of the world. Now my idea was this:

If one thinks of the surface of the earth, not in terms of political divisions (tinted various colours on maps and separated by frontiers), but as regions of varying climates — polar, temperate, Mediterranean, tropical, desert, and so on — with corresponding variations in plant life and human activity, then it would be a useful exercise in geography to traverse each climatic region in turn, starting from where I now was and going southward towards the equator. Thus, in turn, I would cross the tundra, the taiga, or coniferous forest belt of northern latitudes, central Europe, the Mediterranean region, the African desert, the grasslands, till I reached the equatorial forests of central Africa. Accomplish all this, and one would have made a geographical traverse halfway across the world.

I laid a ruler across the map, from Vaitolahti south to Africa. The name of a town on the edge of the Sahara attracted me — Timbuktu, near the upper reaches of the river Niger. From there it was not so much farther to the tropical rain-forests of Sierra Leone. To make such a journey half-way round the globe was a feat which appealed to my imagination. It could be done.

Financing such a journey should not prove too difficult, for I had learned how to travel cheaply. I remembered a conversation with Stephen Graham, an author whose books inspired and encouraged me. We were having tea in his flat in Frith Street, Soho, and the books — *The Gentle Art of Tramping*, *A Tramp's Sketches*, and others — stood on a bookshelf by the table.

"If you have a little money and don't mind roughing it and taking casual jobs, then the whole wide world is yours to explore," Graham remarked, when I told him of my ambitions.

I quoted from his own book: " 'The less you carry the more you will see. The less you spend the more you will experience.' I've already proved the truth of that, sir, by starting off with a few pounds in my pocket to cross Finland and Lapland to the Arctic Ocean."

"I wish you success on your next journey," Graham said as I rose to go. "Young people come to me and say, 'How shall I write?' and I generally reply, 'First you must live. Books should not beget books. Life should beget books. Tramping in search of knowledge and experience is a short cut to reality.' "

Fortune favoured me, and when I reached Kirkenes again a job was waiting for me as steward on a ship loaded with iron ore for Middlesbrough; we reached England ten days later. Faced with the problem of earning money to finance my trip to Africa, I looked round for a place where I could live cheaply while writing magazine articles about my experiences in the Arctic. In a newspaper I read an account of an organisation called the "Grith Pioneers", who were running a camp for unemployed men near Fordingbridge, in the New Forest. This seemed the sort of place I was looking for, so I wrote asking if I might join them. Next spring, with some money saved up, I would find some way of getting cheaply by ship to north Africa, and would then try and hitch-hike southward across the Sahara to the river Niger. The winter months spent at a camp for the unemployed would give me time to read books about geography and archaeology; there were several sites in Morocco and the Sahara which required investigation.

Actually, it did not work out quite as I intended. Part of the camp was burnt down, and I lost my typewriter, books, and manuscripts. Then one of my camp-mates stole money from the lot of us, and so I was left with only about ten shillings in the world. I had to start all over again.

Yet in spite of all the difficulties, early next spring (1936) found me off on my travels. I had discovered that it was possible to travel from London to Gibraltar on a Japanese liner for £3; five shillings would pay one's passage to Tangier, across the strait in Morocco. Roads led southward from Tangier to the High Atlas Mountains, and from a desert town called Tiznit convoys of lorries went across the desert by way of the outposts of Tindouf and Taodeni to Timbuktu.

6

THE ROAD TO THE SAHARA

IT was five o'clock in the morning in ancient Marrakech, some weeks later. In the brilliant sunlight of an African dawn I stood by the "Gate of Skulls" and watched the camel caravans come striding into the city. Then, turning my back on the tawny-hued walls of the old Moroccan city, I looked southward. There before me were the mighty peaks of the High Atlas Mountains, towering more than 12,000 feet into the sky. I looked at them spellbound. A few minutes later they vanished, hidden again behind a barrier of cloud. But the sight had been enough for me. It was time for me to be tramping over the mountains to the mysterious walled city of Taroudant, and then to Tiznit, on the desert's edge, where the caravans left for the Niger.

The first part of my journey had been accomplished. Gibraltar had been reached by Japanese liner; Tangier by coasting steamer. Hitch-hiking had taken me from Rabat to the colourful cities of Fez and Meknes; I had walked quite a lot of the way to Marrakech. Living had been cheap. Bread cost twopence a loaf, cheeses fourpence each, strawberries twopence a pound. Once for fourpence I had bought four eggs, two pounds of potatoes, two oranges, and a pound of tomatoes. Haggling with native dealers in local market-places was fun. Red wine was twopence a pint. Lodgings also cost little. Sometimes I slept at French farmhouses, or country inns, or out in the open. Frequently my travelling expenses had amounted to no more than sixpence a day, for I camped out whenever possible, cooking my meals by the side of the road.

Back at the inn where I had left my rucksack, the realisation came that I would not cross the High Atlas Mountains this year: my journey to the Niger was ended. "Civil War in Spanish Morocco. Fighting still in progress," declared the headlines of a newspaper which was thrust into my hand by old Othman, the inn-keeper. Spanish Morocco was the scene of fierce fighting, I learned, and it was expected that the frontiers would be closed in a few hours. As I had just enough money to get back to Tangier by crossing Spanish Morocco, it would be necessary to return now before the frontier was barred to travellers. My ambition to tramp over the mountains was abandoned.

The sound of gunfire rumbling across the tawny Moroccan plain greeted me as I approached the frontier between French and Spanish Morocco. The driver of a big black Renault, a Frenchman named Raoul, whom I had approached for a lift in Casablanca, had agreed to take me with him. He also wanted to reach Tangier before the closing of the frontier. Some hours previously General Franco had flown from the Canary Islands to raise the standard of revolt in Spanish Morocco, but what was actually happening there now nobody knew.

Rabat was full of rumours when we arrived there, but nobody had definite news. A severe bombardment had taken place: Tetuan was in ruins: Arcila was held by the rebels: Larache was being bombed from the air. So said rumour, but, undaunted, we went on. As we drew near the frontier I found myself getting excited. Should we be allowed to pass?

At the military post of Arbaoua soldiers surrounded our car. They kept us waiting a long time, but finally allowed us to proceed "at our own risk and peril". Looking back, I saw the barrier gates crash shut. The frontier was closed, and now there could be no turning back.

Alcazar, first Spanish town beyond the frontier, showed little sign of conflict. Larache, far from being in ruins, appeared to be making merry. But when I stopped to admire a gorgeous display of purple bougainvillea a rifleman came along and reminded me that there was a war on. There were armed men everywhere, work seemed to have stopped, everybody was waiting for something to happen. Some of the soldiers looked very young — mere boys, who regarded the revolution as an excuse for working off their high spirits. The Moorish troops were less friendly; the sight of their grim, unsmiling faces made me hope I should not fall into their hands.

After a long halt we were allowed to proceed till we reached another barricade across the road, where soldiers took away our passports and escorted Raoul to a near-by building. Time passed, and he did not return. I grew worried, not knowing what to do. Finally a squad of Moorish soldiers, armed with rifles and bayonets, surrounded the car and ordered me to get out. Their leader searched me for weapons; then the men fell in around me, and I was taken into the building.

In an inner room I was cross-examined by a fat little Spanish officer, but as he knew no English and I no Spanish, we did not make much progress. There was no sign of Raoul. Finally, the officer gave his task up as a bad job and ordered the Moors to take me away. They thrust me into a small room with a solitary window set high up in one of the stone walls and slammed shut the heavy, iron-barred door. I was a prisoner.

An hour or so went by; then the door opened, my guards reappeared, and they took me back to the officer. Raoul was there, and we were allowed to have a hasty conversation. "They suspect us of being Government supporters," he explained. Apparently, my clothing was partly responsible; my khaki shirt, riding-breeches, and grey "mackinaw" jacket gave me a semi-military appearance.

"Pay attention," commanded the Spanish officer, banging on the table with his fist.

I told him I knew nothing of Spanish politics, that I was an English student travelling across Morocco to learn something of its geography and history. He replied with more unintelligible questions. It was clear he had not understood a word of what I had said.

"Don't get excited," Raoul advised. "They will not shoot us."

We heard the roar of aircraft engines overhead, then firing. The officer sprang up, shouted out orders, and the Moors rushed us back to our cells. A long time passed. My cell door was unlocked, and the guards motioned to me to come out. They escorted me out of the building, where I found the big Renault waiting, with Raoul at the wheel. It seemed we were free to go.

"*Viva* England!" said the soldier, and saluted.

The barrier across the road swung up,

and we headed north. It was long past midnight, and the stars were blazing like lamps in the dark night sky. Like twin searchlights the powerful headlamps of the car probed the dark roadway ahead. Then something happened. Out of the darkness came a flash of rifle-fire, and the windscreen shivered into fragments.

The car lurched, and threatened to plunge headlong into the trees, but Raoul, with a curse, wrenched the wheel round, and by sheer will-power kept the car on the road. We heard the *tack-tack-tack* of a machine-gun, but it suddenly stopped. Men came dashing through the trees, firing as they came. Raoul shouted to me to crouch down on the floor, and though badly shaken and bleeding, he kept the car going. Luckily the person who had fired off that first premature shot had warned us of the ambush, and so we escaped without serious damage.

Jolting and swaying, the car rushed along, with Raoul clinging grimly to the wheel. Behind us we heard the stammer of the machine-gun again, then it stopped, and there was only the deserted roadway. Why it had all happened — an ambush by

Government forces, a misunderstanding on the part of a rebel patrol — we never learned.

At last a river came into view, a bridge, and the frontier. Beyond was Tangier and safety. There was nothing left to do except cross over to Gibraltar and join a Japanese liner returning to England. Some day, perhaps, I would return and complete my journey to the Sahara.

When I got back to Manchester it looked much the same as when I had last seen it. The "dole office" (labour exchange) in Burton Road was as crowded as ever, with long queues of unemployed men waiting their turn to "sign on" for their weekly dole. There was the same atmosphere of quiet despair, of frustration, of hunger and poverty, of being regarded as unwanted by society. The policemen, the hunger marchers, the lines of Blackshirts shouting "Long live Mosley!" the bands of men singing or playing musical instruments in the streets, the beggars, were the same. Nothing had changed.

Conditions *were* improving, I was told. There were now only two million unemployed. Adolf Hitler was adopting a more conciliatory attitude, so it seemed likely the war with Germany would be postponed for another year or two. Even King Edward was having troubles of his own, because he was not to be allowed to marry the woman he wanted. It would be a pity if he had to abdicate.

I swallowed my pride and went back to my former job as assistant in a green-grocer's shop at a wage of a pound a week. I went back to live with my parents in that red-brick "council house" which was so much like all the other millions of similar houses which covered the English country-side like a red rash. My great plans to learn geography and history, to be an explorer and a writer, all seemed to have come to nothing. Other men might become students at Manchester University, get degrees in geography, but not my kind. For us there were only evening classes, at the end of a tiring day's work. Better to forget my silly ideas and remain content to be a shop-assistant, until I asked my boss for a bigger wage and got the sack.

Later a good friend of mine, Gordon Cooper, author of a hundred books, was to sum it up succinctly: "What a man accomplishes in England depends upon which bedroom he was born in. I was born in the right bedroom." He had been born in a big house in Charlotte Square, Edinburgh, and educated at Charterhouse and Edinburgh University. In five years he had spent over £30,000 left him by his grandfather, the editor of *The Scotsman*, doing many things I should like to have done — travelling round the world, meeting interesting people, writing books.

It was not too bad a life, if you were without ambition. One could endure. At twenty-three my life seemed finished, without hope for the future. Sometimes I marvelled at the things I had done — the voyage in the *Herzogin Cecilie*, the expeditions across Lapland to the Polar Sea, my experiences in Morocco. They might have been accomplished by an entirely different person, and not by me.

Something I could never get used to was living in a big city. The miles and miles of housing estates depressed me. They seemed to go on for ever. Living there was mere existence, slightly better than being dead. Maybe it suited some people, but I was the kind of man who needed high mountains to look at, wide seas to cross, great forests to walk through, plenty of space and air and freedom. Otherwise — why be alive? Whenever possible I got out into the countryside — Cheshire, Derbyshire, Staffordshire — staying at youth hostels, exploring the limestone and gritstone uplands of the Peak District. But it was not enough.

One spring day I recalled my ambition to cross the Sahara and reach the rainforests of West Africa. Why not make a second attempt? An article in the *National Geographic Magazine* attracted my attention, for it described the road known as the Route Impériale which the French had built across the Middle and High Atlas Mountains of Morocco to the mysterious Oasis of Tafilalet in the Sahara. Certain paragraphs in the article intrigued me mightily:

. . . There are regions in the Great Atlas where die-hards still maintain their freedom . . . and in the desert spaces of the Sahara, horsemen and cameleers who ride acknowledging no lord. . . . In the cedar forests there is still need for watch and ward. . . . From here on no one may go except in a caravan protected by armoured cars, and this once only in every ten days. . . . Tafilet remains a closed book, we may not enter there.

Once Tafilalet (also spelled Tafilet) had been a separate kingdom from Morocco, and its capital city of Sijjilmassa had been one of the great trade centres of Africa, for it controlled the caravan route from Tangier to the Niger. French troops had occupied the oasis only in 1932, and so far as I could discover, no Englishman had visited the place since Walter Harris, the correspondent for the London *Times*, travelled there in disguise in 1893. I decided to walk to Tafilalet, and be the second Englishman to explore the ruins of ancient Sijjilmassa. I had some money saved up, acquired by writing magazine articles, giving a radio broadcast or two, by mowing lawns and doing other odd jobs. I could look after myself.

It was a month later (June 1937).
I stood beside a stony track gazing up-

ward at a walled Moslem town which crowned the top of a cliff. The town was Moulay Idriss, reputed to be hostile to Christians, who were not allowed inside the walls when the gates were closed at sunset. Moulay Idriss was still one of the most fanatical towns in Morocco, for in its chief mosque was the tomb of that Moulay Idriss, a descendant of the prophet Mohammed, who established Moslem sovereignty in this part of Africa. The rocky heights on which the town stood appeared to be about three hundred feet above me, and the track I was following led straight up the precipice towards the main gate. I was gasping for breath by the time I had climbed to the top.

It was shortly after dawn, and the landscape was flooded with pale-yellow sunlight. The gate-keepers had opened the heavy wooden gates a short time before, and as there was no choice but to go forward I walked through the gateway, out of the brightness of the sunlight, into the cool dimness of the main street of the town. I hurried along over the cobblestones, past the blank-walled, windowless Moorish houses. So early in the morning few people were astir. The road I was following passed right through the town and out the other side, and not till I had emerged from the far gateway did I begin to breathe more easily.

Ahead of me there was a grand view of high mountains reaching skyward, and a wide green valley where herds of black cattle grazed. Shafts of sunlight played hide-and-seek among the hills, and the wind blew fresh and clear. It was an ideal day for walking, so for some hours I strode out across the wide pasture-lands, until increasing hunger compelled me to stop for a meal. A large red building proved to be a communal cattle-shed, where cattle-drovers could stay on their journeys between the mountains and the Atlantic coast. A party of drovers let me use their fire to cook a pan of porridge, and after eating this I lay down on my cape and slept until late afternoon.

Fifteen days previously I had set out from Sale, the old Moorish city by the Atlantic (reached by train from Tangier), and had walked inland. My destination was Fez, the ancient capital city of Morocco. So far my journey had been interesting but unexciting, walking by day, sleeping at little country inns or camping by the roadside at nights. I did not anticipate any serious difficulties until I began the crossing of the Atlas Mountains. Morocco, I had already discovered, was really two distinct countries. The northern part of the country across which I was walking now was the new Morocco created by the French, with modern towns, hotels, roads, amenities; south of the Atlas Mountains was old Morocco, little touched by modern civilisation, where men lived much as their forefathers had done in the days of Abraham. There the solitary wanderer was liable to be killed on the spot to the greater glory of Allah, and great lords still lived in medieval fashion, in strong castles, surrounded by private armies of fighting-men. The "Zone of Insecurity" the French authorities termed the southern part of Morocco, and permission to enter it was granted to civilian travellers grudgingly.

Tramping onward towards the mountains, later that afternoon, I came to a place where the track divided. Not knowing which way to go, I asked a passing shepherd, and he pointed to the right-hand branch. It led me upward and upward, into wilder and wilder country. I was seeking a small country inn, where I had been assured I could secure accommodation for the night, but this did not seem to me to be the right sort of place to find an inn. Then the track came to an end, and I found myself standing on a mountain spur, with empty space on three sides. There was no sign of an inn — only the high walls and gates of the stronghold of the Kaid (or Lord) of Beni Amar.

The shadows of approaching night were filling the deep valleys below, so I went forward and knocked on the gate with my umbrella. A watchman in a tower above called out to me, and then the gate was opened slightly, and two burly men with black beards, armed with old-fashioned guns, scrutinised me and asked my business. They did not understand my explanation, but orders concerning me must have been already given by someone in authority, for I was allowed to enter. A bespectacled youth who spoke French fluently — Abdeslem Ben Mohammed Ba Azizi by name — took me to meet the Kaid.

The space inside the walls of this mountain stronghold was filled with big crumbling blocks of buildings, separated by narrow, cobblestoned streets. The streets were ankle-deep in dung and rotting refuse and filled with a stink which was almost visible. There were people everywhere — men driving donkeys, sheep, and goats, women carrying earthenware jars or petrol-tins filled with water, hordes of children with nothing better to do than stare at me. It was like stepping back into the Middle Ages — yet Ba Azizi had only recently returned from Paris, where he had been inspecting motor-lorries with a view to starting a haulage business.

The Kaid greeted me courteously, and invited me to be seated. A servant appeared with a tray containing glasses of mint tea, and when this had been consumed the Kaid said that I would be provided with food and lodging for the night, and guides who would escort me to the road to Fez in the morning. He was a dignified old man, with a grim face, and was dressed in a long white robe. The interview took place on a stone-paved space in front of his white-walled house; afterwards a servant conducted me to the guest chamber, where I spent the night on a strip of matting, with a few score fleas for company.

Next morning, after I had breakfasted on coffee, freshly baked bread, and butter, Ba Azizi escorted me back to the gate. Three of the Kaid's retainers who were to act as my guides were waiting for me. Sight of these tough-looking, hard-faced individuals did not inspire me with confidence. We started off in the opposite direction to that I expected, but, knowing how the track twisted and turned, I did not argue, expecting that we should reach the motor-road to Fez lower down. When we plunged into wilder and yet wilder country, however, with no sign of the highway I wanted, I became uneasy.

"Is this the way to Fez?" I asked my guides, and they promptly replied: "Yes — to Fez." Reasoning that they must know the lie of the land better than I did, I plodded on.

At last we came to a motor-road, and with broad grins my three villains pointed at it triumphantly. Very soon my sense of uneasiness returned; there could be no doubt at all now that we were travelling *away* from Fez. My guides were deliberately leading me astray. Not being certain of my whereabouts, I decided to wait a while before demanding an explanation, but when they turned down a narrow path leading towards a tangle of jagged mountain-peaks I halted and refused to follow. The sinister growl in the leader's voice as he snarled "Come!" was not at all reassuring.

Presently a turn in the road told me exactly where I was, for there in the distance was visible the building where I had eaten with the cattle-drovers the day before, and a white kilometre-post clearly stating the fact that instead of going towards Fez I was returning to the holy city of Moulay Idriss. It was time for a show-down, so I halted once more and said to my guides, "You have brought me the wrong way. Fez is not in this direction — it lies over yonder."

Without giving them time to argue I turned on my heel and walked away. Next instant there came the sound of running feet, and then a brawny hand grabbed my shoulder and pulled me round. The three of them barred my way, obviously determined that I should not go to Fez. If I had been uneasy before I now felt downright frightened, but, putting on a bold front, I attempted to push past them. Instantly one man seized my rucksack, another my cape. I did the only thing possible, and punched the leader on the chin, sending him staggering. At once all three sprang at me.

In fiction one Englishman is supposed to be the equal of three "natives", but in actual fact I got the worst of that fight. Remembering the old adage, "He who fights and runs away . . .", I kicked two of them on the shins with my heavy boots, and then ran off down the road. I looked helplessly about me, but there was only the desolate valley devoid of life. I had the odd feeling that this sort of thing happened only in story-books, not in real life, that it could not really be happening — *but it was.*

My three companions made no attempt to follow me, and I soon discovered why. A peculiar whistling call sounded across the valley, and I looked round to see a group of Berber horsemen riding towards me. They spread out in a semicircle, cutting off my retreat, and then came charging down upon me. Not wishing to be cut down by their horses' hooves, I held up my hands in token of surrender. In silence they shepherded me back to where my three guides were waiting. We resumed our journey.

For hour after hour we travelled over a scorched land, under the blazing sun. Parched with thirst and almost dead-beat, I saw once more the walls and gates of Moulay Idriss crowning the hilltop in front of me. To my surprise my companions took me to a French military post not far away, and there the whole misunderstanding was explained. It appeared that the Kaid of Beni Amar had suspected me of being a German spy from Spanish Morocco — my khaki shirt and shorts were to blame for his getting that idea — and he had instructed his men to take me to the French military authorities at Moulay Idriss. As they had been unable to explain this to me, they had pretended to guide me to the road to Fez. It had been a misunderstanding on both sides. They imagined me to be a spy, while I feared I had fallen into the hands of brigands.

The French authorities were quickly satisfied that I was harmless, and I was free to continue my journey — which meant walking back along that hot, desolate mountain valley for yet a third time!

With engines labouring, brakes screeching, enveloped in a cloud of choking, blinding dust, the convoy of heavily laden lorries was crossing the High Atlas Mountains by the seven-thousand-foot Telrhemt Pass. On either side of the road we could see towering mountain-peaks showing starkly against the cloudless blue sky. Rising over all was the giant peak of Djebel Ayachi, long reckoned as the highest mountain in North Africa. "The Mother of Water", as the Berbers termed the mountain, was estimated to reach about fourteen thousand feet in height, and remained snow-covered in summer.

The road we were following was a memorable one. For centuries it had been known as "The Imperial Road", and along it, from times immemorial, caravans had journeyed from Tangier to the river Niger. Along this road the French colonial army had fought its way to conquer the great Saharan oasis of Tafilalet, and until 1934 caravans had been able to pass along it only at ten-day intervals, and then only if protected by armoured cars and cavalry patrols. It was the Khyber Pass of Morocco.

My notebook contained my impressions of a journey along this road:

Along it in days gone by had come the great caravans from Timbuktu, thousands of camels laden with gold, slaves, ostrich feathers, and ivory, guarded by companies of archers, spearmen, and swordsmen, ever watchful for attacks by the veiled fighting men of the central desert. Along it from out of the southern deserts, had come great armies of fanatical men, filled with the lust to convert the world to the Moslem faith, their leaders bent upon conquering Morocco and making themselves Rulers of the Faithful (and Sultans of Morocco, in due course, many of them *did* become).

Along this road marched the French Army to complete the conquest of Morocco and bestow the benefits of civilisation upon the peoples of the Sahara — whether they wanted them or not. Along this road they had all passed: men of the French Foreign Legion striving to bring civilisation and men of the desert tribes who strove with equal energy to prevent its coming. White explorers such as Walter Harris and René Caille, travelling in disguise and often in danger of their lives. Sultans and would-be sultans, great lords and desert sheiks, traders, priests, bandits, and beggars.*

I might have added — *and now me.*
I had walked south from Fez for fifteen days, into a land where forts crowned the hilltops and men carried rifles as a matter of course. Halted at the fort of Itzer by its young French commander, I was informed that the official in Fez who had given me permission to enter the "Zone of Insecurity" had exceeded his authority. Permission would be granted for me to continue my journey south; the crossing of the High Atlas must be made by convoy, since the country was not considered suitable for walking tours just yet.

"One can yet die very quickly in these mountains," the lorry-driver explained. "There was a friend of mine, you understand, who was instructed to convey a very

* *The Land of Mud Castles*, by Jim Ingram (John Long, 1952).

important personage — a colonel of the army — along the road in his *camion*. My friend was driving fast, for one is not anxious to remain for long in the mountain-passes. It was near the settlement of Foum Kheneg — we shall pass there later on — that my friend felt the colonel's head resting on his shoulder, as though asleep. But when he looked again he saw that there was a bullet-hole in the colonel's head. Ah, yes, my friend, the Berber tribesmen who live alongside this road are good shots."

At a height of seven thousand feet a mountain-spur blocked the way so completely that I thought we had come to the end of the road. The black mouth of a tunnel gaped in the grey rock wall. This, I knew, was the famous "Tunnel of the Legion", and I looked out to read the proud inscription carved over the entrance: "THE MOUNTAIN BARRED THE WAY: THE ORDER WAS GIVEN TO PASS: THE LEGION CARRIED IT OUT." The French Foreign Legion had constructed most of the Imperial Road, and along it, as the tides of war ebbed and flowed, had moved the men and munitions without which the conquest of the north-western Sahara would have been impossible. Even now it was the lifeline by means of which the French Colonial Army maintained its hold on the desert outposts to the south.

We emerged from the tunnel into a landscape of breathtaking cliffs and canyons, with a foaming river rushing along perhaps a thousand feet below. The road now followed the valley of the river Ziz, that strange African stream which, rising amid the snows of the High Atlas peaks, is fated never to reach the sea, for its waters die away in a salt marsh amid the thirsty desert sands. This great gorge is indeed Morocco's Khyber Pass; a few hostile riflemen hidden among the rocks could render the road impassable. French forts appeared at long intervals, protected by crenellated walls and barbed-wire entanglements. At one of these we stopped for a drink, and to stretch our legs.

The road continued through a series of terrific gorges, walled in by blood-red cliffs half a mile high, and defended at strategic points by more forts and machine-guns. For twenty miles a continuous line of *postes* and watchtowers guarded the way to the desert, whose hot breath one could already feel. My impression was that this was Africa untamed, and I knew now why it had taken the French no less than eighteen years of fighting to conquer the southern oases.

The great defile of the Ziz Gorge ended at last, and there before us stretched the Sahara. It appeared as a vast tawny-coloured plain stretching into infinity. This was not a desert of great sand-dunes, such as I had expected, but a stony desert, surfaced with boulders and gravel. The heat, especially when one was crouched on a seat in the cab of a big lorry, was like that of an oven. After passing a waterhole called the Blue Pool, where twenty thousand tribesmen once gave battle to the French, we arrived at the settlement of Ksar es Souk, headquarters of the autonomous territory of Tafilalet.

Official permission having been received for me to continue southward to Tafilalet Oasis, I started off on foot the next day. Away from the fast-flowing river Ziz the road led across a yellow sandstone desert, an ochre-tinted plain stretching to the horizon. Beyond was a region of sand-dunes, looking just like a typical desert scene one sees in films of the Sahara. The dunes stretched away in every direction like the waves of the sea. Travelling across this desert gave one the impression of being far out at sea, with the scattered clumps of palm-trees appearing like islands on the wave-swept surface. Among the dunes it felt hotter than ever.

A wind arose from out of nowhere, and I found myself engulfed in a sandstorm. A blinding, stinging, choking mass of whirling sand came sweeping over the desert. The air was filled with sand, so that it was like trying to walk through a wall. This was frightening, if what I had read about sand-storms was true, and it was with much relief that I saw a big lorry approaching me along the road. The driver stopped long enough for me to scramble up on to the seat beside him, then revved up his engine, and drove steadily on.

Some time later we left the region of sand-dunes behind and entered what seemed to be a veritable forest of palm-trees. Ahead of us appeared the battlements of a city wall, and a few minutes later we entered the desert outpost of Erfoud. This was a purely African city, with architecture suggestive of the Sudan. The market-place was a wide, colonnaded structure, surrounded by rectangular blocks of flat-roofed, blank-walled buildings, some surmounted by domes constructed of dried mud. I saw carpets, pottery, rugs, and leatherwork displayed for sale.

Early next morning I started southward again. The yellow-tinted desert was smooth, hard, and level — excellent for walking. The air was very hot, but I experienced no discomfort, and continued to stride steadily southward for mile after mile. There was no road, as the term is understood in civilised countries, but merely a few marks made by wheels and hooves on the bare expanse. Part of the way I was accompanied by a garrulous desert boy and an old man with a long white beard.

After I had been walking for several hours a green line showed up ahead, the outer fringe of the palm forests. Tafilalet Oasis was reached at last, and my ambition to be the second Englishman to reach the place after Walter Harris of *The Times* was now realised. Then the ruins of buildings, half buried in the sand, appeared on either side. I saw crumbling walls and gateways, the remains of towers, a mosque, and other buildings. My archaeologist's instinct was roused at the sight of these ruins, for I knew that they were all that remained of one of north Africa's greatest cities, Sijjilmassa, which had been the capital of Tafilalet for hundreds of years. Of the once-mighty Saharan capital only acres of crumbling ruins stretching along the river Ziz now remain.

The palm forests grew thicker. In an open space appeared the walls of two powerful fortresses. On one side was a yellow-tinted stronghold, the castle of Belgacem N'Gadi, the Berber chieftain, who had made the last stand against the French forces until the final battles which brought the conquest of Morocco to an end in 1934. Artillery and aircraft had blasted holes in the walls of N'Gadi's stronghold, but this was now past history, and the inhabitants appeared to have settled down to peaceful ways.

The other building was Fort Rissani, the headquarters of the governor of Tafilalet. This magenta-tinted fortress had a high turreted gateway and high towers set at the angles of the walls, and several yellow-painted armoured cars were drawn up outside. Native riflemen were guarding the gate when I walked up and asked permission to enter. One of them escorted me inside the fortress, and took me into an office. A man came towards me, dressed in baggy trousers, loose jacket, and sandals, and introduced himself as Captain Henri Brissaud Désmaillet, commander of the fort and governor of the territory south of the Atlas Mountains.

"It is reported that you have walked here from Rabat," he said, after greeting me in excellent English. "That is, save for those occasions when we soldiery have insisted that you travel by motor-vehicle for your health's sake." He smiled. "Regard yourself as our guest. This evening, if you desire it, I will take you for a run across the desert in my new car. You will find much of interest here to investigate."

I went to sleep that night feeling that my dreams were not so impossible after all.

Some weeks later, under the burning July sun, I stood on the rocky banks of a dried-up river in south Morocco. The river was the Dra, and the land beyond was the little-known, little-visited territory of Mauretania. All about me, as far as one could see, was the vast tawny expanse of the Sahara. Oases, widely separated, marked my route there.

Grouped in a line near the river-bank were a number of heavily loaded lorries; their drivers stood about on the sand, smoking and chatting. Where the track led down to the riverbed were three or four yellow-turreted armoured cars, and beside these stood men of the French Foreign Legion. A little distance away a squadron of blue-cloaked Mokhazni, or native cavalrymen, waited for orders. This was the convoy which would shortly depart for the desert outpost of Tindouf on the caravan route to the south. I hoped to accompany it.

Nearly two years had passed since I had acquired the ambition to make a traverse of the world's climatic regions, from the polar ice to the tropical rain-forest of Africa. On this, my second attempt, I hoped to be more successful.

Again I was to be frustrated; I was not to reach the equatorial forests that year. The officer in charge of the convoy made this plain. He was a quick-tempered French major, and he promptly refused to grant me permission to go south to Tindouf with the caravan.

"No — no — no! It would be madness! My superiors would never permit it," he exclaimed. "You must go back!"

"I have come here from Tafilalet Oasis," was my reply. "To get there I walked five hundred miles from Rabat. I can walk five hundred more."

The major looked at me, then pointed to the armoured cars and the waiting cavalry-men.

"We are not here for a pleasure trip, my friend, but because there are those among the Blue Moors who do not like the look of our faces," he explained, "so we must teach them a lesson in manners. Not until we have completed that task can any travellers be allowed to go south by this route. But if you have made the desert crossing from Tafilalet to this place, then you have already done a great deal. Now I order you to return to Tiznit on the lorry which is leaving here in half an hour's time."

Argument was useless. I must accept defeat. If I could not reach central Africa overland, then perhaps I could get there by sea, by taking ship to Dakar or Accra, and then travelling inland. I would get there somehow, some day. Perhaps it had been a crazy venture, anyway, to imagine I could plunge southward across the world's biggest desert, without proper equipment or preparation. To some persons it might have appeared suicide.

Already I had accomplished a very worthwhile journey. I had stayed at forts of the French Foreign Legion and watched the desert tribes come in to make their submission. I had seen walled cities where daily the drums proclaimed the glory of the Sultan, and where ever-watchful riflemen guarded the gates against the attacks of the veiled fighting-men of the central desert. Life had been good.

Maybe I had not been able to get to university, but I had learned some geography.

The *world* was still *my* university!

It may be asked how I managed to accomplish all these difficult journeys — to the Arctic, the Sahara, and others not described here, to Spain, Yugoslavia — when I was so badly handicapped by short-sightedness and a diseased hip. Yet I *did* accomplish them, though it was not easy. I suppose it was a matter of knowing what I wanted and being determined to get it in spite of every obstacle. I wanted more than anything in the world to travel across little-known countries and learn something about their geography and history. If I could do that I was prepared to endure anything — pain, hunger, loneliness, hostility, ridicule, to die, if necessary. Nothing else mattered.

Short-sightedness nearly caused my death several times. After operations for cataract one should wear thick-lensed spectacles to correct the distortion caused by the removal of the lens of your eye. I hated wearing glasses, and it was years before I would wear mine. Nobody bothered. By screwing up my eyes and staring long enough I could focus upon objects until eventually I could tell what they were. I could see a mountain if it was big enough. I have told how, trying to cross a rushing mountain river in Lapland, by hopping from one stone to another, I fell into the water and was nearly swept to my death over a waterfall. Even then I did not start wearing those hateful glasses!

At Meknes, in Morocco, I decided to call upon a member of the French Foreign Legion, who was stationed at the local depot. You might imagine that it was not possible for even the most short-sighted person to miss a fort, complete with gateway and sentries on guard-duty, but I did, and went blundering on until I discovered myself in the middle of the regimental cabbage-patch! It was only when I heard the voice of the commanding officer, declaiming in French about the imbecile behaviour of a certain drunken civilian, that I realised he was talking about me. But still I did not consider it time to start wearing glasses!

Once, crossing the High Atlas Mountains by the Pass of Tizi n'Test, I developed such spasms of pain in my leg that I could have lain down and cried. Later, in the Black Mountains of southern Yugoslavia, my hip hurt so much that it was all I could do to grit my teeth and trudge on. The truth is, I suppose, that we can endure far more pain that we give ourselves credit for. In the Arctic forests or amid the Saharan sands one simply must keep going, pain or no pain. For when it comes to the actual point where death stares you in the face, from somewhere comes the will-power to carry you that little bit farther. Yet there were moments when even courage failed me, and I felt I had reached the end of things.

7

I GO BACK TO SCHOOL

A STRONG smell of chocolate greeted me as I walked down the winding lane to Fircroft College; there was no doubt that I was in Bournville, a place made familiar through the medium of Cadbury's advertisements. To visualise my first sight of the college, that sunny September day in 1937, think of a large, red-brick Victorian house, with other, more modern buildings adjoining it, half hidden by foliage. I looked at the buildings with expectation, for I had come to spend a year there as a student. My last camping-place had been by the river Dra, on the southern frontier of Morocco; it had been a long journey from there to Bournville, by way of Tiznit, Agadir, Casablanca, Gibraltar, London.

In the wide hallway of the college a group of men stood talking; they nodded to me in friendly fashion when I slung my heavy rucksack on to the floor and stared about me. Economics, philosophy, history, geography, politics, and government — to learn something about these subjects I was prepared to give up my wandering life for a while. My future colleagues, I observed, were a cosmopolitan crowd, for as well as English and Welsh there were Germans, Danes, Norwegians, Austrians, even a solitary Icelander.

How does an unemployed man, without money or influence, set about going to college? In a magazine I had read about Fircroft, which provided accommodation and tuition in various subjects, for working-class students. There were many subjects about which I was ill informed — economics, political theory, social history, law and government, subjects which were a key to help me interpret the facts collected during my wanderings. So, before leaving for my trip to the Sahara, I had written a twelve-page letter to Mr. Wulstan Lee, Warden of Fircroft, telling him about myself, my ambitions, my achievements. The result had been a bursary entitling me to spend a year studying at the college. Manchester Education Committee granted me fifty pounds to cover additional expenses.

The idea of adults going back to school was no novelty to me, for though in Britain the majority of working-men cease their education at school-leaving age, in the Scandinavian countries I had met members of adult schools and envied them their opportunities of improving their education. It had been a pleasing discovery to learn that similar colleges existed in England. Fircroft did not provide vocational training, but aimed at giving men who had been working since they left school an opportunity of withdrawing from industry for a time to study subjects which, though they might not help one to earn money, did broaden a man's outlook and make a better citizen of him.

The men standing in the hallway all looked such a neatly dressed, respectable, reliable group that it was hard to realise that many of them were miners, engineers, seamen, farm-labourers. Like myself, they had come to Fircroft to study some of the subjects which they had been denied the opportunity of learning earlier. Looking at them, I realised that I was no longer the roughneck who had tramped alone across a dozen wild countries, one man against the world; now I too must learn to become a respectable member of society, and fit in. Apart from the second-hand suit I was wearing and a rucksack containing some books, papers, underwear, and a clean shirt, my worldly possessions comprised five one pound notes with which to pay sundry expenses during the next three months.

Students at Fircroft shared rooms, and the one which I was to occupy during the coming year proved to be a light, airy apartment with a window overlooking the winding, tree-bordered lane and a green hillside beyond. Two iron bedsteads, two chests of drawers, two writing-tables, two chairs, several pictures of no particular artistic merit, completed the furnishings. My room-mate, when he arrived, proved to be a Norwegian, Trygve Storas, a school-teacher from Alvik, by Hardanger Fjord. He was a tall, softly spoken, gentle man, and we got on well together. After the midday meal I used to lie down for a time to rest my eyes, and would listen to Trygve read from one of H. V. Morton's books, to test his pronunciation of English words.

Fircroft had been founded in 1909 as a place of study for adult workers by George Cadbury and Tom Bryan; the latter became its first warden. The two had been impressed by the Danish high schools, and considered how a college for working-men could be founded in England. It was the function of Fircroft to demonstrate the value of residential colleges as part of the system of adult education, to enlarge men's sympathies, while everything — curriculum, modes of tuition, arrangements for board and lodging — was to be simple and informal.

The teaching at Fircroft was designed to help the working-man as a citizen, to give him guidance in the study of the humanities — literature, history, economics, and so on — in which, it was considered, he had as much right to be interested as anybody else. There was no written examination for admission, and the students were not necessarily those who were most advanced in the ordinary sense of the word; they had to show they possessed certain definite interests. It was not, the two founders were at pains to explain, a matter of fostering a working-class culture separate from, and opposed to, the culture of others; still less of giving to working-men an education considered appropriate to their station life, but rather of helping men to realise the value of their own experiences and the contribution which they could make to society as a whole.

Fircroft, I now discovered, was a member of a group of colleges, nine in number, known as the Selly Oak Colleges, which had some two hundred and fifty students in residence. The aims of each college were distinct and independent; thus Fircroft specialised in economics and literature, Avoncroft in subjects associated with agriculture, Woodbrooke gave prominence to the activities of the Society of Friends; the other colleges were devoted to theological and missionary training. Each college stood in its own grounds and had its own corporate life, but all were linked by a central council, and students could attend lectures at any college or special courses at Birmingham University.

There were four groups of studies

available at the colleges: (1) Social and Economic Studies, including international relations; (2) Literature, Art, and Drama; (3) The Literary and Historical Study of the Bible; (4) Philosophical Studies. My own choice included economics and its theory, history and geography, psychology, and philosophy. When I discovered that written work relating to each subject had to be handed in to one's personal tutor each week I was glad I had not attempted more. When not attending lectures students were expected to devote their time to private study, and at the end of each term one had to produce an essay on some special aspect of one's chief subject. Thus my first essay dealt with the history of the Hudson's Bay Company, to illustrate the development of the joint-stock company. Each student had to take it in turn to act as orderly, to wait at table, serve meals, and wash dishes.

One lecture still sticks in my mind, and is worth describing because it was typical of the way lectures were conducted at Fircroft.

Three of us hurried into the lecture-room that morning conscious that we were nearly late for the start of a lecture on modern philosophy by Dr. H. G. Wood. We found the other students already seated at their desks, and an animated discussion in progress concerning the respective merits of Arsenal and Manchester City. Three students had gone into a huddle in front of the blackboard, demonstrating the correct technique for passing a ball to goal. At the back of the room the Communists and the Socialists were arguing abstruse points of ideology as usual, and as usual the Austrians and the Germans were each accusing the other of being the cause of Hitler's rise to power.

It was the commencement of a normal lecture period at Fircroft.

Before the lecturer arrives take a look around, for you will not see students like these at an ordinary college. Their average age is higher, and what they may lack in book-learning they more than make up for in practical experience. They have enough knowledge to correct a lecturer when he makes a wrong point, for some of them have helped make contemporary history. Look! There is Heinrich Müller, German trade-union leader, a huge figure of a man six feet or so high and as broad-shouldered as an ox; he has the strength of a bull and the kindest heart imaginable. (Three years later, to escape from a German concentration camp he fled to Denmark, and started a chicken farm; later, when the Nazis over-ran Denmark, he was to escape again by swimming across the Sound to Sweden, to start life as a lumberjack.) Beside Heinrich sits my friend Bob, tall and wiry, with a forthright manner and a head of flaming copper-coloured hair. Bob was an engineer, but he gave up this job because he refused to make guns for a future war. It was he who, when I jokingly remarked that I was too poor to buy something I needed, waited until we were alone and then offered to lend me the money. Good old Bob!

Look! There is Sigurd Jannssen, young, blond, boyish-looking, from a farm in Iceland: Albert King, who worked at a Bristol post-office; Alan, a curate, who fears most of us are heading for perdition (wherever that is!). Ole Braevold is from Norway, Albert Data from Denmark, Strasser, a trade-union leader from Austria; Noel was a ship's wireless operator, Bickerstaffe and Watchman were colliers. All these men have either been granted bursaries, or had the year's fees paid for them by their trade union, co-operative society, adult school, or other educational organisation. A few students work at Cadbury's factory, and attend lectures on certain days of the week. Other students come from the Quaker College of Woodbrooke.

The door opens, and Dr. Wood enters. He gives us all the once-over, and comments sardonically about the fug created by somebody's pipe. This observation is allowed to go unchallenged, for we all like Dr. Wood, who is small and bird-like, and who has a droll manner of speech. His is the difficult task of instilling into our thick skulls the elements of ancient and modern philosophy, and, after working our way up from the Greeks and then through Descartes and Spinoza, we are now getting our teeth into Karl Marx. In spite of the fact that this gentleman has been dead for half a century, many of the students can work themselves into a frenzy whenever his name is mentioned, and the wise ones are those who steer clear of the interminable arguments which ensue.

Come to think of it, there must be a number of men here who have witnessed more exciting expositions of Marxism behind the barricades of European cities.

"Now that the atmosphere has cleared somewhat, gentlemen," Dr. Wood observes, "we will examine Chapter Five of *The Introduction to Philosophy*. There is no need for me to dwell upon the preceding material, as I have no doubt you have all grasped its implications. Now, concerning Chapter Five, I think we can agree upon the following conclusions . . ."

He launches into a long-winded discourse, which I, for one, find almost completely unintelligible. There are blank looks upon the faces of the men about me also. The silence lasts for fully five minutes while we slowly digest his remarks, and then the silence is broken by a loud, penetrating voice which says, "You don't know what you are talking about!"

The voice is that of Isaac, a London Jew, with a keen brain full of unco-ordinated knowledge, and an aversion to work. Isaac is small and burly and bald, and seems to know everything — except how to stop talking. One of his chief delights is to ask lecturers questions and then get them tied up in knots when they attempt to explain.

"Wh-what's that?" stammers Dr. Wood, at a loss because his fine discourse has suddenly been cut short.

"What I just said," Isaac persists, ignoring the scowls of the men about him. "How can you attempt to explain Marxism when you begin with the conviction that Marx could not possibly be right?"

"But personal convictions have nothing to do . . ." Dr. Wood begins again, when Isaac cuts him short a second time.

"That's just it — the academic mind again — nibbling at the dry bones of a subject and missing its real implications. You people want to come down from your ivory towers and get your feet on solid ground. Think of events in Russia, Spain, Czechoslovakia. It might happen here."

Once Isaac starts on his favourite hobby-horse he does not know when to stop, so the only thing is to be brutal.

"Shut up, Isaac!" I say, being a crude outlander with no manners. "You'd argue the hind legs off a donkey." Then to Dr. Wood: "This matter of surplus value —

I don't get it. If you could just explain . . ."

Dr. Wood, grateful for my intervention, proceeds to explain the point which puzzles me, and the lecture continues in a more or less orderly fashion. From which it may be gathered that life at Fircroft differed perhaps from life in an ordinary college. Can one smoke or argue or flatly contradict lecturers in public schools or universities, I wonder?

It was a very pleasant life, my year at Fircroft, with so many things to do, so many new experiences to sample. I loved to saunter through the college grounds and see the sunlight glowing on the lawns and trees, and listen to the carillon on Bournville Green chiming the hours, or sit in cosy chairs around the fire in the common-room, chatting with friends. How many wordy battles that common-room witnessed, and how many friendships were born there! One cannot estimate in money the value to a man of a year at Fircroft; the good it does stays with him all his life. And what a lucky city is Birmingham to have the wooded Clent and Lickey Hills on its doorsteps, so that one had only to journey to the end of the tram-tracks to find fresh green woods and hills.

Money to maintain us during the Christmas holidays was earned by working as amateur postmen. I doubt if ever again Bournville post-office witnessed such sights as it beheld that Christmas. There was myself, perched on a high stool, with an enormous mound of letters piled on the bench in front of me, rapidly flicking them into any one of sixty-four pigeonholes, while behind me Wilfred the Welshman stood at the counter going *bang-bang-bang* with the date-stamp, so that his arm bounced up and down as though he suffered from St. Vitus's dance. In the corner of the room Eddie was thrusting bundles of letters into mailbags and sealing them, and Isaac — well, Isaac sat on the edge of the sorting-bin and entertained us by reading out messages scribbled on the backs of Christmas-cards.

"Can you make anything of this card?" I asked Wilfred, pitching it over to him. "It looks like a cipher message."

He grinned. "It is a list of the numbers of the hymns for the parson to give out next Sunday. But Isaac has added them together, multiplied them, found the square root, worked it all out to three places of decimals, and what the original numbers were is now a complete mystery."

"It will give parson something to do in his spare time," said I heartlessly. "Why, look, here is a card from our fellow-student Albert at Bristol post office — and it is addressed to us: 'Hello, chums, what does it feel like to be doing a bit of honest toil for a change?'"

"And by an odd coincidence here is a card from Albert to his girl-friend in Bournville," Wilfred commented. "Give me that pencil and I will add a postscript: 'PS Hey, love, ask him about that other girl he has been meeting in Elm Road.'"

"Chuck it!" I said. "Albert will have the very devil of a job explaining it to her next time they meet."

"It's too late now," Wilfred replied. "It's in the bag."

That evening the postmaster gave me a mailbag, an arm-band, and a key, and told me to go and empty the post-box outside the main gate of Cadbury's factory. It was getting dark when I arrived, and a gentle rain was falling. Could I get that pillar-box to open? I could not. I twisted the key in all directions, I shoved and pushed and cursed, but the post-box door remained closed. Nothing I did would induce it to open. All the small boys in creation suddenly appeared as if from nowhere and stood round me in a ring, making such useful comments as "Can't yer get it open, mister?" and workers coming out of the factory eyed me suspiciously, and the rain trickled down the back of my neck.

From somewhere near-by came the measured tread of a policeman hurrying to investigate matters. I wondered whether to ask him for help, or whether to take the pillar-box back to the post-office with me (tucked under my arm), and at that moment my pal Wilfred arrived on the scene. The Postmaster had given me up for lost, and sent out a patrol to look for me. Was I glad to see Wilfred! He tried, and I tried, but the door stuck fast; then suddenly it shot open and hundreds of letters all tumbled out on to the wet pavement. We gathered them up hastily and stuffed them into my bag, while the policeman stood and looked at us, as if considering which breach of the regulations we might be charged with. Abashed, I slunk away from there as quickly as possible.

My room-mate during the second term at Fircroft was a tall, solidly built, confident man named Wills (a name I associated with tobacco), who had worked in a tin-mine in Malaya and also been an air pilot, before coming to Fircroft to study social science. I envied his public-school manner of calm self-possession and authority; he proved to be a friendly, helpful person with none of the patronising manner which his class often exhibit towards working people. During the eleven weeks we shared that room together I cannot recall a single disagreement.

I sometimes reflected that there was something about Fircroft which set it apart from other colleges, something which bred an aggressive spirit among its students, making them inclined to indulge in flamboyant and dramatic gestures, so that to local people they often appeared more bumptious and cocky than was really the case. Whatever leanings a man had towards extremes of opinion seemed to become more exaggerated here. Sometimes it needed only a chance word or phrase, uttered during a discussion in the common-room, to strike a spark that roused the bitterness of the angry young men of our generation.

A chance remark by Wills once struck fire out of my friend Wilfred. Wilfred had the Welshman's capacity for sudden transition from exuberance to melancholy, the Welsh gift of brilliant but often inconsistent rhetoric. He was always ready to champion any cause, or help a lame dog over a stile. One might be infuriated by his actions, but never bored.

"How can your kind know anything about our kind?" Wilfred demanded. "We are the disinherited. We ought to share in the wealth and leisure and opportunities which modern economic organisation could provide for everybody, but we don't get the chance. As long as we are content to keep our places and do as our masters say, then we are considered good fellows, deserving of a pat on the back, but if we get ideas above our station, if we demand equal opportunities with public-school and university men, then we are laughed at." He laughed moodily. "Maybe it would be better if they could breed workers with no brains at all, willing to do their jobs and live like contented cows."

Once I had experienced such fierce resentments myself, but now, after several years wandering alone across wild countries, I wondered whether such an attitude might not be unreasonable. Going to public school or university did not necessarily provide you with a soft job for life, I knew; public-school men I had met had done their share of hard, dirty work and had to suffer similar disappointments and indifference as I had.

I remembered some words spoken to me by Richard Perry, author of *Lundy, Isle of Puffins, A Naturalist on Lindisfarne,* and other books about bird life, whom I had encountered while working on a farm on Holy Island, off the coast of Northumberland.

"I know it must be heart-breaking for a working-man to be unemployed for a long time, especially if he wants to make something of his life," Perry declared, "but have you ever considered the plight of the public-school man in the same situation?

Not all of us have rich relatives to support us, you know. You will find that despite his educational advantages the public-school man is often no better off than the youth who left school at fourteen.

"Take my own case," he continued. "I wanted to study birds and write books about them. But when I left Cambridge the only job I could get was selling ladies' stockings, and I only stuck it for two days. I was unemployed for three years. So don't imagine that the working class is the only one which suffers."

Finally, he had taken a job as shepherd on a farm in the Scottish Highlands, in order to have the opportunity of following the pursuit he really desired — to study the behaviour of wild birds.

This brief sketch of life at Fircroft cannot be concluded without reference to a most important topic — wash-day. Those students who could not afford to pay laundry bills washed their own clothes in the college's wash-house, and what a scene of activity this place appeared towards weekend, when most men needed a clean shirt or trousers pressing! There, in an atmosphere of steam and soap-suds and hot water, husky young fellows who were probably quite useful in a machine-shop or at the coal-face could be seen solemnly thumping away with a flat-iron, muttering sundry oaths about the appearance of scorch-marks on their one remaining decent shirt, while other young men, shirt-sleeves rolled up, would be rubbing away at various garments in the wash-tub and making caustic comments about their inability to get their "smalls" as white as they wished. Should one boil clothes or only steep them ? Were the various washing powders and soap-flakes as good as the advertisements made them out to be ? How could one prevent woollens from shrinking ? Week after week these same questions were bandied about in the college wash-house.

Socks were the cause of continual heart-burning, for these useful items of apparel seemed to possess an inherent faculty for acquiring holes, and unless one was handy with a darning-needle it was necessary to be acquainted with some person capable of eliminating holes in socks. The more personable or more knowing students solved the problem by getting girl-friends at a neighbouring college to darn their socks for them; but the rest of us, who possessed neither girl-friends nor knowledge, were content to wear our socks to shreds and then buy new ones.

The most important lesson I learned at Fircroft was that there were other people in the world beside myself. Friendless, alone, often with books as my only companions, before coming to Fircroft I had lived in a sort of dream-world, with little contact with the world about me. My physical handicaps had set me apart from other people, and I was content to let things remain that way. It took me a long time to realise that although I was disabled, I could do the things that fit people did, live the sort of life they did. Fircroft taught me to have confidence in myself.

One fact must be stressed. The reader of this book may get the impression, after learning of my adventures in wild countries, that I was one of those tough, adventurous characters one sometimes reads about, who deliberately seek excitement, even trouble.

Such an impression would be quite false, for I was not that kind of person at all. I was crippled, shy, diffident; often I felt very helpless. If excitement and adventure came my way they were not of my choosing; they simply happened. What I *did* possess, and strongly, was a terrific driving force which compelled me to go on and on across wide seas and lonely lands to find out what the world was like. Often I was ragged, hungry, penniless, but always there was this urge to find out what lay beyond the skyline. The difficulty was that I was so poorly equipped for such a quest.

Of all the tough camps at which I stayed during those years, toughest of all was the archaeological camp at Eddisbury Hill, Cheshire, to which I made my way after leaving Fircroft. My reason for going there in the summer of 1938 was to acquire some practical experience of large-scale excavation; I also gained some practical knowledge of life with thirty Irishmen, many of them spoiling for a fight. A Dr. W. J. Varley of the Geography Department of Liverpool University was excavating an Iron Age fort on top of the hill; in reply to an inquiry of mine he invited me to join them.

I walked from Manchester to Dr. Varley's home, near Frodsham, to ask him where the camp was situated. He was not at home, but it seemed Eddisbury lay ten miles to the south. I was glad to get a lift on a bus, which deposited me at a crossroads in the heart of Delamere Forest. Cheshire is not entirely the flat, pastoral countryside many persons imagine it to be; here were high sandstone escarpments, and valleys filled with oaks, larches, and beeches.

Sight of a long, grass-covered ridge rising above the tree-tops made me quicken my pace, for I guessed this was Eddisbury Hill. I still had to reach the camp, so I made inquiries at the post-office in the straggling hamlet of Delamere and was told to follow a stony lane leading uphill. This old road was hewn out of solid red rock in places, and was the original Roman road called North Watling Street, though I did not know this at the time. Seeing a cluster of bell tents and a big marquee in a field ahead of me, I guessed that this was the camp.

A light streamed from the open door of a wooden shed, so I walked up to it and looked inside. A pleasant-faced man, middle-aged, who was writing at an improvised table consisting of two empty tea-chests placed side by side, greeted me cheerfully.

"Good-evening. You must be the new recruit Dr. Varley told me about," he said. "My name is Harrison — I am the camp Warden."

He told me that most of the men at the camp were unemployed and "on the dole". The Bickerton Camp Scheme, as it was known, had been started three years earlier with the idea of giving unemployed men from Liverpool the chance to spend a few weeks in the country. The plan was for them to co-operate with undergraduates from Liverpool University in the excavation of various Cheshire hill-forts. The digging season lasted six weeks, and parties of thirty unemployed men replaced each other at fortnightly intervals. The unemployed men did the manual work, digging and clearing sites, removing earth and rubbish, under the direction of undergraduates.

A clean-looking compactly built young fellow named Bob Sandison took me to the tent where I was to sleep, and introduced me to some of my fellow-diggers. They were known by such varied nicknames as Sailor, Crummy, Stash, and there was also a Tom, a Walter, and a Charlie. Bob told me to make up my bed on a palliasse between himself and Sailor and store my rucksack behind it. By the time this was done supper was ready, and there was a wild dash to the dining-tent to secure seats at the long wooden tables. Mugs of cocoa, plates of bread and cheese, and dishes of jam were passed round. I observed that most of my workmates appeared to be Irish — navvies, dockers, and labourers, for the most part — a husky, quarrelsome, argumentative crowd.

When supper was over most of the men disappeared in the direction of the public-house in Delamere. I went along to the store-hut to be fitted with a pair of shorts and working-boots. By then it was ten o'clock, and bed seemed the best place to me, so I picked up a hurricane lamp and went along to my tent. It was empty, so I spent a few minutes removing earwigs from my mattress, stretched myself out, and almost immediately was asleep. I had slept the previous night on a bed of bracken under a hazel-bush, and now looked forward to a good night's sleep.

I remained asleep for nearly two hours, but about midnight was awakened by the sound of drunken singing coming towards the camp. Then the tent was suddenly filled with a crowd of heavy-footed individuals who kept falling over me in their efforts to remain upright. I lay still, pretending to be asleep. They then made the very dickens of a row "shushing" each other so as not to awaken me. Last of all Sailor came stumping in. He proceeded to shake me by the shoulder, so at last in sheer self-defence I sat up and asked him what the blazes he thought he was doing.

"Brought a bot'l' beer f'r you," Sailor hiccoughed gravely. "Missed y' at the pub tonight and didn't wan y' to feel out of it."

Somewhat mollified by this kindly thought, I put the bottle of beer under my pillow, thanked him, and turned over to go to sleep again. What a hope! The gang turned the hurricane lamp up as high as it would go, put the glaring light down on the floor just in front of my eyes, and then squatted down on their mattresses in a circle.

"What the hell are you lot up to now?" I demanded, intrigued in spite of myself.

"We're jush going t' have a lil game o'cardsh," Crummy explained.

"Cards! At this time of night?"

"Sure, it's early yet!" they all chorused.

My hopes of a good night's rest vanished, but deliverance — of a sort — was at hand. Suddenly the whole tent shook as several figures hurled themselves against the laced-up door-flap. "Come out of it, you Belfast bastards!" shouted a voice. My companions accepted the challenge with a roar, unlaced the door-flap, and went charging outside. I heard the sound of a violent struggle, then blows and groans. Presently Sailor came reeling back, clutching his forehead.

"Some so-and-so biffed me on the head with a bat," he muttered.

By now a battle royal was raging outside. Despairing of getting any sleep, I crawled to the door-opening and looked out. In the darkness outside, lighted only by the flickering red glare from several hurricane lamps, was a surging, struggling, heaving mass of men's bodies locked in mortal combat. With cries and curses they grappled and struggled, lashing out with fists and pieces of wood. Every now and again a man would reel back from the whirling mass and collapse on the grass. The tent facing ours went down with a crash. Its occupants, clad only in their shirts, came charging out to do battle. Two fighters fell over a lantern, sending the red flames streaking up into the dark night sky, so that I expected to see the tent go up in flames.

As I stood watching this fantastic scene with sleep-bemused eyes, a burly Irish figure loomed up in front of me out of the darkness. He was clad only in a pair of khaki shorts, and with his bulging arms and massive chest he looked as big and strong as a gorilla. He swung a blow at my face with a ham-like fist, which, if it had hit me, would have knocked me off my feet. But he was too drunk to aim straight, and as his fist went whistling past my ear I grabbed hold of his arm and pulled him suddenly forward so that he fell flat on his face in some mud. He sprang up with a roar and came at me a second time, but

Sandison caught him by the shoulders and flung him backward into the wreckage of the other tent.

"That was Corrigan," Sandison remarked unperturbed. "You'll meet him in the morning. He's a kind of foreman round here."

"Something must have upset them all tonight, eh?" I remarked.

"Oh, no, we have this sort of thing pretty often," Sandison replied calmly. "Bedtime now, I think."

He sat down on his mattress, unlaced his boots, pulled his blankets over him, and within a few minutes was asleep. Meanwhile I was wondering what sort of crazy establishment it was I had come to. But sure enough, within fifteen minutes, everything was quiet again. In the morning I awoke before the others, felt the need for refreshment, and reached out for the bottle of beer which Sailor had insisted on giving me. It was an empty bottle! During breakfast I gathered that the previous night's fight had broken out because on the way back from the public-house a Belfast man had been indiscreet enough to make a discourteous remark to a Dublin man. The battle had ended honours even, but it was the ambition of all concerned to bring it to an honourable conclusion during the coming night.

After breakfast a gong sounded summoning us to work. Imagine thirty or forty men, clad in khaki shorts and shirts, or perhaps without shirts, tramping along a winding road cut out of the solid red rock of the hillside. Above us was the steep southern spur of the ridge known as Merrick's Hill, and as we drew nearer I saw that the top was covered with ruined buildings. Halfway up the hill, cut out of the rock, was a deep ditch, V-shaped in outline.

"That ditch was dug to defend the Iron Age fort," Sandison explained. "You see how steep the hill is. They cut the ditch out of the solid rock and put sharpened stakes in the bottom so that if anybody tried to climb up they would fall on the stakes and be impaled."

"And there would be spearmen and archers on top, I suppose, shooting down all the time," I said. "Men with slings, too."

"Yes, there are stone ramparts on top.

There are firebays, too, as in a modern trench system, and even little places cut in the rock for archers to drop spare arrow-heads in. But those ruins you see on the top do not belong to the Iron Age fort. They are much later and belong to the Middle Ages."

When we arrived on the top of Merrick's Hill we found the scientific members of the party already at work. There were several young men and women, undergraduates, and one or two older people who were acting as supervisors. The unemployed men were split up into a number of working parties, each in charge of one or two supervisors. The men went along to a wooden hut, which served as work-room and laboratory, chose the tools they wanted from a collection of spades and pick-axes, and went off to the various sites which were being excavated. One party was opening up the Iron Age ditch, others were excavating the medieval buildings on top of the hill, a third party was investigating the stretch of Roman road which ran below the ramparts, while a fourth party was uncovering one of the gates of the fort.

By now all the other men were at work, and I was left alone. Numbered posts had been thrust into the ground here and there, indicating working sites, and the university students were hurrying about armed with tape-measures and drawing-boards. Another student moved about taking photographs. Dr. Varley, the director of the excavations, stood outside the wooden hut with a sheaf of plans in his hands, giving instructions to his subordinates. Every so often he would be interrupted by one of the supervisors coming up to him with a problem to be solved. From all round came the clatter of shovels and pick-axes, and lines of men pushing wheelbarrows constantly passed and repassed.

"What we are hoping to do now," Dr. Varley was telling a visiting newspaper reporter, "is to uncover the south-eastern entrance to the fort and get occupational material of the original builders, and then to obtain a complete plan of the prehistoric fortifications around Eddisbury Hill."

Nobody took any notice of me, so I looked around for a working party to which I could attach myself. The same gangs worked together each day, and discouraged outsiders from joining them. I found two of my tent-mates working in the half-exposed guard-chamber of one of the gateways of the fort, under the direction of a woman student, so I collected a pick and shovel and joined them. The gates are the most used and most vulnerable part of a fortification, and the part where there are most likely to have been repairs or reconstruction, so archaeologists usually try to excavate at such a spot, as it provides them with the maximum amount of information for the minimum expense of time and labour. From my own point of view, there was a peculiar thrill in standing in the gateway of a walled prehistoric town, which had been hidden from the sight of man for two thousand years.

By the time work finished for the day we had cleared the gateway down to bedrock, and found part of the original oak gate still in position. The entrance in which we were working had been camouflaged to mislead an invading force. A sunken way led up the steep slope of the hill to a defile cut out of the rock, to simulate an inturned entrance. To complete the illusion, the inner portion of this sham gateway had been lined with drystone walling applied to the face of the rock. The real gateway had been spanned by an oaken bridge carried on two massive supports, behind which was the gate itself, likewise slung on two oak posts, one of which was still preserved complete with its unique iron ferrule. The road leading up to the gateway was metalled, and that it had been used a long time was evident from the fact that it had been rebuilt and enlarged several times.

That evening, as a result of a conversation with Dr. Varley and from pamphlets which he gave me, I learnt that there had been an Iron Age fortress erected on the Eddisbury ridge probably in the first century before Christ, and that later, perhaps on the eve of the Roman conquest, it had been enlarged and strengthened. The fort had been unable to stem the Roman advance; they had dismantled the ramparts, filled up the ditches, and blocked or dismantled the gateways. Towards the end of the Roman occupation of Britain a group of people had built a settlement of wattle-and-daub huts on the site of the dismantled ramparts.

Still later, probably in the seventh century, a Saxon built a house in one of the silted-up ditches; perhaps this was the man Ead who most likely gave his name to the hill. According to the *Mercian Register* (a document incorporated in the *Anglo-Saxon Chronicle*), Ethelfleda, the warlike daughter of King Alfred, built a "burh", or fortified town, at Eddisbury in the year 914. Much later, in 1337, John Done, the Forester of Mara (the present Delamere Forest), built on Eddisbury Hill a hunting-lodge known as the "Chamber in the Forest". This served as the meeting-place of the Hundred Court, and possibly of the Forest Court. There were believed to be traces of seven different cultures occupying the top of the hill.

By the time work finished for the day I had acquired an aching back, any number of blisters, and an added respect for the men who dig ditches and excavate the foundations of buildings. But it had been pleasant working up there on top of the hill, in the bright sunshine, with the knowledge that at any moment your spade might disclose some relics of a bygone race.

For me there is a peculiar fascination in standing on the site of a vanished town or fortification, whose buildings have sometimes disappeared so completely that hardly any trace of them is left. The mentality of the archaeologist is this — that he feels an urge to dig down into the ground, to clear away the covering of earth and disclose what lies underneath, the crumbling and hidden remains of a vanished *place*, and from this ghostly outline recreate, if only for a fleeting moment, something of the lives and loves and laughter of the shadowy inhabitants who peopled it so many centuries ago, and then abandoned it to the wind and the rain. This is one of the most exciting forms of exploration still left to us — Exploration into Time.

After tea I decided to go for a walk through the forest, but happening to lie down on my mattress for a few minutes I fell asleep, and it was supper-time before I awoke. It was well I did so, for hardly had I gone to bed after a short stroll with the Warden, when a violent commotion broke out in one of the other tents. The nightly battle was just beginning! I gave up any hope of getting to sleep, and crawled outside to watch the fun.

In the lurid glow of a hurricane lamp I saw a man come out of a tent beating his chest like a gorilla and announcing to all and sundry that he could thrash any half-dozen of us knock-kneed, slab-sided, cross-eyed, bald-headed, flat-chested, spindle-legged, blue-nosed, miserable runts single-handed — nay, with one hand tied behind him. I did not feel inclined to take up this challenge myself, but my tent-mates were not so backward. They sprang upon the challenger in a body, and he went down amid a wild tangle of arms and legs.

One after another the tents went crashing down. A wild mob of men, most of them drunk, led by a red-headed fellow brandishing a mallet, came charging up to our tent, which was the only one left standing. Sandison, Sailor, Charlie, and I locked shoulders to prevent them charging through, while Stash bounded forward flourishing a cricket-bat and explained in sanguinary terms what would happen to anyone who so much as laid a finger on our tent. At this challenge the redheaded man leapt forward with a roar, so Stash tapped him smartly on the head with the bat, and he fell limply backward into the arms of his tent-mates. They looked at him and they looked at our faces, and then they decided to leave us alone and went off to wreck the cook-house instead.

8

THE
AMATEUR ARCHAEOLOGISTS

"ARE you looking for a job, Jim? I could do with some help."

It was the following morning. Bob Sandison had seen me prowling about the site, looking for a work-party to join, and was calling to me. I liked Sandison, who was a keen worker and possessed a sense of humour, so walked over to join him. Mr. Gregg, the supervisor, greeted me cheerfully and explained they hoped to uncover medieval remains supposed to exist on the hilltop.

As I worked, exposing an old cobbled pavement, the thought came to me that archaeology is a many-sided subject. In lands such as Britain only excavation can reveal remains left by bygone peoples (unlike some countries where ancient buildings survive above ground-level). By seeing places and handling things one can learn much, for, after all, archaeology is the study of ancient *things*. Just as history is the narrative of events, so archaeology is mainly the study of things which man has employed to express his needs and emotions. Such things as tools, weapons, buildings, ornaments, religious symbols, trackways, are all evidence of man's past activity.

The soil removed from the medieval building was being tipped into the rock-cut ditch which ran round Eddisbury Hill.

When it came my turn to wheel the barrow-loads of earth into the great ditch of the old fortress the size of it impressed me. I marvelled that men with such primitive tools as the Iron Age peoples had possessed had been able to execute such a laborious undertaking. The builders had made deliberate provision for the manning of the defences by laying down a series of clay floors, occupation sites, behind the inner ramparts.

I wondered who the people had been who built the fort, and how they had lived and where they had come from. Probably they had belonged to the second wave of Celtic migration from Europe — the

Brythonic Celts from whom the Welsh derive their language. It is believed they were an upland people, and as the Romans advanced towards the lower Severn Valley they followed the hill-ranges from Shropshire into Cheshire. But though one did not know their name or history, one could see where they had lived, the tools they used, the hearths at which they did their cooking.

I had discovered by now that Eddisbury Hill was a flat-topped plateau of Keuper sandstone, covered with two or three feet of glacial drift. Its flat top and steep sides made it an ideal site for a defended settlement, for it dominated the whole of Delamere Forest as well as the pass which carried the Roman road from Chester to Manchester. The northern spur of the hill was known as the Old Pale Heights, and between it and Eddisbury Hill proper lay Old Pale Farm. Around the hill on the north and east ran a great double line of defences, quarried out of the solid rock and separated by a deep, rock-cut ditch. These big ramparts were the first things you saw when climbing the hill, for they rose eighteen feet above the silted-up ditch. The total area enclosed within the ramparts was over sixteen acres. There were four gateways, one on the north and one on the east, the other two on the west.

Work had been in progress for nearly a fortnight when I arrived, following on the excavations of the previous season. Dr. Varley told me that there were three problems which he hoped to solve this season; one was to discover the course of the Iron Age defences around Merrick's Hill, another to locate the Saxon town built by Queen Ethelfleda, and the third to investigate the supposedly medieval remains and discover whether they were part of the hunting-lodge known as the "Chamber in the Forest". This season's excavations had already proved that the prehistoric defences encircled the hill, by disclosing to view the series of magnificent rock-cut ditches which I was now helping to fill in.

When our work-party had filled in the exposed part of the ditch we commenced digging up the hard earth floor inside one of the ruined buildings. This had apparently been a two-roomed structure, each room being about twelve feet square. At present only two or three feet of stone walling showed above the surface. Since, up till now, there had not been found any trace of the Saxon town built by Queen Ethelfleda in the tenth century, we hoped that underneath the rubbish we were wheeling away we should find the ruins of the "burh aet Eadesbyrig" which she ordered to be built.

Or perhaps these ruins were part of the "Chamber in the Forest" built by John Done, though it was evident that the building must have undergone many changes between the fourteenth and eighteenth centuries. It was believed that later the hunting-lodge may have been converted into a farmhouse. I thought of these things as, sometimes, I paused to rest my aching back, and looked across the interior of the old fortress, now occupied by a field of waving corn. Was the Saxon town hidden out of sight beneath that field?

"Always keep a level floor surface," Sandison counselled, watching me dig. "Keep clearing the surface which you are cutting right down to floor-level. It makes a neater-looking job and gives you room to put your feet."

I was finding a navvy's job not so easy as it looked. What well-known authority declared that all art is dependent upon the art of the navvy? Most of my mates had been brought up to pick-and-shovel work, and it came easy to them. They had a deceptively casual manner of handling their tools, which appeared effortless — until you tried it yourself. Sandison was an unemployed builder's labourer, and I owed what knowledge of practical archaeology I possessed to his kindly advice and criticism.

"Don't let the handle of your spade fall in the muck," he advised me a few minutes later. "If it gets wet it will chafe your hands, and then you will find it hurts to dig."

For several days we continued our work in the ruined building. Some distance below the surface we came upon pieces of broken pottery which were carefully collected and handed over to Dr. Varley. It resembled the earliest Iron Age pottery of south-east England, this demonstrating what was previously guessed at — namely, that types of pottery made in that part of England as early as the fourth century before Christ continued to be made in northern England as late as the eve of the Roman conquest. A series of five cooking hearths was found inside the rampart. They were bean-shaped slabs of baked clay, burned red and black by fire, and were bounded with sandstone kerbs. Some had been rebuilt as many as four times, indicating the lengthy occupation of the site. Lower down we came upon quantities of ash and broken pottery, fragments of stone tools, and burnt animal bones.

I was now engaged in wheeling barrow-loads of earth from the site where Sandison was digging, and tipping them into another part of the excavations. Liverpool University was under an obligation to fill in the excavations before leaving, and the quickest method of doing this was to fill up one hole with earth removed from another hole being dug. In this way at the end of the season there would be little left on the ground to show that it had been excavated, though the results would be recorded in plans and photographs and museum specimens. Meanwhile the prehistoric and medieval remains would be preserved underground for posterity.

Corrigan, the burly Irishman whom I had encountered during my first night at the camp, got tired of working with his own party — or they tired of him! — and came over and joined us. This resulted in frequent arguments between him and myself, for I worked too fast for his liking. I wanted to get on with the job, to learn archaeology and perhaps make discoveries. Corrigan's idea was to take things steadily, very steadily. He used to wheel his barrow so slowly that it made me impatient to watch him.

"Stop pushing your barrow so fast, young fellow," he growled at me. "And don't fill it so full. Take your time, get down under a bush and have a smoke, take things easy. We don't mean to kill ourselves on this job."

"You do it your way and I'll do it my way," was my response.

"Remind me to cut your throat some time, twerp," he replied, running a dirty finger across his stubbly chin.

Nevertheless I studied the men about me and saw that they set their own pace, and nothing would make them go any faster. If you tried, things started to go wrong: a barrow would break, or a wall would collapse, or the whole party would disappear in the direction of the lavatories for a smoke. I was being watched myself — by Corrigan.

"I'm warning you, fellow," he growled. "You turn that barrow upside down and run it empty a few times and give us time to breathe. Or something will happen to you — see!"

I "saw", and slowed down my pace to that of the others, not wishing to be pushed "accidentally" off a wall into a ditch.

We had a fight a night the first three nights I was at the camp, but the fourth night there were two fights. The usual indescribable din began about eleven o'clock, some of the tents got knocked down, a few men were bashed, and, speaking generally, a good time was had by all. The Warden never attempted to interfere or to maintain order, which was probably just as well, as the crowd would most likely have thrown him into the water-trough. He just retired to his own tent and left them to it.

That night I had finally dozed off, but was awakened by a second outburst at some ungodly hour in the morning. Looking at the tent across from ours, I saw a red-headed man called Ginger come running out in his nightshirt, pursued by a big fellow flourishing a wooden club, who was clad in nothing at all. Ginger sought refuge in the tent next to ours, thereby bringing down the wrath of its occupants upon his head. Apparently as one man, they all rose up in a rage, intending to throw him out, but in the ensuing confusion they threw the wrong man outside. Then they discovered their mistake and threw Ginger out as well. The man with the club was still making a nuisance of himself, so they hauled him back to his own tent by his arms and legs and flung him inside. This precipitated another battle, which would have continued indefinitely, had not somebody shouted out:

"Jasus, you fellows! Look at the time. We've got to get ready for Mass!"

It was Sunday morning. The fight stopped immediately. The late adversaries picked themselves off the ground and brushed each other down. They dressed, washed, then dashed around looking for bicycles to take them to the church a few miles away. The rest of us turned over with a sigh of relief and went to sleep again. For some nights after that, also, we slept in peace, and one of my immediate problems was solved, for I had been wondering whether I could stick this life long enough to learn anything about archaeology.

When they were not fighting they were snoring — and such snoring! I used to lie awake at nights marvelling at it, and picturing the whole camp rising and falling to its sonorous rhythm. As fresh parties of men arrived it began to get uncomfortably crowded in the bell-tents, and often I awoke to find my head on somebody else's mattress, or that the fellow next to me was using my behind as a pillow. Most of the university people slept elsewhere and had little contact with the ordinary workers. One undergraduate named Foster shared a tent with Corrigan, Ginger, and other high-spirited individuals, and to judge by the weird sounds emanating from it at times it seemed they were leading him a dog's life.

A fortnight went by. Life at the camp became quieter, and the work of excavation progressed smoothly. We were still burrowing down into the buildings on Merrick's Hill. Our illusions were shattered when we learned that instead of an ancient Saxon fortress or even a romantic "Chamber in the Forest" the place we were uncovering was probably an eighteenth-century cowshed. But below these remains we came upon more walls, made of huge blocks of dressed stone, showing much better workmanship than the buildings above. Was this part of the hunting-lodge built by the old Forester of Mara? It was an exciting moment when my spade went into a layer of ash and bones, which covered the ground everywhere to a depth of several inches. It did not require much imagination to picture a great fire, some time back in history, devastating the buildings on the hilltop. Always there was the feeling that if only you penetrated a little farther there was something exciting waiting to be discovered.

Altogether I spent more than a month on the hilltop, and when the time came for me to leave I felt that the experience had taught me far more of the practical details of archaeology than any amount of reading or listening to lectures. A would-be archaeologist could hardly have chosen a better site to begin his apprenticeship in learning the techniques of excavation. There are certain places which seem to epitomise the entire history of England, and Eddisbury Hill is such a one. Celts, Romans, Saxons, and people of the Middle Ages have all left some evidence of their way of life for anyone skilled enough to uncover and interpret it. How true it is that the history of England can be visualised in her buildings and her countryside!

Of the three questions which it had been hoped this year's excavations would solve, only the first had been answered: it had now been proved that the prehistoric Celtic defences completely encircled Eddisbury Hill. But we had met with no success in locating the site of the tenth-century town supposed to have been erected by the Saxon queen Ethelfleda. In view of the amount of building and rebuilding which had gone on during the centuries this was, perhaps, not surprising. But what was curious was the fact that, although cultural evidence of every other period in the history of the site had been discovered, no trace at all had been found of the Saxon occupation. The layer of earth which might have been equated with the Saxon period was found to be completely sterile.

Our work among the ruins on Merrick's Hill had proved that the medieval hunting-lodge known as the "Chamber in the Forest" no longer existed in its original form, but that the buildings we had been excavating had been constructed of stones which might have formed part of a much earlier building. But it was clear that the stones were not in their original position, and had been used several times over. Objects recovered from beneath the ruins suggested that the site had been occupied for many centuries, but that the present ruins appeared to be those of a farmhouse and its outbuildings, which had been destroyed about the beginning of the nineteenth century.

The last two days at the camp passed very quickly. There were still last-minute jobs waiting to be done. As fast as we shovelled dirt into one excavation, excited undergraduates dashed around with parties of helpers opening up fresh sites, in a frantic attempt to gain a little extra knowledge before the site was finally closed for good. It was the last season they would be digging at Eddisbury; next year they would move on to a new site.

"If you want to get any sleep tonight you had better go somewhere else," Sandison advised me on our last night. "All the men will get roaring drunk to celebrate the breaking up of the camp, and life won't be worth living."

"Thank you for the tip," I told him. "I'll take my blankets and sleep in the old fort. It looks like being a fine night."

At sundown I slung my blankets over my shoulder and climbed up to the old fortress. From the ramparts I looked down upon the world below. Soon everything down there became dim and shadowy, but on the hilltop it was still light. The far-reaching forest was a sea of shadows, with motor-car headlamps moving along like the lights of passing vessels. How often had I tramped these grass-grown ramparts in the evenings, watching the sun go down and darkness creep over the world! The dark, ancient place seemed to call out to me, and I had the feeling that up here that which men call time was so tenuous that I could almost peer through it and see my ancestors. It seemed to me that if only my dull brain could work a little faster I would grasp the simple key which would admit me to that other world and see those ancient people moving about me.

I walked along the sunken road to the gate of the fort. On either side of me were rough stone walls, and under my feet was solid rock; ahead of me, through the opening, I could see a stone-walled guard-chamber. Inside this on a stone bench covered with bracken I made my bed, and when the blankets were tucked firmly about me I lay there looking up at the dark sky. The roof of the guard-chamber had gone centuries ago, so it seemed as if the sky was only a little way above me, with the stars just out of reach. I was awakened some time later by strange noises which came drifting up from the tents below — shrieks and moans, the sound of devilry by night. I chuckled, and went to sleep again.

It must have been after midnight when raindrops splashing on my face awakened me from the confused dream of a meeting with a tall man wearing a curious-looking helmet. I wrapped my big cape about me and tried to go to sleep again. The rain became heavier, water cascaded down the stone wall and formed a pool about me, so I was compelled, very reluctantly, to realise that I had better move to a more sheltered spot. But there was no shelter nearer than the camp in the meadow below. The storm was increasing in violence every minute, and I did not like the prospect of climbing down the steep slopes of the hill in the darkness.

With the blankets slung over my shoulder I groped my way through the gateway of the fort, expecting every moment to stumble over a wall or fall into a pit. At one place the ditch was crossed by a couple of planks, and somehow I managed to negotiate these by feeling the wood with my feet. It was so dark I could not see my hand in front of me, and the thought of climbing down the rampart made my hair stand on end. Meanwhile the storm was raging round me. Thunder boomed across the heavens, and lightning flashed from rock to rock. I started to climb downhill, trying to avoid the steepest slope, for if once I started slipping there would be nothing to check my fall until I hit the stones below.

I groped about with my feet for the

sloping path running below the rampart, but could not find it; instead, the slope got steeper and steeper. I clutched at some boulders, and they started moving and went crashing past me in the darkness. Then I remembered that part of the rock-cut ditch was not yet filled in, and must be just in front of me. In my efforts to avoid this chasm I blundered into a heap of gravel. My feet shot from under me, and I rolled over and over down the hill till I landed with a crash against a wire fence. Even while falling I clung grimly to my pile of blankets, and these saved me from the worst effects of the fall.

I picked myself up, breathless, and with the storm still roaring in my ears set off for the roadway leading to the camp. Some time later, in driving rain, I reached an open shed where hay was stacked. Deciding to spend the rest of the night there, I made myself a bed in the hay — by the feeble light of my electric torch — and crawled into it. Not even sodden clothing and blankets kept me awake. Some time later I was awakened by a light being flashed into my eyes and a husky voice exclaiming:

"By Jasus! Now there is a sight for you!

The lad says he doesn't drink, and then goes off by himself and gets so tight he can't even crawl back to his tent!"

The Second World War came and went. The Army did not want a lame man, so I spent some years working on farms in different parts of England and Wales. It was a good life and I enjoyed it, but gradually I was compelled to realise that it was not the life for me. After all, I *was* disabled, much as I would have liked to forget it. One day as I was harnessing a horse to a cart the animal reared up suddenly and flung me against a stone wall. The accident damaged my crippled leg, and for days I moved in great pain. It was plain that I should have to give up farmwork. What kind of job should I do next?

A white-walled building with a red-tiled roof stands by a rushing little river in a wooded valley a couple of miles north of Scarborough, on the Yorkshire coast. Once the building was a water-mill, but the triangular green sign on the wall proclaims that it is now that most modern of hostelries — a youth hostel. If you were to visit the place you would find it thronged with a crowd of young people, sensibly clad in nothing much, engaged in cooking meals, studying maps, repairing bicycles, or holding a sing-song. They would be a friendly, cheerful crowd, gathered there from every part of the British Isles, from various countries of Europe, America, and the Antipodes. About them there would be that air of casual comradeship which exists among people who walk or cycle, climb or canoe, about the countryside for the fun of it.

You might have seen me there also, sitting at a table collecting membership-cards and allocating beds to new arrivals, or in the kitchen helping to cook and serve breakfasts and suppers. Scarborough youth hostel was my home from 1943 until 1947, when I worked there as Assistant Warden, and some of the happiest memories of my life are associated with that old building. Travel abroad was not possible until the War was over, so the next best thing was to work among people with the same interests as myself.

The hostel was open seven days of the week, and for several months of the year was never empty, with people coming and going all the time, so that we who worked there had very little free time. Yet in spite of the long hours and hard work and poor pay I enjoyed the life there. One of the principal sources of enjoyment was the daily meeting with people who were interested in the world about them, people who had hobbies, and who could talk intelligently about a wide variety of subjects.

It was the policy of the Warden, Colin Beech, in the evenings after the supper-table had been cleared and the dishes washed, to get out maps and books and pictures and try to arouse the interest of the younger hostelers in the scenic and historical attractions of the Scarborough district. "Why trouble to cycle all the way to Scarborough if all you can think of doing when you get here is to go to the cinema?" he would ask, and would then proceed to point out on a map features of interest within easy cycling or walking distance — cliffs and caves, old villages, prehistoric remains. To give the young people their due, they could show themselves interested enough, if somebody gave them guidance. Many were the animated discussions which developed round a roaring log fire in the common-room. The hostel was visited by men and women on leave from the Forces, by young factory workers, by university students, by schoolteachers and headmasters, too. In trying to teach them something of the history and geography of the district we found that we were teaching ourselves quite a lot also.

One evening after supper I was pointing out on a map an interesting route to Bridlington for a couple of cyclists to follow, when a voice remarked:

"The Warden tells me you are interested in archaeology. I do a bit of field-work in our area — near Kirkby Moorside."

Looking up from the map, I saw a tall, rangy individual with a weatherbeaten face and an engaging smile. He introduced himself as Raymond Hayes, professional photographer, now engaged upon warwork in a Kirkby Moorside factory. I listened fascinated as he told me of his activities as an amateur archaeologist, of tracing Roman roads across the moorlands of east Yorkshire, of exploring the burial mounds of the New Stone and Bronze Age peoples. Bedtime came, and we were still talking; by then Raymond Hayes was my friend for life.

"I will send you some books about archaeology which you may find useful," he said to me next morning, when the time came for him to leave. "I took some of the photographs, and they deal with sites you might find it worthwhile to visit."

I took little notice of this remark, for it was my experience that many people make promises, but few people carry them out; therefore Raymond Hayes went up in my estimation when, a few days later, the postman handed me a parcel containing several books and an invitation: "Come and spend a few days at my place when you are not so busy at the hostel. We have some interesting sites in our area which you should visit — Cawthorn Roman camps, the Roman road across Wheeldale Moor, and any number of earthworks and tumuli. Maybe we could do some work together."

I wrote back at once to say that I should visit him as soon as possible, but it was September before I could start off on my bicycle to visit the village in which Raymond lived. As I cycled westward from Scarborough along the foot of the escarpment which marks the southern extremity of the moorlands of north-east Yorkshire, I was delighted by the succession of little villages with mellow stone walls and red pantiled roofs through which I passed. I, who had seen some of the grandest scenery on earth, from the icy peaks of the Arctic to the sun-scorched sands of the Sahara, now felt the strong appeal of these English hills and valleys. The northern forest makes a strong impression on the human mind, but it is the appeal of a vast, lonely land where nothing has happened. It is a land without history; whereas almost every mile of English soil holds something of the past. Everywhere you go in England there are old churches and castles, storied towns and villages, places where for centuries men have lived and worked and died. I was to realise that without people a place is nothing.

Raymond's village is one of the prettiest in Yorkshire. It lies in a wooded hollow surrounded by hills and moors. Its peculiar charm is due to the fact that a stream flows in a little green valley through the centre of the village, much as a main street runs through the centre of other villages; the buildings — well-built stone houses, village hall, post-office and general store, school — face each other across a wide expanse of greensward, with small, white, wooden foot-bridges connecting one side of the village with the other. Motor-vehicles have to splash their way across fords, and woe betide their drivers if the little river is in flood, for then they may find themselves with engines stalled in the middle of the stream.

Raymond, who was a bachelor, lived in a bungalow on the edge of the village. A studio, in which his photographic business was carried on, stood near the house; as soon as he was released from war service he planned to return to his job of photographing local weddings, shows, festivities, and other happenings. The interior of the studio betrayed its owner's chief interests; scattered about were maps and books, pieces of Roman and prehistoric pottery, boxes of bones and flint implements, and in the corner stood a pair of skis, for Raymond found these the best means of traversing the snow-clad moorlands in winter.

"Glad to see you, Jim," he greeted me. "Look at this."

He spread a map of Roman Yorkshire on the table-top and began to point out various features of interest. I knew already that the scenery of east Yorkshire could be divided into two distinct types — the rolling chalk hills known as the Yorkshire Wolds in the southern part, and to the north the more level-topped Yorkshire Moors, trenched by narrow, winding dales. Wolds and moors were separated by the wide, green Vale of Pickering. Upon these physical features Raymond now proceeded to outline the pattern of human activity — ancient British settlements on the moors and near the coast, Roman forts and camps at York, Malton, and elsewhere, signal stations at various points along the coast, linked by a system of Roman roads, though the courses of many of these, it appeared, were based largely upon conjecture.

"The trouble is that many people interested in archaeology are content to speculate about things which puzzle them, but only a few are prepared to get out into the country and see what evidence they can discover on the ground," Raymond said. "Even in a comparatively small area like this there is a vast amount waiting to be

234

discovered, and field-archaeology is the means of finding out."

"Maybe people will be more interested after the War," I suggested. "There will be more time, more money, more petrol then."

"This is the job I am doing now, in my spare time," Raymond said, pointing to the map. "Out on Wheeldale Moor there is a stretch of Roman road called Wade's Causeway. It is in good condition, stone pavement, kerbstones, culverts, still in position. It appears to point towards Whitby, but if it is not leading there, then where does it go? And where does it come from? From York? To find the answers to these questions we need to explore the ground between York and the sea. Have you seen the remains of the Roman signal-station at Scarborough?"

"Inside the castle walls, on the edge of the cliff," I replied. "Somebody told me that a high tower stood there, and when the Roman soldiers on guard-duty saw Saxon warships approaching they sent signals to the fort at Malton to summon the help of the cavalry stationed there."

"Where are the roads which linked all

the signal stations?" Raymond went on. "Where are the remains of the other Roman villas? There must be many clues hidden in the ground if only we could find them."

His enthusiasm made me wonder what England had looked like in Roman times. Now I seemed to view Yorkshire as it once was — the red-roofed Roman country houses surrounded by yellow cornfields, the walled towns with their houses, workshops, and markets, the harbours on the coast where Roman patrol ships docked, and linking all these Roman roads stretching like the fingers of one's hand from the great legionary fortress at York.

Listening to Raymond, I realised the possibilities open to anyone interested in archaeology. Instead of being disgruntled because one could not go to university to study the subject, here was an activity one could undertake *now* — field-archaeology, the investigating and recording of the remains of the past which were to be found everywhere. Excavation of towns, forts, big buildings, was a task requiring a large labour force and a considerable amount of money; but the tasks which the field-archaeologist could undertake — tracing ancient roads, measuring and mapping earthworks, locating almost vanished historical sites — could be accomplished by anyone with some knowledge of the subject, either alone or with a small working party. In every district of Britain there was a vast amount of archaeological field-work waiting to be done.

Raymond's nature differed from mine in that, where I had a tremendous urge to explore as much of the earth's surface as possible, he had the desire to discover all that was to be known about the particular area in which he lived. His was the patient, lifelong accumulation of facts, by personal investigation, in the manner of Gilbert White of Selborne or Canon Atkinson of Cleveland, two tireless investigators of the kind to which certain branches of science owe so much. During the years I lived in Yorkshire I was to discover how one small portion of the earth's surface could claim a man's heart, and that a lifetime was all too short in which to discover everything that was to be known about it.

"You make it all sound very exciting," I exclaimed. "How can one make a start? What jobs want tackling first?"

"The first job is to trace the course of Wade's Causeway — the Roman road leading from York to the sea," Raymond replied. "After that, the job of locating Bibo House."

"What's that?" I demanded.

"A Roman pub," Raymond replied with a grin. "And then there is the Lost Roman Villa to find — out there on the edge of the moors. That should be enough to be going on with."

Wade's Causeway, Bibo House, the Lost Villa!

Those three archaeological problems were to dominate our thoughts for years to come. Whenever we had any free time we would arrange a meeting, either at Raymond's home or some convenient youth hostel, and pick up the threads of the investigation where they had been left on a former occasion. During the course of our wanderings we explored much of east Yorkshire, on foot or bicycle, so that ultimately the Vale of Pickering and the hills lying north and south became familiar background. The War came to an end, Raymond returned to his job as a photographer, conditions became easier at the

Scarborough hostel, and some of our ambitions were achieved.

One of the first things I did, after leaving Raymond's home one sunny October day, was to cycle to a hamlet called Stape to examine Wade's Causeway. Raymond had told me that Stape was as primitive a place as could be found in England, that the people rode about on donkeys and burnt peat for fuel, and, sure enough, the very first man I saw was jogging along the dilapidated road on a donkey and thin blue columns of peat smoke could be seen rising from the isolated cottages. It was all very much as one imagines the west of Ireland to be, the whole scene, by some trick of the light or perspective, having that atmosphere of remoteness and forlornness which one associates with Celtic lands. Even the road seemed to grow weary and come to an end, and I had to ford little streams which flowed everywhere or cross them by little plank bridges.

Then ahead of me, curving away across gentle undulations, I saw the road, the Roman Road, looking at first sight much as it must have done when the legions abandoned it to the wind and the rain so many centuries ago. It is one of the most interesting specimens of actual Roman road to be found in England, for it retains its old stone paving, kerbstones, and culverts; a section of it has been excavated by the Ministry of Works and left open for public inspection. It was a thought-provoking experience to see the old stone road running across the heathery moorland, until its course was lost to sight near Wheeldale hostel. What happened to it after that? That was the problem.

During the winter months my services were not needed at Scarborough hostel, so I bought a small caravan parked in a field a couple of miles away, and fitted it up with an iron stove, bookshelves, and table, so that I could write a book about Cheshire. This task kept me busy until it was time to start work at the hostel again. Not till later could time be found for field-archaeology. One of the stumbling-blocks which confront workers in this field is the little matter of having to earn a living, and Raymond and I often reflected that we could get a lot more done if some kind person would only present us with a private income — say, £500 a year.

Trying to trace the course of a Roman road is an arduous business, we discovered. With the exposed section of old stone road on Wheeldale Moor as a starting-point, we worked seaward, but lost all trace of it before reaching Whitby hostel, perched on its windswept cliff-top over-looking the river Esk. (The hostel is housed in the stables of the old abbey, and from the common-room window there is a marvellous view over the North Sea.) Working from the opposite end of the stone road, we found ourselves clueless in the middle of the wide, green Vale of Pickering. A hill rose in front of us, Rise-borough Hill, once an island, in the days when the Vale had been a lake, and curving round the side of the hill was a clay cause-way — the road we were seeking. We followed it as far as a railway cutting, and then lost it.

"The thing to do is to start at York and work back in this direction," Raymond said.

We met some time later at York hostel. A big house standing in a wooded garden above the river Ouse, it was one of the finest youth hostels in England. It had for neighbour Mr. Peter Rowntree's private residence, and visitors were likely to find him busy in the hostel, for as chairman of this region of the Youth Hostels Association he took an active part in running them. A wooden plaque in the common-room commemorates the generosity of the American trade unions, who provided over £7000 to help the establishment of this and several other hostels. Note the little wooden mouse carved on the plaque, the trade-mark of Mr. Robert Thompson, the wood-carver of Kilburn.

The following morning, as we were cycling out through the city gate called Monk Bar, Raymond suggested that one of the towers of the Roman city should be near-by. We parked our bicycles, climbed to the top of the city wall, and walked along it for a short distance. Yes, there was the Roman tower, still standing twenty feet high in places, buried among under-growth. It was not possible to reach it from the top of the city wall, so while Raymond took photographs I went back the way we had come and asked a joiner's permission to go through his yard to the waste bit of land on which the Roman tower stood.

Sight of the grey stones of the tower thrilled me, and I was so busy sketching and measuring the ruin that I failed to observe that the joiner had locked the gate of the yard and gone away. Unable to return the way I had come, for the fence was too high to climb, there was nothing for it but to scale the city wall. I scrambled up the base of a medieval tower, while Raymond stretched himself out on top of the wall and tried to hoist me up. As my fingers clutched the edge of the rampart Raymond slipped and let go of me, and I was left with my legs dangling into space, a sight which must have provided any passing citizens of York with considerable amusement.

Awheel again, we headed north-west into the golden sunshine, over Strensall Common, by winding by-ways towards the Howardian Hills. A signpost marked High Stittenham beckoned us uphill to a few isolated farmhouses, and there in a field I saw something which made my heart leap — a long, low, green mound. Was it the Roman road? Roman cooking vessels had been found in this vicinity, and when we inquired at various houses we learned that some old coins had been dug up. A frantic search by a housewife failed to reveal the whereabouts of the coins, so we had to leave the question of their identity unsolved.

Pushing and carrying our bicycles, we crossed lovely wooded, hilly country, remote and little-visited. We forded Bulmer Beck, and followed cart-ways towards Castle Howard. At Brandreth Farm we found the last authentic piece of Roman road which had been recorded, with the big stone pavement slabs lying where they had been left when excavated by the late Dr. F. Elgee in 1928. Though we searched every other field in the neighbourhood, we found no other traces of the road. Between York and the hills all knowledge and evidence of the road seemed to have vanished completely, but we hoped to find some clue which would encourage us to dig a trench and possibly locate the old road surface. Buried somewhere under the green meadows and pastures lay the Roman road, perhaps robbed of its stone paving years ago to build field boundaries, perhaps ploughed almost to its foundations, but enough of it should be left for an archaeologist to say, "Here the Roman road once ran." But where to start looking?

We cycled north again, through Castle Howard Park. At a place called Braygate Street we found traces of the Roman road again, but it did not fall into line with the other two pieces we had seen. The proverbial straightness of a Roman road is misleading, however, for they bend considerably when circumstances demand it. We found the road running across a potato field, almost ploughed out, and in an adjoining garden a man was actually hacking a trench for celery through it, and complaining of the number of stones he kept encountering!

We free-wheeled downhill into a region of marshy water-meadows, the Vale of Pickering, which in Roman times was a vast swamp or lake. To reach the moorlands to the north the road must have followed various hills and ridges rising about a hundred feet above the marshes. At a bridge over the river Rye we stopped to talk to an old man who had lived there sixty years. He told us of a reputed Roman ford near his house, and we promised to return later to investigate this. At Normanby we called at the vicarage for information, and were given a piece of Roman pottery.

By now my legs were nearly crying out with weariness, for we had been on the trail eleven hours; Raymond appeared to be tireless. Such is the spell of archaeology that, tired though I was, I agreed we ought to interview one more man. He proved uncommunicative, so, feeling that we had done enough for one day, we mounted our bicycles again and went on to Hutton-le-Hole. We had found two sections of Roman road and a probable third, interviewed ten people, and explored country which had previously been a blank. Altogether it had been a satisfactory day's work.

I have described this day at some length, for it is typical of many such days spent tracing the Roman roads of east Yorkshire. We followed false clues, wasted time over misleading reports, but gradually extended our knowledge of the road northward beyond the river Esk and southward into the Howardian Hills. We acquired much first-hand information about Roman road construction, discovering that road surfaces might be of stone, gravel, solid clay, or even, perhaps, of turf. Materials and surfaces seemed to vary with the type of country crossed.

We interviewed any old people who might have childhood recollections of an old road, since destroyed, we asked all farmers and land-workers to report to us the discovery of anything unusual encountered in their fields while ploughing, we dug trial-trenches along the probable line of the road until we nearly cried with weariness. We unearthed prehistoric burial mounds, the sites of forgotten villages, castles, and earthworks whose function puzzled us completely. We realised the wealth of archaeological material which lies buried under English soil, only awaiting someone with keenness and muscles to unearth it. We had started out to find solutions to three problems; now the various remains which we kept encountering presented us with so many other problems that we eventually came to realise that no two men working only in their spare time could ever hope to deal with them. Things which puzzled us must be left to other workers for solution.

Where was Bibo House? This was

another question which was to occupy our thoughts for a long time. Searches for Roman forts and villas are common enough, but who ever heard of anyone going in search of a Roman "pub"? Yet there were references to such a building in the neighbourhood of Pickering (and in Gordon Home's *The Evolution of an English Town*). The name Bibo was supposed to be derived from the Latin word for drinking, though how the name could have survived through the centuries which had passed since the Roman occupation was something which nobody could explain.

In our search for the Roman tavern we ranged the countryside from Newton Dale to Farndale, and from the Esk Valley to Malton, by the river Derwent, obtaining clues and following them, only to find that they were false. Bibo House was here, Bibo House was there; old inhabitants of this village or that village clearly remembered certain places which had been pointed out as the reputed site of the Roman inn.

What would a Roman tavern in the wilds of Yorkshire look like, anyway? It would not look like a modern public-house obviously, but like one of the Roman posting-stations, a *mansio*, with inn, stables, other buildings, perhaps, and earthworks. Obviously such a hostelry in such a location would need to be fortified. So we started looking for earthworks of the sort which might surround a posting-station. I even went as far afield as Hardham, in Sussex, to examine the reputed site of a Roman posting-station, in order to make a comparison with the earthworks seen in Yorkshire.

We explored a great many earthworks, measuring and drawing them. We found the sites of "lost" villages on the Wolds, of old manor-houses, of Saxon and Romano-British settlements, but never of that Roman "pub". Again and again we experienced the excitement of almost solving the problem, and at last we found what we thought might be the site. In an earthwork of Roman pattern, surrounded by a wide ditch, was a heap of crumbling stone-work, which may have marked the last vestiges of the ancient tavern where our Romano-British ancestors quaffed the equivalent of a pint of ale.

Before solving this problem, however,

we had become involved in another, and even more fascinating one, locating the Lost Villa. That is the difficulty with field-archaeology; one problem leads to another and you soon find yourself with more puzzles than you can handle.

At Sleights, in the Esk Valley, Raymond heard a curious story. An old man, now blind, told how as a boy he had been taken on a Sunday outing from Whitby to a relative's farm on the moors. Talk turned to the Romans, and the farmer remarked, "Why, this farm is built over a Roman house," and lifting up some floorboards he revealed to them a mosaic pavement, embellished with a peacock design, underneath. Taking them round to the cowsheds, he showed them pieces of mosaic being shovelled into a cart along with the muck. The farmhouse was indeed built on the foundations of a Roman building.

The boy returned home to Whitby with his father, grew to manhood, became an old man, but he never forgot that sight of the Roman house. Blind now, he could not guide anybody to the farm, but he remembered that they had gone to a rail-way-station, walked along a footpath, and reached a cross-roads. This story roused our curiosity, for study of the map of Roman Britain showed that no Roman villas had been located north of the Vale of Pickering. The site of a Roman villa located at Gargrave, near Skipton, was considered (1945) to be the most northerly villa discovered in England, but if the blind man's story was true, then this lost Roman house was even farther north still.

"The most northerly house in the Roman Empire" — that phrase was to haunt us for months, for years even. Where in the vastness of Yorkshire was it? To cut a long story short, we located the railway-station the old man described, we — though the finding was more Raymond's than mine — located the footpath and the cross-roads. That left us with a piece of country about two miles square, containing several farms. Under one of these farm-houses, if the story *was* true, was the mosaic floor with the peacock on it, which would prove or disprove the story. One by one we investigated these farms.

Astonished farmers, confronted with a request that we might remove the wooden floors of their sitting-room and look underneath, promised to oblige. How many tidily minded Yorkshire housewives were chagrined to discover their best sitting-room carpets and furniture moved to one side while their husbands laboured with screw-drivers and chisels, we do not know, but we must have left a trail of woe behind us. At last the search narrowed down to two farms. Both were occupied, and both tenants were unco-operative, so all we could do was wait.

Suddenly one farm became vacant, and we swooped, having obtained the owner's permission to investigate the foundations. To our dismay, the sitting-room did not contain a small trap-door screwed down into position, as described in the blind man's story. The floor was quite solid, so we were baffled again. We questioned some of the oldest inhabitants in the neighbourhood, who might remember the names of people who had tenanted the house at the time of the boy's visit, sixty years before.

One old man provided us with an exciting clue. The present floor of the sitting-room had been fitted some years before the last war; before that, he thought, the floor had contained a small trap-door. Excited by this discovery, we returned to the farm-house, but new tenants had moved in, and they did not take kindly to the idea of having their sitting-room floor disturbed. So there the matter rests, and we must wait until the house becomes empty again. Then perhaps the mystery of the most northerly house in the Roman Empire may be solved.

9

I'M ALL RIGHT, JACK

"TO continue with the classification of ancient monuments — so far I have dealt with rectilinear earthworks. These are often hard to diagnose by inspection, as those of you who have sometimes found yourself mistaken are no doubt aware."

The speaker paused, and looked at us belligerently. From the desk where I was sitting, pencil poised above notebook, his face was clearly visible. There was the bristling moustache, the spectacles slipping slightly forward towards the tip of the nose, so that the eyes behind them seemed to be staring at you over rather than through the lens, the high forehead with the hair somewhat disarrayed, all the features characteristic of Professor Gordon Childe, Director of the Institute of Archaeology of the University of London. His voice continued:

"Of these earthworks the most curious are the so-called *cursûs*. As the more knowledgeable of you may be aware, *cursûs* is a Latin noun of the fourth declension, so that its plural is *cursûs*, but those of you who are inured to riding in omnibuses may not mind watching races in *cursûses*!"

Later I was to realise that this cut-and-thrust style of lecturing was typical of Professor Childe. While I was struggling to remember if *cursûs did* mean "circus" (for such Latin as I had learned at school had been forgotten years ago), the Professor had passed on to an entirely different topic:

"Comparison should be made with the earthwork excavated at Trelleborg, on the Danish island of Zealand," he was saying. "Here we have a fortified camp where young sailors of the Viking fleet were quartered in boat-shaped houses each accommodating the crew of one longship."

This statement appeared to have no connection with those made previously, but it was woe betide the student who missed the gist of what Professor Childe was talking about; if your thoughts lagged behind, then you were lost indeed. A pity I had missed his comments on Scandinavian earthworks, for Raymond Hayes and I had come to the conclusion that certain mysterious earthworks we had discovered in Yorkshire could only be explained by the presence of settlers from Denmark. Maybe one of my fellow-students would let me see his notes; it was more than one's life was worth to interrupt the Professor in the middle of his discourse by asking a question.

"That will be all for today, gentlemen," Professor Childe concluded. "I am glad to see that you have all grasped what I was saying. I wish you good-day."

Now, this was taking place in the lecture-room of the Institute of Archaeology, in Regent's Park London, and I was one of a small group of students which the Professor was addressing. In that lecture-room and in the library adjoining I had spent several pleasant weeks acquiring some knowledge of the aims and methods of modern archaeology. Yes, I was actually a student at a university, studying a subject which had enthralled me for years, under the guidance of some of England's leading archaeologists. True, it was only for a limited period of time, a month or two, perhaps three; but a little of something was better than nothing at all.

It had begun three months before, when I had read an article in the *Strand Magazine* by Dr. Kathleen Kenyon, who was the secretary of the Institute of Archaeology; the article was called "Learning History with a Spade". Now for some time past I had been aware that my knowledge of history and archaeology was very disjointed and incoherent; it needed disciplining. Jumbled up in my mind were chunks of information about the Neolithic Age in Canada, Roman and Moorish remains in North Africa, the exploration of the Arctic seas, prehistoric and Roman archaeology in England. My mind was a ragbag of disconnected items of information, so that what was needed was to spend some time studying archaeology under skilled supervision.

In reply to a letter of mine Dr. Kenyon told me that it was possible to attend lectures at the Institute, even without studying for a degree. Lectures could be paid for as and when the money for them had been earned. This was good enough for me. My services were not needed at Scarborough youth hostel in winter, for few hostelers came to stay there except at Christmas-party time, so I was free to do as I pleased. I had some money saved up, some pieces of writing commissioned; now was the time to undergo the discipline of university education. If I could earn some more money while I was in London I could attend lectures at the Institute that much longer. It was as simple as that.

In those days the Institute of Archae-ology was housed in a building in the Inner Circle in Regent's Park. Picture me making my way there one dark November evening, with a batch of admission cards to lectures in my jacket pocket. My rucksack had been left at the youth hostel in Great Ormond Street, where I was staying until I could rent a room. This evening, in the darkness, the Institute building was effectively concealed, and for a time I perambulated helplessly round and round the deserted spaces of the park. A faint gleam of light, coming from a dark shape outlined in the gloom, encouraged me to think this might be the place I sought. Blocks of stone, ancient statuary, standing in the front hallway confirmed my guess. Stumbling, blinking, into a brightly lit office, I found myself being greeted by Dr. Kenyon herself.

The lecture had already started, so I slipped into a back seat, trying to guess who the lecturer might be — Professor Childe, Professor Zeuner, perhaps some other well-known archaeologist. To meet educated people — professors, doctors, leading historians, geographers, scientists — had been a will-o'-the-wisp which had lured me on since boyhood. Twice I had been thwarted in my youthful attempt to go to university; now, grasping at any straw, even two or three months at the Institute of Archaeology would be better than nothing.

The speaker was Professor F. E. Zeuner, one of whose books on environmental archaeology I had been trying to read in my spare time. Some portion of what he was saying was quite beyond my comprehension; but it was gratifying to discover that I could understand something, at least, of the subject-matter. When I got back to Yorkshire I could discuss some of the complexities of the subject with Raymond Hayes.

My life during the next two months was that of freelance journalist-cum-student of archaeology. My batch of tickets admitting me to lectures covered the whole range of the archaeology of Western Europe — Stone Age, Bronze Age, Iron Age, Roman — with the emphasis upon the geographical background and the various raw materials used by ancient man to make his tools and weapons. The geography of bygone landscapes was a study filled with fascination, as were the lectures on the repair and preservation of objects found in graves and settlement-sites. Whatever the topic of the lecture, I lapped it up as a cat laps up cream.

In the new year my money ran out, and I had to quit. My studies at the Institute came to an end, and I returned to Scarborough youth hostel. The time and money spent attending lectures had not been wasted, for though it had been but a little taste of studies which other young people obtained without difficulty, at least it was something towards the furtherance of my ambitions. One way and another I was gaining some knowledge of archaeology. There had been Dr. Varley's "dig" on Eddisbury Hill, in Cheshire. There was Mr. Gilyard-Beer's excavation of a Roman villa in Yorkshire, which turned out to be a miniature Bath. There were other jobs where I had played a part — helping to uncover the civil annexe to a Roman fort, helping to dig a Romano-British settlement, helping to trace a Saxon settlement, locating Roman roads. The results of these "digs" were recorded in professional papers in newspaper accounts, in my own notebooks.

Although that crippled leg of mine was continually giving me trouble now, so that I was frequently in pain, I refused to let it bar me from taking part in archaeological field-work. "Knowledge is not to be had by reading alone," counselled one of those handy volumes on prehistory published by Penguin Books. "The proper order is: text, sites, museums, texts. Go out into the country and *see*, and, where possible, *handle*." O. G. S. Crawford, Editor of *Antiquity*, had written:

One can learn more about a vanished race by handling the things their hands have made, their pottery, their stone and bronze implements, their ornaments; by walking along the roads which have grown up under their tread, by climbing the grassy slopes of their abandoned earthworks, or resting in the shadow of their mighty buildings; one can learn more in this intimate way than by reading all the books which have ever been written.

Years later, when I read his autobiography, I was to realise how much amateur archaeologists such as myself owed to O. G. S. Crawford, and how much his writings had influenced my life. From the time when, as a boy, I had first bought a sixpenny copy of his little book on the techniques of field-archaeology, to later years when I made use of the series of historical maps which he produced as Archaeology Officer of the Ordnance Survey, I and many others were in his debt.

Life during these years was exciting, busy, filled with interest, yet it had its bleaker moments. Yearly the pain in my right leg and hip was growing greater, and it was becoming more and more of a struggle for me to remain on my feet, to make my wilful muscles obey me. What the trouble was I did not know, and it never occurred to me to go to hospital to find out. I had been born crippled, and that was the end of it, I supposed; I would continue to be crippled until I died. Always at the back of my mind was the fear that one day my legs would fail me completely, so that I should be absolutely helpless. Unable to earn my living, the only future for me was a miserable existence in some institution for the disabled and the senile. So much for my dreams of becoming a writer, an explorer, and an archaeologist. Once again in my life I seemed to be facing a blank wall, without hope or encouragement.

These thoughts came to me only in my blackest moments, after a particularly bitter struggle with that stupid leg of mine. At other times life was exciting, gay, cheerful. That sense of wonder, that intense, childlike curiosity concerning the world about me, was still mine. The urge which I had experienced as a child was still as strong as ever — "to see strange lands from under the white-arched sails of ships", as Longfellow expressed it. Wonder is "something that arrests the attention or strikes the mind by its novelty, grandeur or inexplicableness: something unusual or strange: something that is extraordinary or not well understood." That dictionary definition explained my desire to spend part of each year in visiting lands beyond the skyline.

My spirit craved landscapes which appealed directly to my sense of awe and wonder — cliffs, gorges, caves, big trees, waterfalls. To see the *biggest*, the *highest*, the *deepest*, the *oldest* of anything — mountain, rock formation, ancient building, prehistoric monument, natural wonder. Those were the things which inspired me. Niagara Falls, Stonehenge, Pompeii, the Dead Sea, the Midnight Sun, Rome, the Sahara, the volcano Stromboli. If a thing could be described in superlatives, then it was worth visiting.

A problem which I had successfully evaded for a number of years now threatened to become all-important.

For more than a dozen years I had led a casual sort of life. Apart from times when I worked at Scarborough youth hostel, or was a student at Fircroft College, my life had been that of a wanderer, always moving on. From the Arctic to the Sahara, from Spain to Yugoslavia, I had wandered, tackling any job offered. Always to be moving on, seeing new places and faces, having new experiences — what other sort of life could compare with it? A lonely life, yes, for there was no time to make lasting friendships, but a disabled man learns to be alone. A lone wolf, going where and when I pleased, that was my ideal.

As for women, I had met all sorts, and liked some of them. But love now, that was different, for I liked my lone-wolf life and fought shy of entanglements. Love meant marriage, settling down, living in a house and having a family, and working regularly for a wage — how could *I* fit into such a life? No, I was content to be a spectator of life, watching other people get married and struggle with the problems of civilised existence. The life of a lone wolf was good enough for me.

Yet, as I grew older I became aware of a

feeling of dissatisfaction, became aware of a longing which was more than the mere desire for friendship with a woman. The idea came to me that man was not meant to live alone; he needs a woman to share life with him. He needs her not merely for reasons of sex, but because without her his life is not complete. In two books of travel which I wrote I tried to express the power of the wanderlust to drive a man on and on, from one strange experience to another. Suddenly the wandering man wakes up, as it were, and realises that most other men have settled down, have homes and families of their own, and that he is left like a stray dog whom nobody wants. A man gets the feeling that he does not fit in anywhere, that he does not belong.

To find the place where he belongs; that is what a man needs to do most of all.

For several years there had been this conflict, this struggle between two opposing points of view. On the one hand was the call of the world outdoors, away from city life — the call of the wild places and the open road, with its free, irresponsible life without commitments, always moving on in search of something new. Surely it was better to be a spectator of life than to become entangled in emotional complications? If a man's wants were few and his standard of living low it was possible to live simply and have time to do the things which interested him.

On the other hand, as I grew older, there was the call of my fellow-men, the desire to be like them and have a home and wife and family of my own. Yet this called for more money, a higher standard of living, being tied to a regular job, and hence was the exact opposite of the life of the lone-wolf adventurer. The wandering man would have to learn to fit into society; the question was whether the wanderlust could be overcome, whether the wanderer could change himself from being a lone dog who eyed all the world askance to a conventional respectable husband and father.

Women, so it was said, wanted a home, security, babies; and whether such things could be fitted into a wanderer's life was a problem. How could a man's wish for adventure be reconciled with a woman's desire for security?

The whole problem resolved itself very naturally. Life continued to be full and interesting, with hostel activities and archaeological investigation in my spare time, and then one day I looked up and saw a woman in front of me — Joyce was her name — and looking at her I knew we would be married and would start a new life together. Always at the back of my mind was the thought that some day I should meet a woman who would be everything in the world to me, and sure enough this *did* happen.

Something which had puzzled me was how, in books, a man had only to look at a girl to know at once that she was the only woman in the world for him. I had often wondered how anyone could be so certain that a stranger met by chance was destined to be one's wife. And yet it happened to me. I could not have explained how, but I *knew* that I was going to marry Joyce. Something inside me told me.

Days drifted by as we wandered along the cliff-tops together, picking wild flowers and blackberries, exploring little hidden valleys. The three days which Joyce had planned to spend at the hostel became a week, a fortnight. It was time for her to return home to Sheffield. The night before she was due to leave, panic-stricken that I might lose her, I could hardly wait till the day's work was over before taking her to our favourite haunt by Scalby Ness, so that I might ask the fateful question:

"Darling, will you marry me?"

And though I was so sure I knew her answer, it was still a relief to receive her reply: "Please."

Joyce went back to Sheffield, and I was left, an engaged man now, with two problems to solve — how to earn my living as a married man and how to get a house for us to live in. After working at the hostel for four years I wanted to obtain a new job, suited to a physically handicapped man. A job which left me with some free time for studying and travelling, I reflected. What kinds of job were open to a crippled man? My life had been an unusual and exciting one. Could I earn my living by writing and lecturing about the places and peoples of which I had first-hand knowledge? To be a writer had been an early ambition of mine, though up to now it had been a spare-time activity.

One evening I was sitting at the table in the common-room, with a pile of books and maps about me, explaining to some hostelers how to reach various places of interest near Scarborough, when I had a feeling that I was being watched; turning my head, I discovered a big, pleasant-faced man watching me.

"Tell me," he asked. "Do you do much of this kind of thing — teaching young people to read maps and explore the countryside?"

"It was the Warden's idea originally," I explained. "We try to get hostelers interested in the out-of-doors. It seems such a waste that they should cycle all this way and then have nothing better to do than go to a cinema."

His next question surprised me.

"Have you ever thought of becoming a teacher?"

"Me — a teacher," I said, shaking my head. "I've never thought of such a thing."

"I should say you have the makings of a good teacher in you," he remarked. "A teacher must be capable of arousing children's interest in things, and you seem able to do that."

To be a teacher, I mused, to help children

realise the wonder of the world in which they live. As a child there had grown up within me three ideas which were to influence my life — a sense of wonder and a desire to explore the world about me, and then *to tell other people about it*. The joy of discovery is doubled if it can be shared with others. Children possess this sense of wonder; often, by the time they have reached maturity, they have lost it. How to help them retain that sense of wonder throughout life, that was the problem. Writing books and lecturing was one way; teaching could be another.

How strange, the thought came to me, if youth hostels, having provided me with a wife, were now also providing me with a way of earning my living! My companion — headmaster of a school in Manchester, it appeared — was explaining that there was going to be a shortage of teachers, and that a man could become a qualified teacher by undergoing a two-year course of instruction at a training college. All this was news to me.

"What about my lame leg?" I asked. "Maybe they won't let a crippled man become a teacher?"

"Could you not go into hospital and have your leg straightened?" the headmaster asked. "Surgeons can do quite wonderful things nowadays."

"I have always regarded being crippled as something which one has to put up with," I told him. "It is not easy to get into hospital nowadays, you know, unless you are nearly dying."

"Why not see what can be done?" he suggested. "And do not forget my advice about taking up teaching as a career."

"Get married, go to hospital, become a teacher," I mused. "It looks as if I am in for a busy time."

And so Joyce and I were married early in 1948.

We began our married life in a caravan measuring ten feet by six, parked in a field two miles north of Scarborough. We had a water-tap two yards away and a large barn in which we could keep our bicycles and spare possessions; we were happy enough. The idea was that we could take part-time jobs in a catering establishment (my job at the youth hostel had come to an end), which would leave me free to write books. My first book, about Cheshire, was selling well, and we hoped to be able to save enough money to get a house to live in and furnish it. That was what we hoped to do . . . but actually it didn't work out in that way at all.

First we were ordered to move the caravan from the field by the local council (since people were not allowed to live in caravans), and we then discovered that there was no place where you were allowed to put a van. You could only move on — or be moved on by the police. So we and other caravan-dwellers were moved on — and on. We all finished up in the only parking site where living was permissible, in a field by the municipal refuse dump. This unlovely site was a place of stinks and flies and no water. To get away from this horrible place we took jobs as cooks at various holiday camps, only to discover that we were expected to work ourselves to death for low wages. Coping with all these setbacks left me no time for writing books; writing had to wait until we were both out of work. We had to live on our savings, and these dwindled away.

We decided to have a honeymoon. We had been married over five months, and had been so busy surmounting one difficulty after another that there had been no time for a honeymoon. Now was the time to fulfil a promise I had made to Joyce, that I would show her the two greatest waterfalls in England — High Force and Cauldron Snout, in the valley of the river Tees, where Yorkshire and Durham met. And so we started off, packs on back, glad to escape for a while from the fumes and flies of Scarborough's rubbish dump.

How it rained in England that summer! As we went across Yorkshire, by way of Ampleforth and Ripon, Askrigg and Barnard Castle — that friendly little town with its magnificent château-like Bowes Museum filled with some of the best of the world's art — the rain went with us all the way. In driving rain we made our way up the wooded valley of the Tees (which, with the valley of the Dove in Derbyshire, I placed above all others in England), to the isolated youth hostel at Langdon Beck. This hostel was a simple wooden structure, and we were the only visitors there, so we foraged for fuel and food, and cooked meals, and sat huddled by the stove while the rain poured down outside, and were quite happy together.

And we saw High Force and Cauldron Snout, where the river Tees plunges down from the uplands in two majestic cataracts. High Force drops a sheer eighty feet over a cliff of black basalt, a wall of foaming white, and is a sight to inspire awe in heavy rain, even though one had to pay sixpence at a turnstile in order to view it. But Cauldron Snout in the rain was sheer undiluted savagery, for it is located out in the wilderness miles from anywhere, just a great waterfall thundering down the mountainside in the loneliness. The Tees flings itself over a series of rock-ledges in a huge cascade two hundred feet high, forming a sort of gigantic staircase with the river descending in great bounds, to plunge in a welter of spray and foam into the pool at the bottom. The roar of it was a sound worth listening to.

From the falls it is not much farther to High Cup Nick, a mountain-pass walled in by high cliffs without a road through; the sight of it is enough to make your hair stand on end if you try to pass through it in the rain and mist. But this we did not try to do, but only looked, and then, soaking wet, turned back towards civilisation. So it will be seen that we brought back some vivid memories of our honeymoon.

And when we got back to our caravan there was a letter waiting for us; someone was actually offering us a house to live in!

As the train bore us westward across Yorkshire towards the smoky pall of the coalfields I read for the dozenth time a letter from my friend Reginald which had reached us a few hours before. "You are looking for a house," he wrote. "I have a cottage here to rent, if you are interested. Fifteen shillings a week, and it's a nice little place. This area is not quite up to the standard of Scarborough for scenic beauty, but parts of it are not too bad. Of course, the house may not suit you, so if you do not want it, just let me know." *If we do not want it !* We would not have said no to any house, and we caught the first train to Wakefield. How curious, I thought, that Reg, who had been a butcher in Manchester, near the greengrocer's shop where I had worked as a boy, nearly twenty years before, should now be the medium by which our marriage was to have a chance to survive! Reg, it seemed, had turned from butchering to market-gardening, and, having bought an old farmhouse five miles from Wakefield, planned to supply eggs and vegetables for the local market.

Now the train was passing through an unlovely region of slag-heaps and colliery winding-gear and stagnant pools and railway sidings. Our hearts sank when we saw this dismal landscape under a leaden sky, but we knew now that a house near the beautiful sea-coast and moorlands was not for us. A bus took us away from Wakefield towards a long, low ridge whose summit was outlined in the red glow of coke-ovens. Stark against the sky showed the outlines of pithead gear, and the men who boarded the bus wore metal helmets and had black faces. A stink of gas was everywhere, and the countryside about us seemed to be a black waste of colliery tippings. We felt worse than ever.

Then we passed through a gate in a brick wall and found ourselves in a little secluded garden, and our spirits rose immediately, for there in the midst of the coal-workings was a little oasis of peace and beauty, a place with a green lawn and hedges and rose-bushes, red and cream, and tall pink hollyhocks, and masses of marigolds and other flowers. Behind the garden was a house, with spacious rooms, and such amenities as electric light, taps from which one could draw any number of buckets of water, gas, and a coal-range, and, best of all, a bathroom in which one could splash about to one's heart's content. If we had been offered our choice of houses we could hardly have found one better suited to our taste, and it was ours for the taking!

Now that we had got our house, the next thing was to furnish it. This was no easy task, for shopkeepers would not sell you, for example, a carpet unless you bought several hundred pounds worth of furniture — and paid cash. Eventually we acquired various suites of furniture — living-room, bedroom, dining-room — sundry carpets, tables, bookshelves. But for three months we slept on camp-beds, ate our meals from a folding table, and cooked over a Primus stove. The day when we actually acquired a gas cooker was a day of triumph. Our savings dwindled rapidly; two cheques for royalties on my first book, each for one hundred and twenty-five pounds, did not go far. When my daughter Anne was born I had little more than five pounds left, and had to leave immediately for London, to urge my creditors to pay more promptly and to secure contracts for more books. With difficulty I got my income up to £10 a week.

There were few jobs open to a crippled man with bad eye-sight, so that it seemed for the time being I must become a writer whether I willed or no. Always at the back of my mind was the suggestion made by the headmaster I had encountered at Scarborough youth hostel, that I go to a training college and become a teacher, but how my wife and baby daughter were to be maintained during the two-year period of training was a problem nobody could answer. Several books published and bringing in royalties at six-monthly intervals was one solution. But the biggest problem was that silly leg of mine, which was continually giving me pain, and making it difficult for me to walk. Sooner or later I should be compelled to go to hospital and ask the doctors to discover what the trouble was. But hospital also was out of the question until I had some money to keep my family while I was undergoing treatment.

So I embarked upon a career as an author, with an old washstand for a desk and my books piled in heaps on the floor about me, so that whenever I wished to check a reference I had to dash frantically from one pile to another to find the volume I needed. Novels were what I wanted to write, but they were too chancy a proposition for a man with little capital who had to have money coming in as quickly as possible; I decided that non-fiction books offered better prospects of success. Books of travel and adventure, books about natural history and country life, books telling the English people of the fascinating places to be discovered within the boundaries of their own country. It seemed to me that there ought to be a living to be made from writing this sort of book, together with magazine articles and radio broadcasts.

It appears to be almost a convention of fiction that the unknown author, after an initial period of struggle, produces a book which is an immediate success, which sells in thousands, so that the writer is then embarked upon a career as a successful author for life. Probably there were writers in the 1950's who achieved immediate success with one book, but no author I know did this. They had to write quite a number of books to achieve even a modest success, and even with a couple of dozen books to their credit were still liable to have their next effort rejected by publishers.

Authorship today, stripped of its glamour, is a highly disciplined profession. Authors cannot write to please themselves, but have to write what publishers think will sell. In an instructive article in *The Writer* Ethel Mannin pointed out that the ordinary writer who has not a private income must have a big annual output to be able to secure even a modest return. A writer must be prepared to tackle any job offered — books, radio, articles, advertising, reviewing, ghosting. My target was to write a thousand words a day during a year, and in my first year I produced

353,000 words. I did not reach the total I aimed at because I had to stop work for a fortnight after the birth of my daughter, to help with the housework and shopping.

A thousand words a day may not sound much, but I could not afford to pay for the services of a typist, and retyped everything myself. And the material I wrote was not imaginative writing, but factual matter, so that long journeys were required to collect the facts. Joyce and the baby were often left alone while I traversed the British Isles, from Kent to Northern Ireland, from Cornwall to the Lake District. My plan to write a book about the islands off the coast of England and Wales, which had already taken me to Holy Isle and the Farne Islands, off the coast of Northumberland, now took me to East Anglia and Kent, and then along the south coast, by way of the Isle of Wight, to Land's End. The Bristol Channel coasts were visited in snowstorms and bitter cold, and my principal memory of the Welsh coasts is of high winds. So I came again to the Hilbre Islands, at the mouth of the river Dee (which I had first seen so long ago as a boy), and the journey to islands round Morecambe Bay was comparatively easy.

As time passed the pain and discomfort associated with my damaged hip became more and more severe, and our future became correspondingly more and more menacing. What was to become of us? I did not know, for it was only by my working seven days a week that we were able to keep going. If I had to stop writing there was no other way of earning my living. I should be finished. Living in an isolated colliery village in Yorkshire meant that I was too far from markets for my kind of writing; one had to rely on conducting business by correspondence, and waiting for acceptances could tax one's patience to the utmost. One needed to live near London, in order to keep in personal contact with editors. Yet, by working hard, I sold several books and radio scripts, and a fair number of magazine articles. Fellow-writers told me I was doing well.

Life as a writer, then, was bitter-sweet. Periods of worrying and typing for ten or twelve hours a day and increasing pain made me despair. Other times, rarer, when contracts and cheques were gained without too much difficulty, brought happiness, and the sun shone. In our own poor way we were happy, for there was pleasure in being able to leave one's work at will, and with Joyce and baby Anne in her pram go for walks along the country lanes which still existed like oases of greenery amid the smoke and blackness of the colliery landscape. For it is one of the anomalies of the coalfield that though at one moment you may be in a landscape which resembles the infernal regions — smoke and flames, blackness and acres of slag-deserts where nothing grows — a little later you may be in some of the most charming scenery imaginable. Within walking distance of our home was a long winding lake, surrounded by wooded hills, whose slopes in springtime were shaded deep blue with myriad bluebells. Walk in the other direction, and you emerged upon the summit of a breezy moorland, where heather and bracken grew.

We often filled Anne's pram with baskets and jars, and went collecting blackberries, or anything edible. There were people who had apples, pears, or rhubarb they wanted to get rid of, and there were elder-berries and rose-hips to collect. In the wood beyond the lake we came upon a ruined house with a walled garden, deserted for many years, and here we found rasp-berry and blackcurrant bushes, with fruit ready for the picking. Joyce filled dozens of preserving jars with fruit, enough to last us from one year's end to another. The butcher sold us sheep's heads at sixpence a time, and they made nourishing soup, and sliced sheep's tongue, with salad from the garden, was worth eating. Marrow bones, too, made many a tasty meal. Joyce baked bread, cakes, confectionery. We did without entertainments, news-papers, drinks, cigarettes.

So we lived cheaply, happily.

10

THE PROBLEM OF PAIN

IT was in a consulting room in Pinder-fields Hospital, Wakefield, that the next phase in my battle against pain took place. Clad in a dressing-gown and not much else, I lay on a couch and listened to Miss Pearson, FRCS, diagnose my trouble.

"Now, Mr. Ingram, we've examined that hip and leg of yours and can tell you what the trouble is: it's osteo-arthritis. It is rather far advanced, so it is no wonder that you have been in such pain for the past few years. Why did you not come to see us earlier?"

There was a cold feeling in the pit of my stomach. Although one may have suffered pain for years, to the point of virtually becoming a helpless invalid, it is still an unpleasant experience to have a doctor tell you that your worst fears are true. I did not know then that arthritis does not kill, but merely tortures, and had visions of being confined to bed for the rest of my life, unable to earn my living or mix with other people. Arthritis was an old person's disease, and I was not that old, only thirty-six.

"Have you been involved in an accident?" Miss Pearson asked. "That hip looks as though it has been messed about — quite a number of years ago, I should imagine."

"My mother fell downstairs just before I was born," was my reply. "She said the doctors gave me only a week to live."

"I have known a number of people who were expected to live for only a week," Miss Pearson remarked cheerfully. "They will be drawing their old-age pensions presently."

"We can do something about that hip," she went on briskly. "It will take an operation, but there will be an end to the pain. You will not be able to do all a normal person can do, but you will have a better sort of life than the one you are living now."

"Then the sooner the better," I said. "I am tired of living like this."

The prospect of undergoing a major surgical operation did not distress me; I had spent plenty of time in hospital. Any operation was better than this miserable half-life I had endured during the past few years. The operation did offer some hope of a pleasanter life in the future.

When I left the consulting-room it was with the knowledge that I should be operated on as soon as the hospital had a vacant bed for me. Then, within a few months or a year, I should be able to walk about without pain. Instead of the pain-filled, helpless future I had visualised was a future bright with opportunity. If I could be cured and made fit again, then I could do as the headmaster at Scarborough youth hostel had suggested two years before: I could go to a training college and learn to become a teacher. That should be an interesting job, for with my first-hand knowledge of far-off lands I could bring the wonder of the world into my classroom, and help children to keep their sense of mystery of the world about them. Authorship was a good life if one could write books which would stir the world; there was no particular merit in spending one's life churning out the mediocre.

I returned home, and waited for the message which would tell me the hospital had a bed for me. I waited a long time, but no message came. Weeks went by, then months, and still there seemed no chance of my getting to hospital to undergo that most vital operation. The pain in my leg and hip grew worse. The time came when it was no longer possible for me to venture outside, for my leg would no longer obey me. I spent hours lying on a couch in our living-room, with my typewriter placed on a piece of wood so that I could at least make some attempt at earning my living. As I waited the thoughts which filled my mind were very grim ones. In this world one was alone, and could expect no help from anyone. Some words from the Bible haunted me: "Unto him that hath shall be given, and from him that hath not shall be taken away that which he hath." Certainly some of us had very, very little, and even that little we were liable to have taken away from us.

What was the encyclopedia definition of osteo-arthritis?

A degenerative disease of the joints, affecting the hips, knees and shoulders. It usually attacks people over middle age and the elderly. It seems to occur in those joints which during the course of life have been subjected to the most strain and stress. The cartilage of the joints wears away, the corroded bone ends being left to grate one on the other. There is pain on movement and at night when the protective muscular spasm relaxes.

So that was osteo-arthritis; it seemed as though I had been fighting the disease all my life, though at first its slow, relentless advance had been undramatic. From an early age I had learned about disability, for as a child I had become accustomed to speaking of "my bad leg" and "that silly leg of mine", and passing the pain off with a wry grimace. As I grew older I was subjected to sudden, occasional attacks of pain, which would pass and leave me free, maybe for months or a year. Sometimes the pain was barely noticeable, sometimes it was a nagging, gnawing pain, and sometimes it darted along my leg like a red-hot poker. As well as pain there was something else, even more frightening — the gradual loss of movement in my right hip and leg. As I grew older it required immense concentration to make my legs do what I wanted them to do.

The slow, gradual approach to complete disability took years, but it came relentlessly. One came to accept it fatalistically; *what can't be cured must be endured*. Born damned; die damned. You were either lucky or unlucky in this world, and if you were one of the unlucky ones, then Christ help you. One became like a dumb animal, impassive, without hope, waiting for the future. The future was slow death.

Yet in spite of the pain and increasing disability I accomplished the experiences described in this book — the long journeys, often on foot, across Lapland, Yugoslavia, Morocco, the hard work in camps and hostels. Looking back now, I wonder how I accomplished it all, and there were moments when even my courage failed me, and I felt that I had reached the end of things.

Of recent years the pain and discomfort had grown so great that when it came to walking I could take only a few steps at a time, and would then have to stop and think — standing on one leg and holding on to a door or table — of how to take the next few steps. By the time I had solved that problem I would have forgotten what I had intended doing, anyway. Sitting down and then getting up again became a major difficulty. Sometimes one got into a position where one was completely im-mobile, and then there was nothing to be done but grit your teeth and force your reluctant muscles to obey you. Pain then was worse than anything I had experienced before, so that whatever action I was trying to perform would go completely out of my mind.

Once in Belfast, where I had gone to collect some facts for a magazine article, I started to cross a wide street. I saw a motorbus a long way off, but so slow was my progress that the vehicle had time to traverse the whole length of the street and reach me before I could get my leg muscles to work. I stood there in the middle of the street, looking stupidly about me, horribly frightened, while the brakes of the bus screeched as the big vehicle skidded round me. The driver, who could not know that it was muscle-seizure which made it impossible for me to move backward or forward, shouted out something about damned drunks who went to sleep in the roadway.

Later, as the muscle-spasms increased in intensity, I came to dread trying to get on or off vehicles, or to cross streets, for it seemed only a matter of time before I was knocked down. Looking at myself in a mirror one day, it came as a shock to see how twisted my body had become, and what a misshapen humpback I must appear to other people, with one hip stuck out at an odd angle. How ungainly I appeared, and how people looked at me as though it made them uncomfortable to have a cripple around!

Yet I still had my living to earn somehow or other, for so far as I knew a man and his family could starve to death if he was unable to work. National Assistance and charity were things I had not heard of; all I had to guide me were some precepts instilled in me during childhood, in Canada. Look after yourself and expect help from no-one. Stand on your own feet. Fight your own battles or go under. In this world the weakest must go to the wall.

This grim period of waiting seemed to go on for a long time. But one day the postman delivered the message for which I had been waiting so long: there was a vacant bed at the hospital for me. Now the next phase in my battle against pain and immobility could begin.

I opened my eyes. Bright lights blazed into them, making me blink. The atmosphere about me was intensely hot, so that it was difficult to breathe. I seemed to be in a low tunnel, but when I tried to move out of the way of the lights nothing happened. Not a muscle in my body obeyed me, and it was only with the greatest difficulty that my head could be moved from one side to the other. The heat and glare made me, for one quick moment, wonder whether I was dead and in hell. This seemed to be the sort of experience one would meet with there. I was still puzzling over this when blackness engulfed me.

When I came to again I was still in the tunnel, but the lights were not so bright and it was less hot. I could lift my head, and looking about me I saw Joyce. She said something, but what it was I was unable to make out. *Did I want a drink?* I took a sip of water from the cup she held out for me, and was promptly sick. Another voice, a nurse's, joined my wife's, but I felt too wretched to reply. But it was good to feel Joyce was there and I was still alive. Then the darkness came back.

When I came to again I was no longer in the tunnel. I was lying in an ordinary hospital bed, with the blankets raised above my legs by means of a metal framework. On either side of me were other beds with figures lying in queer attitudes. Some looked as though they were stretched out on a rack; one patient appeared as though he was being crucified. A man with a broken neck sat bolt upright. But they all called out cheery greetings to me, and somebody shouted to an orderly that the patient in Bed 9 was conscious and waiting for his dinner!

My body still remained immobile, though I could turn my head from side to side. The thought came to me: I'm in hospital, I've had an operation, I can't move, what the hell have they done to me? I slid one hand down my side to where my right hip should have been, but my groping fingers encountered only a warm, solid substance which covered my entire body. Some time passed before I realised that I was encased in plaster from my chest to my toes. Small wonder that I could not move! The tunnel, it seemed, was a piece of apparatus which is placed over a patient after an operation to dry out the plaster as quickly as possible. It amused me to think of myself wearing a suit of armour.

How long am I going to spend like this? came the thought, and at once the answer came — twelve weeks. The surgeon had said she would examine the hip in three months' time; until then there was nothing to do except wait. After that — it would take time before the muscles started working again. Say, a year before the leg was in good working order. The operation *was* a success, I suppose?

Nothing to do except wait. Doctors never tell you anything. Why worry, when one felt so tired; best go to sleep again. Sleep and wait. Time would pass. The darkness came again, and once more I was plunged into a world of queer, disturbed dreams.

A week went by, and another and another. Like a log I lay there, unmoving, almost indifferent to my surroundings. My body seemed to crave sleep, as though still recovering from the shock of the operation. I ate the food which was given me, used a bed-pan when one was needed, chatted with the men in the beds round me, yet only with part of my mind; the other part seemed completely detached from it all.

The solid casing of plaster no longer bothered me; rather it felt somehow comforting, so that I would have suddenly felt naked if it had been removed. I could manipulate my arms and shoulders now, reach for things from my locker, even write, using the plaster on my chest as a writing-table. Now and again sudden stabs of red-hot pain would dart through my hip and leg, making me scream out loud at times, but nobody took any notice; this was a good sign, that the hip-bones were knitting together after the operation, so they told me. I felt cheered by the news.

A month or six weeks had passed now,

and it was time for me to be thinking of doing something useful with my time. My stay in hospital might last another four or five months, so perhaps the enforced leisure could be made profitable. Could I do some writing? Could I learn something? This was an opportunity to improve myself. I had time on my hands and nowhere to go, I reflected grimly.

I enrolled for a correspondence course in English language, and when this was completed enrolled for another course in short-story writing. I completed part of a book called *I Found Adventure*, which had to be written in long-hand, for I could not bend to reach a typewriter balanced on my chest. Conscious of gaps in my education, I read all the books available — books dealing with English literature, science, history, and geography. Friends sent me parcels of books; a friend paid for a subscription to a weekly magazine. Three months passed fairly quickly, but after that I began to get impatient and bored.

To get any writing done involved me in a continual battle with Matron. My manuscripts, lessons, text-books, were kept in a brief-case, and in order to be able to reach them with my right hand I asked Eric, the orderly, to suspend the case from the side of my locker by an S-hook. If the locker was turned at an angle to the side of my bed I could just manage to remove papers from the case with my right hand, but if the locker was kept straight, then I could not reach the things I needed. It happened that Matron insisted that all lockers in the ward be kept in the one position, which made it impossible for me to reach mine. No amount of explanation would persuade her to relax the rule, so whenever she was suspected to be in the neighbourhood my writing activities had to be postponed until she had departed.

Even lying encased in plaster in a hospital bed one can have new experiences, undergo the thrill of discovery. One day, reading an article in a magazine by Albert Schweitzer, I was struck by one of his statements: "If you have been delivered from bodily anguish, you must not think you are free. From that moment on, you feel bound to help to bring others to deliverance. If an operation has saved you from death or torture, do your part to make it possible for medical science to reach some other place where death and agony still rule unhindered." This idea was new to me. Was it true?

To what extent does the individual owe a debt to those less fortunate than himself? Does the crippled man who has had his ability to walk restored to him have any responsibility towards those who will never be able to walk properly? Does the blind person whose sight has been restored owe anything to those who cannot see? Albert Schweitzer had no doubts about the matter; "Your Second Job" was how he phrased it. The idea gripped my imagination.

The idea of becoming a teacher, as I have recalled, had been in my mind for some time. Now that my operation was behind me — and if all went right I would be able to walk fairly well again — I could plan for the future. To be a teacher, yes, but not just an ordinary teacher, rather a teacher in a school for physically handicapped children. As one who had suffered from physical handicaps myself and overcome them, I was the sort of person who could show crippled children how to overcome their own difficulties and find life worth living. My experiences could be an example to them, so that a disabled child could say, "I've had a bad start in life and things looked pretty hopeless, but Mr. Ingram was crippled also and see what he has managed to do." I could help to give them the courage to continue when they felt disheartened.

Not all of us could be Albert Schweitzers and go to Central Africa, but we could start trying to help persons less fortunate than ourselves, wherever we might be.

The end of my stay in hospital, when at long last it arrived, came quickly. There was the great day when my plaster was removed — a real carpenter's job this, with much sawing and banging — and then there was exposed to view a thin, wasted object which I hardly recognised as *my* leg. Humph, thought I, to imagine I will ever walk on that thing again! But when Miss Pearson examined it she appeared pleased and remarked what a good job had been done. The day came when I was allowed to sit up in bed and dangle my leg over the side. Then there was my first attempt to put my feet to the floor, and, oh, dear, how dizzy the effort made me! The first time I tried to get those wasted muscles working — it was agony! But within a fortnight the muscles *were* working, and within a week or two after that I was walking — first with crutches, then with two sticks.

It was good to be able to hobble about on one's own two feet, even if one's first progression along the corridors was slow and painful; even the bleak winter landscape outside was a change from hospital walls. But now there was a sense of urgency to be away from hospital, to get back home again, to be working at my typewriter so that we should have some money coming in to keep us during the next year or two. To be a teacher involved having that leg of mine in as good working order as it was possible to be. Two years was the time which Miss Pearson said was needed before the leg-bones would set in the hip sufficiently solidly for the operation to be considered finally completed. That would be Autumn 1952. Only then could I apply for admission to a training college, so in the meantime

I must still continue to earn my living as best I could. Another three months of lying on the couch in the living-room would be needed before my legs would bear my weight sufficiently for me to venture farther afield, so it was a case of back to the typewriter and somehow of making a living by the only method which was open to me — writing.

One advantage I possessed, which was of great value to a man struggling to earn a livelihood by authorship: I had several good friends who were also writers, who were able to give me information about markets and to write letters of encouragement when my manuscripts were returned. To four such men I owe a great deal for the friendship and practical help which they gave. While a student at Fircroft College I had made the acquaintance of a Mr. and Mrs. Wilson, who lived in a lovely old half-timbered house named "Four Ashes" standing in wooded, green countryside some miles south of Birmingham. They allowed me the freedom of their home, and for this I was very grateful, for theirs was a way of life which I had never experienced before; but, even more than this, I came to know the author of a piece of writing I admired — John Hampson and his *Saturday Night at the Greyhound*. John Hampson worked as companion to the son of the house, and during my visits there I learned from him something of the technique of writing novels.

Then there was Rex Hardinge, who lived in an old house overlooking Chichester Harbour, who made a living by writing books of travel and adventure. A tall, wiry-looking, silvery-haired fellow-wanderer who greeted me like a long-lost brother. From our very first meeting, in a big room decorated with crossed African spears and old guns, we talked as though we had known each other all our lives. Hardinge had just returned from a trip into the bush country of West Africa, where he had nearly met his death in a cannibal's cooking-pot, as he described with gusto in his book *Gambia and Beyond*. Meeting him made me conscious of the warm spirit of comradeship which exists between men who have roughed it in the far corners of the earth. It was good to have known such men.

In a flat in Belgrave Square, in London,

I met another man who was destined to become a good and helpful friend. This was the author and traveller Gordon Cooper, a row of whose books faces me on the shelf as I type this. *Roving round the World, I searched the World for Death, Life's a Short Summer, The Globetrotter's Bedside Book*, which he dedicated to "Barclays Bank, that anonymous but indispensable friend". A big man, who paced the room restlessly as he talked, he described far-away places — the Grand Canyon and the Big Trees in the United States, the ruined city of Angkor in Indo-China, and Zimbabwe in Rhodesia — in a way which made them seem just around the corner. Our friendship was to last twenty-five years, till his death in 1963.

It was near Frome, in Somerset, that I first met another writer who was to be a staunch friend for close on twenty years. This was Frank Stuart, who after years as a working journalist in Fleet Street had settled down in the country to make a living by writing novels — *Remember Me*, a story of the "lost years" in William Shakespeare's life, and *Elephant in Jet*, a tale of the lost Indus civilisation; his first novel, *Caravan for China*, had just sold over 100,000 copies in the United States. A tall, spare-framed man with a keen, friendly face and laughing, kindly eyes, he opened the door of his house to me and welcomed me into his life and the lives of his family. In such books as *A Seal's World*, *Wild Wings*, and *City of the Bees* he combined acute observation of wildlife with mastery of the written word. Reading his books, you were carried away from the drab, everyday world into a magic world where creatures such as bees and ducks and seals underwent breathtaking experiences following their destinies in the wonderland of Nature.

"They fulfil God's purpose, just as we do," was the way he explained it.

A sincere Christian, he demonstrated by his actions, in a quiet, unobtrusive way, his belief that Christ's teachings were just as applicable now, under modern conditions, as when the Sermon on the Mount was first preached nearly two thousand years ago. He was to be the best friend a man could ever have, a man to whom one could always turn when in trouble, and never be let down. When he died in 1955 something went out of my life which could never be replaced.

Meeting such men as these helped to give me a balanced view of life. The manner in which they offered friendship and help, without a hint of patronage, made me consider the English public-school system again, for it seemed to produce a fine type of human being. The working-man, struggling to make something of his life, deprived of opportunities of education and advancement, is apt to feel that all the social system is "agin" him, that he is being deliberately kept down in his "proper place", but I never experienced anything of this sort myself, and found men friendly enough, without regard to one's origins.

This was the case with other men I met, writers most of them. In a big, rather dark room overlooking a narrow, noisy street in Soho I met Stephen Graham, the author whose writings had influenced me in my decision to start off from Manchester with a pack on my back to find out for myself what the world was like. Stephen Graham was another big, quietly spoken man, author of *The Gentle*

Art of Tramping, which had encouraged me to wander along the roads of the world. Seated in a chair, I watched him pace the length of the room and back, while listening to tales of his tramps across Russia, to Jerusalem with the pilgrims, over the American Rockies with the poet Vachel Lindsay. All these experiences were described in fascinating volumes — *A Tramp's Sketches*, *The Moving Tent*, *A Tramp's Anthology*.

Other men I had met — Crichton Porteous, farmhand-cum-author, who wrote *Teamsman*, *Land Truant*, and other good books; Richard Perry, author of *Lundy, Isle of Puffins* and *A Naturalist on Lindisfarne*; R. M. Lockley, whose book *The Way to an Island* once started me off in search of an island of my own on which I could live; and Ralph Whitlock, known for his broadcasts about "Cowleaze Farm" in Children's Hour. Between them all these men helped my mental horizons to expand, for they taught me much about many things.

11

GIVE GOD A CHANCE

SEATED at my desk in our cottage in the Yorkshire mining village, back at home after months in hospital, I wrestled with a problem; what was I going to do next? Did I or did I not want to become a writer? Yes, I did want to be a writer, a novelist. To be a writer in the great tradition of the past, to write novels whose message would go thundering round the world, that was to be a writer indeed!

But there did not appear to be an opportunity for authors to write that kind of novel in England now. There was only the eternal triangle in ten thousand manifestations, crime, sex, school stories, romances for women's magazines — the work of competent, business-like writers, but not of great writers. The writing of today was petty writing, without fire and without a cause. There was nothing left to write about nowadays — no great social injustices, no fights against tyranny, no struggles for freedom. These were not themes for English writers, but for the novelists of the new countries, writers in Africa and Asia. I was a writer without a cause.

There was no particular merit in writing for the commercial market; in fact, there was no point in being a writer at all. Therefore, if one could not write the kind of books one wanted, and could not honestly write the kind of stories for which there was a demand, the answer was to be something else. To be a teacher, a teacher of disabled children.

That was the answer.

That involved a second problem — that silly leg of mine.

It was more than a year since I had come out of hospital and, with a couple of sticks to help me along, had attempted to resume my life where it had been so rudely broken off. A one-man business such as authorship suffers when illness compels you to stop work for a year; markets are lost and cannot be regained, money flows out and little comes in. And my leg presented me with many difficulties — simple things like sitting down on a chair, putting on my boots, using a toilet, climbing stairs. Once, by the boating-lake in the park, I said to Joyce and Anne, "Come on, we'll get a boat out, and I'll take you for a row." Then I realised that with a rigid hip, unable to bend, sitting down in a rowing-boat was no longer possible. I would never row a boat again, or ride a horse, or go cycling. Never again would I do lots of things which once I had taken for granted.

But I was grateful, as I knew that the operation on my hip had made me better off — the results had been just as Miss Pearson had forecast — as she later told me, "I am proud of that operation. You should be thankful."

And I was, although it took some time to reconcile myself to my handicaps, at last the pain had gone.

That brought me to my third problem — the house we were living in and the mining district in which it stood. In the beginning we were so desperate to get any sort of house that we would not have spurned a hovel, but though our cottage had appeared a desirable residence at first, after living in it for several years its defects were beginning to make life unbearable. Joyce suffered more than I, for she was a house-proud woman. The roof leaked, the walls streamed with moisture because there was no damp-course, subsidence was causing parts of the house to sink into the ground, and try as we might we could not get rid of the mice with which it was overrun. Only a short distance away the coke-ovens and by-products plant poured out gas and smoke and dirt, so that toil as Joyce might she could not keep the house clean.

Fate, ironically enough, had placed her in the worst possible environment for a woman of her temperament. She scrubbed and cleaned and dusted day after day, but she could not keep the house clean. Daily, dirt and smoke filled the house, and yet she slogged away, determined to die rather than admit that conditions were getting the better of her. Gradually the difficulties of keeping that dilapidated old house clean were getting her down. There are some houses which seem to like people, happy houses, and there are houses which hate people, houses which nobody loves. This was such a house.

And so we were both becoming very

disgruntled people. My problem was that of earning enough money to keep us during the next year or so, until I could apply for a place at a teachers' training college, and Joyce's problem was that of living in a wretched old house which threatened to break her heart. Yet somehow we found the strength to keep going, even to laugh at times. And meanwhile young Anne was growing up into a strong, healthy child, so that it was a joy to watch her development. Living only a few hundred yards from a coal-mine was not stopping her growth, and she was as strong and healthy as we could wish.

Struggling to earn a living and keep Joyce happy, I frequently felt frustrated, baffled. Problems arose which seemed insurmountable; as fast as I solved one difficulty another rose in its place. If I could have quit I would. I prayed for help, for someone to extend to us a helping hand, but little help came. We felt that we were the forgotten of God, yet later we realised that the problems *had* been surmounted and that we had managed without help from anyone. Where had the strength to keep going come from?

In my despair, I wondered whether the Christian faith might not be the source of such strength. I did not consider myself to be a religious sort of person, but just an ordinary man who was too busy getting a living to bother about the state of his soul. All my life I had had little contact with organised religion, had never talked with a parson. I would not have known even how to approach one. Years earlier I had written, "Religion is man's expression of inadequacy when confronted by powers superior to his own," and "Christianity is dead, and flogging a dead horse will not bring it back, but the principles of decency and justice which existed centuries before Christ's birth and which will continue to exist long after his name is forgotten, these live on."

This statement had caused my friend Frank Stuart to write back vehemently, "You are wrong, you know; Christ lives on, and one day I hope you will live to acknowledge this." Now I was not so sure myself; a non-believer can disparage Christianity, if he so desires, and yet a faith which has inspired people for nearly two thousand years and which has caused many people to do great deeds, surely it merited examination? So many people over so many centuries could not *all* be wrong!

One of the disadvantages which confront a married couple who have a young child is that it cuts one off from social contacts. Unless the couple are fortunate in having friends or relatives who can look after the child now and again, they cannot go out by themselves, unless they take the child with them. And dragging a small child with you everywhere is not conducive to peace of mind. So Joyce and I had to wait till Anne was old enough to go to Sunday School before we could go to church. It was good to sit there quietly and listen to the service and think over the words uttered by the minister, though hard wooden pews are not made for crippled men whose hips won't bend, and many a time I was squirming with pain and discomfort long before the service ended.

Although I had been fortunate in having as friends a number of persons who assisted in the development of various facets of my personality, it was my misfortune that they lived a long way from where I did;

for much of the time our friendships had to be maintained by correspondence. Not the least of these friends were Frank Stuart, and his wife Phyllis. They were, indeed, real Christians, who practised what they preached.

Only occasionally, when Anne was taken to Manchester to stay with her grandmother so that we could have a few days' holiday together, were we able to visit Frank and Phyllis at their home near Stroud, in Gloucestershire. Sometimes with them we attended the Meeting of the Society of Friends at Nailsworth. Much of my instruction in Christian belief was obtained by sporadic visits to church and from letters in which Frank tried to answer some of the questions which puzzled me. When, told that I should have to go into hospital for a long time to undergo some operations on my hip and leg, I wrote to him saying that I had read the Book of Job, but had gained little help from it, back came a reply in Frank's characteristic style:

Do stop reading Job — it worries me. His idea was very largely to just put up with it all. Fine in a way. But the New Testa-

ment tells us that if we can believe COM-
PLETELY we can beat anything. It's
true, though I haven't the guts to do it
properly. But trying and getting some of
the way is better than resignation. I think
you'd adjust a lot if you read the Bible
several times and kept on reading and
praying. Sounds like a Salvation Army
lassie, I know; sorry I can't make it seem
less sanctimonious. It's real enough when
you get the feel of it, despite rebellions,
pessimisms, hates, fears. They don't stop,
but one gets the strength to plough
through them.

Don't think me intrusive, but I'd have
gone under long ago but for praying, not
only at night as a regular thing, but at any
time of day for any small or big things,
current at the moment. All prayers aren't
granted, of course; I don't know why,
though often I've realised afterwards that
denial meant infinitely more happiness to
me. It's hard, especially at first, to pray
and apparently get no answer, to pray to
what seems blankness. But after a time one
gets a little wisdom and so many prayers
are granted, many that seem impossible
altogether.

I had remarked that it seemed to me that the present crisis in world affairs was due to man's attitude to life, to a wrong sense of values upon which a great part of society based its life, and the end might be the downfall not only of present-day society in Britain, but of Western civilisation. Back came Frank's reply:

You say you want faith in England to make people put their backs into it. Into what? There is only one thing that matters — the faith that makes the individual man want to try to be more like Christ, to try to follow more nearly Christ's teachings. The Four Gospels, prayer, struggle, constant failure, trying again. That is life — the only life worth living at all. The only life.

For a long time the solution to one particular problem had baffled me. Why do some persons have more than their share of trouble, while others are allowed to live comparatively easy lives? Why are some of us born blind and crippled, and have to endure suffering and hardship all our lives, while others are allowed to be fit and healthy and do the work they please? Where is the justice in it? If God is master of all things, why does He allow such injustice? If it is the work of the Devil, what purpose is achieved by giving allegiance to God. No one I had met could give me a satisfactory answer to these questions.

"Don't despise the forces of evil," Frank wrote.

They are just as solid and real as the forces of good. There really *was* a struggle (for the older generation), between good and evil! There really is! It is the texture of life, that struggle between good and evil. Nothing else is living — nothing else at all. Observe, and you'll agree.

Later, in another letter, he wrote:

I think the Gospels explain something of the reason for pain and disappointment and worry. Not all of it (to me) but some. We are told over and over again that if we try to live by Christian principles we shall risk persecution, pain, death. It is made clear that people (often well-intentioned) will harry those who try to live as

319

Christians: "They that seek to kill you shall think they do God service," and many advices like that. I believe it is evident perhaps with some Eastern imagery (since Christ was speaking to Easterns in their own idiom, which is always fanciful) that we should suffer pain and death from spiritual evil forces trying to wear and break down our efforts to live as Christians.

I think when people have some hereditary and inexplicable illnesses and disabilities, sometimes it must be that the forces of evil which Christ warned us were *dominant* in this world (He said it so often one imagines this may be Hell) are picking on that person because he or she might otherwise do rather too much good. Look at Stevenson and Chopin. You yourself — though you may be the first to protest — struggle to live in a way which accords to Gospel directions (of course, we all fail much or most of the time), and some of your trouble is due to the fact that this world has not much time for anyone who tries to do that.

Perhaps your spirit when it came from God was a fine one; the evil of the world gave you a nip in the leg and a sock in the eyes, and marshalled the powers of crassness always to be waiting for you, so that you should be hurt plenty as you went along. Some of us (or so we feel) might be pretty good Christians if we had perfect bodies and easy lives. Or perhaps we are wrong, and the divine spark might have been smothered out by fat living instead of being fanned by the bitter, cold blasts of sorrow and struggle we have to face. I'd love to think that Old Adversary was barking up the wrong tree all the time.

God guides us always. His love is there, urging us back to the way it is best for us to go, like a voice gently and inexorably urging us on, telling us in our hearts when we have wandered out of the way, asking us to go back. When we are wrong we know it in no uncertain manner by perpetual dissatisfaction. Then we must seek, try, experiment, till a less restless feeling results. Eventually, if we work on our characters enough, we can — it is a promise — find the peace of God which passeth all understanding. So I think. And we can never escape from the finger of God, neither we, nor a murderer, nor Stalin nor Churchill nor anyone. This is

His Classroom; some pupils learn quickly and pleasantly, some desperately hard, and it seems unfair, but the Teacher keeps teaching us just the same.

For Heaven's sake don't say there'll be Frank Stuart's teachings in anything you do — remember what Paul said when the heathens tried to worship him: "We are men even as ye are." The teachings are those of Jesus Christ; all anyone else can do is to point back to them.

Later, when my legs failed me altogether, and I had to spend nearly a year lying down, and the future was very black, he wrote:

Here's an idea — if it makes one miserable and savage and hurt to think too much on unhappy things, on war news, poverty, political swindles, etc. — try cutting them out, even if it means not reading a paper; try (when you feel savage) setting your thoughts on beauty, on eternal strength and love, on kindness, on music, on what one has that is nice. Old Paul said it so much better: "Rejoice in the Lord always, and again I say rejoice and fear not. Let your moderation be known to all men. The Lord is near. Be careful for nothing (meaning 'full of cares'), but in everything by prayer let your requests be known unto God; and the peace of God which passeth all understanding shall (eventually) keep your hearts and minds. Finally, brethren, whatsoever things are honest, whatsoever things are just, whatsoever things are pure, whatsoever things are lovely, whatsoever things are of good report, if there be any virtue, if there be any praise, think on these things." (And by inference *not* on their converses.)

It's the most golden advice I know, but it takes a lot of practice before one begins to feel the absolute and comforting genius of it, and how utterly true and helpful it is.

And later:

It's wonderful news to me that in spite of your sorrows and difficulties you are beginning to feel a sort of contentment. It is "the peace of God which passeth all understanding". We only feel it by very slow degrees, and often it seems to be gone and we feel desperate and hateful and as if it is all a myth or swindle. But it comes stealing back, a tiny bit stronger than before. Presently, I know, it will be greater than pain, greater than all the agonies of worry and disappointment. I know from experience that it grows gently, a tiny bit each year — mainly by the amount one has the courage to say with Paul: "Having food and raiment I will be therewith content," and not worrying about tomorrow, knowing that God makes tomorrow His way, whether we worry or not.

In such words, by means of many letters, Frank helped me to realise that the essential truths which Christ taught are as true now as they were nineteen hundred years ago, and as simple. In one letter he wrote:

It requires a considerable effort to realise the simple truth that we cannot set the world right by ourselves — that we must realise our limitations and simply do our best and leave the rest to God. The New Testament tells us that if we can believe this fact we can beat anything. This reliance upon a Higher Power is something which we have to find out for ourselves — nobody else can teach us, though they can point out the way.

It takes a bit of understanding and believing at times — the worldly part of one's mind is usually far more concerned with food and money and paying the rent and earning a living (mine is, anyway), but by steadily pegging away and reading a bit of the New Testament each day, one comes at last to a realisation that God IS, that He exists and vitalises everything, from the air and the stars down to our own thoughts, and that trusting in Him is, in a sense, like trusting to a bicycle when you learn to ride, or to the sea when you swim. You can fall off, you can sink, but it will hold you up if only you believe in it. Till you believe in it, it can't.

And later:

Courage and confidence and the ability to keep on — these things help, but one thing helps far more — training oneself to believe the New Testament promise that God knows our wants and will do what is really best for us. Although we may rebel and cry out like children, and lose faith, dimly one can feel the hand of God guiding our movements, often making happen that which we disliked, but which, in the end, proved better for us. Nothing in the world helps so much as this gradual and reluctant shifting of the weight of one's burden on to God who alone is strong enough to help us with it.

I am sure God guides us always, but His guidance is not like a rein but rather like a directional radio beam which an aircraft uses — when we are "on the beam" our hearts tell us so, and when we are "off the beam" we know it in no uncertain manner, by a feeling of perpetual dissatisfaction.

I believe it is true that there is an infinite source of Power to help us, if only we care to ask for help, and quietly keep on asking in the face of difficulties and disappointments. Often we may be puzzled because what we ask for is not granted, or the help we ask for in prayer does not always come in the form we ask, but perfectly plainly over the course of the years one sees that the help *has* come, often more strangely and miraculously than in the form we asked.

Reading these words I seemed to find the explanation of certain happenings which had befallen me when on various vagabonding journeys. I had often marvelled at the way chains of circumstances occurred, as if to guide my journey in a certain direction. Often one event seemed to follow another in what appeared a providential manner, so that they seemed to be, not mere meaningless and unrelated happenings, but something which had been arranged by some Power superior to man. Gradually I acquired a feeling of being looked after: if I was in difficulties somebody would help me; no matter what trouble I might be in, something would turn up to save me.

I proved this time and time again. On two occasions when I needed to work my passage back to England I made for the nearest little seaport, and there was a ship waiting to take me home. On several occasions when I desperately needed money the first person whom I asked handed over the cash without hesitation. Others proffered help without being asked. A surprising number of times — when I have felt desperate — my prayers have been answered.

This feeling of being guided, this proof of being looked after, seemed to operate even more when the time came for me to go to college to learn to be a teacher.

We were walking along a road. It was a road with a surface of yellow gravel, and there were tall pine-trees on every side. Ahead of us the road curved up towards a range of hills whose bare, rocky summits rose above the forest. A few miles back these hills had appeared smoky purple in colour, but now one could see them for what they were — grey granite heights, streaked with snow. Against the greyness of the hills the trees showed dark green. The ground on either side of the road was green also, the pale green of reindeer-moss. Yellow sunlight blazed down out of a cloudless blue sky. It was early summer in Arctic Lapland.

Joyce and I walked hand in hand, like two children let out of school. In a sense that is what we were, for the colliery village in Yorkshire in which we had our home was far, far away, and this was the Great Arctic Highway we were following, that same highway which had led me to the Polar Sea nearly twenty years before. Now it was 1951.

Often during the years I had wanted to go back to the Arctic, to see the northern forests and rivers again, the gaily-coloured Lapp nomads with their reindeer herds, the blood-red Midnight Sun; but this time I wanted to take Joyce with me. While lying soul-sick in hospital my greatest delight had been to turn the pages of an atlas, so that the outlines of far-off lands appeared before my eyes — North America, Asia, Africa, the Arctic. To go back — somehow. What fun to watch my wife succumb to the lure of the colourful lands which lie beyond the Arctic Circle! Hospitals and operations and the struggle to make a living had combined to make life too grim; *somehow* I would get away from it all and go back to Lapland, where some of the happiest days of my life had been spent.

My old desire to live a vagabonding life was dead; I liked being a married man and had no desire to return to my former life. But a life without some travel in it was not life at all. Somehow a compromise must be found, which enabled me to spend some part of every year in moving on and on to new places. This was vital, otherwise one's spirit died. The sea, the mountains, the wilderness, and the desert still called out to me. I would live in a house eleven months of the year if I could spend the twelfth month really *living*. How well Philip James Bailey, the Nottingham poet, had expressed it:

We live in deeds, not years; in thoughts
    not breaths;
In feelings, not in fingers on a dial.
We should count time by heart-throbs;
    he most lives
Who thinks most, feels the noblest,
    acts the best.

Life is not measured by the number of years we have lived, but by the outstanding episodes which have aided our development. Months or years can go by when nothing much happens, and we breathe, eat, sleep, work, pass the time, in ant-like routine. Then something happens — marriage, birth, death, war, good luck or bad luck, something exciting — and those experiences make us conscious we are alive. If we total up these moments when we were really conscious of being alive, then they constitute our life. Thus the whole of a lifetime could be compressed into a few days or weeks. Those were the times when we really *lived*; the rest was mere existence.

So now — with Joyce and myself, walking along this road. We were learning how to live again.

A way to solve our problems had been found. A commission for a travel book could be obtained, newspaper articles written (the Olympic Games were to be held in Finland in 1952), free travel could be obtained from friendly Government officials; a journey to the Far North was possible. So Anne was left at a children's boarding school near York, and then we travelled by way of Copenhagen — Stockholm — Helsinki — Rovaniemi, on the Arctic Circle — travelling north, north, north — to here. And so again I saw the Great Arctic Highway winding its way through the forest towards the mountains, as if but a few months, and not nearly two decades, had passed.

A deep, tree-filled valley appeared beside the road, and we looked down and saw a river, a swift, tempestuous stream, dropping down in foam-flecked falls and rapids. Yes, there was the Ivalo river again, and the track leading to Laanila goldfield, where presently we would try our luck as gold prospectors. Nothing had changed. And out on the fells beyond the river was the land of the nomad Lapps, from where there came a far-off cry which might have been the howling of a wolf. It was good to be back.

"See those mountains," I said to Joyce, pointing. "They are the great dividing range of Arctic Lapland. From there the rivers flow south towards the Baltic Sea, and from the other side the rivers flow north — north to the Arctic Ocean."

"And what lies over that way?" Joyce asked, staring across the forest towards the east.

"Only empty wilderness," was my reply. "Forest for hundreds of miles, and swamps, and mountains without names. There's over a thousand square miles of country, and only about half a dozen houses in it. This road is the edge of civilisation; beyond it there are no more settlements."

"The edge of civilisation — I like the sound of that phrase," Joyce said. "I've always longed to see something like this — something wild and far away. I'm glad you brought me here."

I realised then, as I had done so many times before, the kind of woman I had married — patient, enduring, undergoing the ups-and-downs of life without complaint, adapting herself readily to new environments, whether in an English city or Arctic wilderness. She was the best companion I could ever have.

A forest ranger whom we had met at a hostel a few miles away had told us he spent his spare time washing for gold along the Ivalo; if we cared to try our luck we would find the necessary equipment hidden in a tree. So after we had admired the view of the river rushing along through its rocky channel we located the tree and found the tools we needed — a pick, a shovel, a metal basin, a long wooden sluice-box. I showed Joyce how to arrange wooden cleats inside the sluice-box, which was then placed with one end in the river, so that a continuous stream of water flowed through.

Shovelfuls of gravel were then tipped into the box, so that the flowing water washed the gravel away and left the gold-bearing sand collected in the wooden cleats. Then I showed her how to squat down on her haunches and swirl the pan round and round, in the hope that a few flakes of yellow gold might be left. Truth compels me to state, however, that though we went through all the necessary motions a number of times, we did not find any gold.

Afterwards we sat down by the river-bank and ate our sandwiches, and I pointed out the place where Bill the sailor and I had crossed so many years ago when we journeyed westward to find the nomad Lapps and their reindeer herds. That was one exploit I would be unable to repeat; my stiff hip had put an end to such feats. But I doubted if the Lapps were still living out there on the fells in the primitive condition we had observed in the 1930's. Times had changed even among the Lapps, I knew, for we had met various parties of Lapps on the hundred-and-fifty-mile journey north from the Arctic Circle. These had been much more sophisticated Lapps than those I had known in years gone by.

Nowadays for many miles the Great Arctic Highway is lined with high wooden fences, enclosing huge reindeer corrals, and parties of Lapps with lassos slung over their shoulders could be seen "rounding up" the deer. In a world that was short of meat the slaughtering and shipping southward of reindeer carcasses had become a profitable business. Rich Lapps, owners of many deer, could be seen using chequebooks instead of money, and making entries in their ledgers with the latest types of fountain-pens.

The business of reindeer-herding was now run on modern lines. Each owner had to be registered with a reindeer association, to which he paid an annual subscription. These associations used the funds thus obtained to pay for grazing rights in the State forests and to compensate farmers for the damage caused to crops by the deer. The associations also kept a register of the different marks by which the owners identified their animals. We were told that nowadays walkie-talkie radio and light aircraft were used to help round up the deer.

We passed a number of reindeer as we walked back to the Arctic Highway, but they went bounding away before we could approach them closely. The thought came to me that it would be fun to tell children about the life lived by the Lapp reindeer herdsmen, when I realised that we had left the forest behind and were climbing up the bare, grey-green flanks of Kaunis-pääs Mountain. White snowdrifts were piled two yards deep on either side of the Highway; above the snow, with the blue sky for background, rose the grey, dome-like summit of the mountain. I felt a sudden urge to climb to the top.

"Come on," I said to Joyce. "Let's climb up there — it is our last chance. Tomorrow we must turn back."

Some time later we sat on the rocky summit, under a sunny sky, gazing down upon a vast bluish-green lansdcape of forest and lake below. Blobs of red among the green, on the edge of the forest, might have been the colourful tunics of Lapp herdsmen. A column of thin, blue smoke rose above the treetops, indicating the existence of some isolated settlement; otherwise there was nothing to disturb the silence and the loneliness.

"I shall remember this when I am at the teachers' training college," I said. "It was good to have seen it all once again."

"The Lapps — the reindeer — the wolves howling in the forest — the wildness," remarked my wife dreamily. "I will remember it all as long as I live."

What thoughts were mine as I first surveyed the battlemented front of the Teachers' Training College in September 1952, with the sunlight glinting on its windows, and saw the crowds of students streaming towards the main entrance from all directions. The feeling came to me that I was going to enjoy being at college, for there was a homely atmosphere about the place. One felt that the people there were friendly and had one's welfare at heart.

My memory of those first days was of wandering about from room to room, among dozens of other new students, collecting sheets of paper containing printed instructions, and listening to a sequence of lecturers talking about the attractions of their various subjects. In the way that these things happen, I found myself one of a small group of older students, all men, whose age and varied experience of life set them apart from the average student. John had been out in Burma, and had then worked with the Groundnut Scheme in East Africa; Colin had been in the Navy, and had returned to England after a visit to Japan; Bill was an ex-pilot of the Royal Australian Air Force. The companionship of these men was to help to make life endurable during the next two years.

Our first two or three mornings at college were spent in wandering from one subject-room to another, listening to the various lecturers, for all the world like so many hucksters in a market-place, each extolling the virtues of his particular subject, so that new students could have some idea of its attractions before deciding to take it at either an Advanced or Ordinary level. See, here is Mr. Good, tall and lean and beaming over the top of his spectacles, declaiming about geography to all who will care to stop and listen, while a few yards away Miss Framley is expounding advanced mathematics so cleverly that most of what she says is above our heads, and we resolve that whatever subjects we may choose, higher maths will not be among them.

Down in the woodwork shop Mr. Gates is talking about the qualities which make a good woodworker, illustrating his remarks by showing specimens of cupboards, bookshelves, and sideboards made by last year's students, and when we observe the quality of the workmanship displayed we realise sadly that woodwork also is not for us.

And see, over there is the religious knowledge lecturer, who is talking, not so much in the airy-fairy manner of many Bible-punchers, but in a down-to-earth manner which later will help us to make sense of some of the more puzzling passages of the Bible. He brings God and Christ out of the pages of the Bible, and helps to make them more understandable. I wish I had more time to study the Bible, I reflect, and how I wish I could take biology also, for I like the lecturer's forthright manner; but though we puzzle over the time-table together it just cannot be done.

So it all goes on, this market-place atmosphere — *who'll buy my oranges?* — who wants history, geography, biology? — *ripe pears, juicy and mellow!* — this way for English, science, physical education — *buy, buy, buy!*

First, every new student had to make a decision — whether he or she wanted to teach infants or junior or senior children. Infant-teaching was a woman's job, and did not concern us men, so we had to decide whether we wished to teach children under eleven years of age, in a primary school, or children over eleven, in a secondary modern school. Teachers for grammar and technical schools were usually university graduates.

Next we learned that we should have to take certain compulsory subjects, but would have a free choice with regard to others. Education, in one form or another, would occupy the greater part of the college course; all students were required to attend lectures in this, the chief subject. We would have to pass examinations in the philosophy of education, the history of education, the psychology of education, child development, and health education. In addition to lectures there would be seminars bearing on all these subjects. Professional studies included lectures on teaching methods, and there would be film demonstrations, and visits to schools of various types; later, there would be periods of teaching practice, when we would spend several weeks as student-teachers in different kinds of schools. Essays dealing with all these activities would be required of us at frequent intervals.

After the compulsory subjects we could choose two subjects which interested us, and study one to an Advanced and the other to the Ordinary level. My own choice was Advanced geography, Ordinary history. Students who had not chosen to take such subjects as English, mathematics, art and craft, religious knowledge, music, at either Advanced or Ordinary level were compelled to take them at "basic level". We quickly discovered that a two-year course was far too short for us to study all the subjects which interested us; there was simply not time left for such fascinating topics as printing, book-binding, puppetry, metal-work, or nature study. Oh, for a three-year course at training colleges!*

As the days, the weeks, the months, eventually a year, sped by one realised almost imperceptibly that one had fitted into the routine of college life, so that the buildings, lecture-rooms, corridors, common-rooms, staff, one's fellow-students, had all become so familiar as to be taken for granted. It required a real effort of will to turn back one's thoughts to those first few days when everything was novel and unknown, and there were so many idiosyncracies of persons and organisation to be learned.

What is it like for a man approaching forty to go back to school, for that is what the two-year course of training at college amounted to in my case? I was to encounter far less difficulty than I had anticipated, as a number of troubles I had expected failed to materialise, while other problems, undreamt of, developed in their place. My physical handicaps — even sitting at a desk in a lecture-room for any length of

* Training-college students now undertake a three-year course.

time — presented a problem. Also, I was about eighteen years older than the average student, and again, it was more than twenty years since I had been in a school, or studied for an examination. Lastly, I had a wife and small daughter dependent upon me.

It was true that I had certain advantages. Several years working at Scarborough youth hostel had given me some knowledge of young people. Years as an author and journalist had given me an orderly mind and a capacity for study; I was to find that the actual routine for attending lectures daily, of reading textbooks and writing essays, was not very different from that in my previous job. What success I had achieved as a writer had been due to the fact that I had trained myself to work to a time-table, with a daily allocation of work to be accomplished.

"You ask me what I think of your chances?" Professor W. R. Niblett, Director of the Institute of Education at Leeds University, had remarked. "Well, I should say that for a married man with a family to support to get through a university course is very nearly impossible, and that for you to manage two years at a training college will be very difficult."

I had asked for an interview with Professor Niblett because it seemed to me that by attending a training college for two years a person like myself, who was above the average age of the students there, might provide sociological workers with useful data regarding the capabilities of older persons to adjust themselves to new tasks and new situations. Much is said and written nowadays of the increasing age of the population of Britain, and of the need for older persons to work longer, and of the need also for alternative types of work to be provided for older persons, different from that for which they were originally trained.

Researches carried out by members of the Institute of Education at Leeds University had disproved the fallacious saying "Too Old at Forty", showing it to be merely a catch-phrase invented and circulated by certain American social scientists in the 1920's and 1930's, when there was massive unemployment in the United States. The catch-phrase had been circulated by employers so that they and the

Government could avoid the responsibility of providing training or alternative forms of employment for men out of work. Bad coinage can be a long time in circulation!

Modern experiments showed the reverse to be the case, that though there might be a slowing up of certain faculties among older persons, this was compensated for by the development of other useful qualities not possessed by younger people owing to the fact that they were younger.

12

TOO OLD AT FORTY?

SEATED at my little desk in a corner of the classroom, with the window behind me and the door leading into the corridor on one side, I covertly eye the children working at the rows of desks in front of me. A sudden quietness has fallen upon the room, but I have no illusions that this is due to my capabilities as a teacher, but rather to the fact that when they are interested in the job they are doing children will work without being urged. There are thirty-nine children in front of me, boys and girls of various sizes, shapes, ages, colours of hair and skin, but apart from knowing that Bill Woodson and Donald Graham are trouble-makers, I have had very little opportunity of discovering what they are like individually.

For this is just the beginning of my second week as a student teacher at Bogglethorpe Secondary School, and I have only the information that this is Senior Three "C" stream and some textbook knowledge to guide me.

Moments for meditation are rare in a classroom, for usually hardly a lesson goes by without some interruptions — the nurse, doctor, or dentist wanting to see certain children, part of the class wanted for sewing, or cooking, or sports, somebody coming along to fill inkwells, or collect money, or heaven knows what else — so this is the first time I have had to get my second wind, as it were, and give a thought to the circumstances which placed me there.

This school, for example, although referred to as Secondary Modern, bears little resemblance to those smart-looking, new streamlined schools whose walls appear to be mostly glass, which are making their appearance in various parts of the English landscape. It is probably fifty years old — a solidly built structure of grey stone, with the long, narrow windows and high-pointed roofs and gables reminiscent of the Victorian era. The upper storey is reached by several winding staircases, and the ramifications of the corridors which connect the various rooms and wings are so confusing that I still lose my way. The windows of my classroom look out across the playground and some green fields to the bright red-brick homes of the new housing estate, and when the sun shines my lessons have to compete in interest with the countryside beckoning outside.

A week ago I came with six other students from the Training College, and the headmaster brought me to this room. I still remember the look on George the class-teacher's face when informed that I was to take over his class. "Gawd help him, then, poor devil!" was his pungent comment. And, looking for the first time at the faces of the children whom I was to teach, I felt inclined to agree with him, for that row of grim, unsmiling faces, sandwiched between shocks of untidy brown hair and grubby-looking scarves, made me think of nothing so much as a row of miniature editions of Bill Sikes. They looked the toughest bunch of little thugs I had ever seen. And what the teacher had to say concerning them was not reassuring.

"I don't know how the hell you will deal with my mob. Half of them are problem children and need special treatment. They broke the heart of the last student who came here, and they'll have a damn' good try to break yours."

I murmured polite platitudes, hoping that the consternation I felt did not show in my face.

"Brought up in Canada, weren't you?" he went on. "I expect that's why the boss sent you here — it may help. But don't worry if you fail — it's asking a lot of a student."

These remarks were conveyed to me, not in the classroom, but in the corridor outside, while he sat on a table-top smoking and glancing through the half-open doorway to see that the class continued with the work it had been ordered to do.

How often had I encountered such an attitude towards children, and heard such opinions expressed! I still recalled the words with which I had been greeted at the last school in which I had taught as a student: "Anyone who comes to this place needs his head examining." I may have been unfortunate, but in three schools I visited I encountered only a cynical attitude towards the children being taught. I wonder if those teachers realised the effect their words might have on new entrants to the profession? Did they consciously wish to discourage students?

That had been a week ago; this was the second week.

On the whole the class is quiet for a moment, and I can reflect about the sorts of homes the children come from. For this is one of the grim northern industrial cities in which I am teaching, with its mills and factories and workshops jammed tightly together in a wide valley which once had been beautiful, but was now desecrated by the dilapidated products of nineteenth-century builders' skill. For miles the landscape shows nothing but dingy houses, shops, pubs, and smoking chimneys. There is no beauty here, only dirt and smoke and narrow streets and railway-sidings and rubbish-tips. The school, located farther out and on a grassy hillside, looks down upon the city from which many of its pupils come; the rest live in the near-by housing estate.

I become aware that three of the girls are talking about subjects entirely un-connected with school work, and that two or three of the boys are shuffling about at the back of the class. It is time to deal with them. Others have stopped work and are eyeing me cautiously, for they are fully aware of the fact that I am not the regular class-teacher, but merely a student from a training college, engaged in that peculiar undertaking known as "school practice" or "teaching practice". Baiting students is a recognised form of entertainment for school-children during this period, which occurs twice yearly in a number of schools in England and Wales. My class is wary, however, for it is known that I was reared in Canada, and there is a danger that I may prove as heavy-fisted as certain characters in Wild West films. It is not my intention to disillusion the class on this point.

I am considering admonishing the class when there is a diversion. A tall, lean man with a bald head, a stranger to me, but not to the boys, who obviously recognise him as a teacher, comes striding into the room and walking up to my desk demands in a loud voice:

"Hey, thee! Where's thy cane? I want to tan one o' thy lads!"

Nonplussed, prepared for almost any eventuality save this, I gazed helplessly about me. Am I to confess that I have not the slightest knowledge of the whereabouts of the cane, or even whether one exists? The class is more knowledgeable, and the cane makes its appearance from out of a cupboard. It is actually made of cane, I observe, and appears to be nearly a yard long, and if memory of distant schooldays does not serve me wrong, half a dozen cuts from such an instrument should prove painful.

The stranger flexes the cane between his hands a few times, and flicks it lightly across one palm; the class, very still and quiet now, watches these manoeuvres with a sort of horrible fascination. Then he beckons a finger to one of the boys, who leaves his desk as reluctantly as a snail leaves its shell.

"Now, then, Brown, I've told you before about fighting on the school bus," he declares. "Hold your hand out! (*Swish.*) I'm not going to tell you again! (*Swish, swish.*) If I catch you again — hold your other hand out! (*Swish, swish.*) — I'll give you something you won't forget in a hurry!" (*Swish.*)

Suddenly all is quiet again. The stranger is gone, and the cane is back in the cupboard, and there is only a startled, attentive class and a boy sobbing quietly over his desk. I collect my wits and recall that I was just starting a lesson in religious knowledge when the interruption began. Is it professionally correct, I wonder, for another teacher to come into my classroom and act in such a manner without so much as by your leave? The lesson proceeds. A few minutes later I am surprised to observe that Brown, the painful episode apparently already forgotten, is laughing over some private joke with his cronies in adjoining desks. Boys are surprising creatures, I reflect, and who can predict how they will act next?

Whatever may be said of "school practice" one thing is certain: it is never dull. There is always something happening, and usually it is something calculated to demonstrate to the student what an ignoramus he is in the art of teaching. Ministry of Education regulations ordain that each student attending a teachers' training college must, during the course of his or her two-year period of training, spend at least twelve weeks actually in a school, in order to gain some practical experience of teaching. So twice during his first year and twice during his second year the student duly hies himself off to a school selected for him by the college officials and spends periods of three weeks coping more or less successfully with a class which considers him fair game for any variety of mischief their innocent young minds can devise. Not until the four three-week periods of teaching practice have been completed can the student be considered eligible to obtain his teacher's certificate, without which he will not be qualified to teach; and, of course, there is also the little matter of passing his final examinations.

School practice is a peculiar experience since it is, of necessity, conducted under artificial conditions. The student is not actually a member of the staff, with its privileges and responsibilities, nor is he merely an onlooker watching somebody

354

else do the job. He is something in between, and, being neither fish, fowl, nor good red herring, possesses no particular status, except that he is the recipient of criticism on the part of the staff and headmaster, and of jokes from the children.

Consider what is expected of him. He is sent straight from college into a strange classroom, presided over by a teacher who is a complete stranger to him, and after a few hours or a day or so of watching that teacher at work, he is expected to take complete control of that class and instruct it in any subject from English history to music, or from religious knowledge to art and craft. In this unfamiliar environment he is expected to maintain discipline, to prepare, conduct, and mark lessons, and to deal with the various vicissitudes which constantly confront the class-teacher in the course of his daily duties.

If he does not accomplish all that is required of him in a satisfactory manner he will get a bad mark when the headmaster sends in a report to the training college about him. For all his work has to be accomplished under the friendly (or otherwise) jurisdiction of the headmaster, under the periodical scrutiny of the class-teacher, under the equally watchful scrutiny of the college lecturer assigned to the task of supervising him, and under the sometimes intolerant gaze of such of Her Majesty's Inspectors as may happen to call, since at any moment any or all of these personages is liable to step into his classroom.

The student on "school practice" is not allowed to use corporal punishment, so that if the class starts bombarding him with pieces of Plasticine — as happened to me — or clouting him on the head — as happened to a friend of mine — he cannot use the cane to restore order. The class is aware of this fact, and also aware that he is a student and only there for three weeks, so that consequently they can get away with actions which their own teacher would not tolerate for one moment. Therefore at times the general aim of the class is to play merry hell with the student's lessons, by indulging in horseplay or by ignoring him altogether. Upon how quickly the student can make the class realise that this is a misapprehension depends not only the mark which he will be allocated by the headmaster, but also whether he will continue with his ambition to become a teacher, or decide instead to go in for some occupation a little less strenuous — say, in a steelworks or in the Army.

Before starting school practice the student pays a preliminary visit to the school and spends a day eyeing the class and discussing with the teacher the lessons which he must give during the next three weeks. Several days are then spent in a hectic rush preparing these lessons. A scheme of work for the three weeks must be worked out and some sample lessons in each subject prepared, ready for inspection by the headmaster, the supervisor, and anyone else who may care to inspect them.

If the student is taking every subject in the timetable as it comes, at least four or five lessons for each day must be carefully prepared beforehand, which, by the end of three weeks amounts to some sixty or seventy lessons. (Experienced teachers can spend much less time on lesson preparation, as they carry most of the details in their heads.) To get through all the work involved in teaching the class during the day, correcting exercises, and preparing next day's lessons means that the student is frequently working until late at night. There is little wonder that a vast sigh of relief echoes through the training colleges of England when each period of school practice is ended.

The bell rings for the next lesson. I tell the class to stop what they are doing, put their books away, and sit up and listen while I explain what I want them to do. The sinking feeling in the stomach which the student experiences in his first few days out from college has gone, to be replaced by a more wary attitude akin to that developed by the big-game hunter who is prepared to discover at any moment that the lion which he is supposed to be stalking is in actual fact stalking *him*. What will those kids do next? Will the head come in during the lesson? Will the college supervisor suddenly appear, and, notebook in hand, take his seat at the back of the room and observe the student's actions with critical eyes? With all or any of these eventualities the student must be prepared to deal.

The lesson is geography, which I love,

and I am dealing with Greece, a country which I visited during the long vacation. Yet first-hand knowledge has its pitfalls, as George, my own class-teacher, has illustrated by telling a story against himself. Recently back from two years in North Africa — "with the sand in my boots", as he described it — he thought he could give a good geography lesson about that country, if about nothing else. So he gave his lesson, with the head standing silently by, and when he had finished the head said, "So you think you have taught them something about Africa, eh? Well, we shall see." He turned to the class: "Smith, tell me — is Africa a very big place?"

"No, sir, not so big."

"About how big would you say? As big as London?"

"Oh, no, sir!"

"As big as Manchester, then?"

"No, sir, about as big as Oldham, I'd say."

"And what sort of animals would you expect to find in Africa?"

"Lions and tigers, sir, and camels."

"What about polar bears?"

"Oh, yes, sir, and polar bears."

"Whereabouts in Africa would you expect to find polar bears?"

"In the parts where it is very cold, sir."

The head turned to the new class-teacher. "Well, mister, what do you think of your lesson now?" he asked.

I am anxious to avoid this situation, so I hold up a pair of straw sandals bought in the market-place of Athens. The class is attentive at once, so after discussing these, and currants from Corinth, and tobacco from Macedonia and Corfu, the Duke of Edinburgh's birthplace, I guide the lesson into a discussion of the geographical features of Greece. I am describing the irregular coastline, the high mountains, the dry, dusty plains, when the head walks in. A minute or two earlier he would have heard me explain that many of the rivers of Greece are without water in summer, so that only the dry river-beds are left.

I like the head, who is small and round and amiable, and who, if strict, is helpful; so consequently I am not put out when he says, "Mind if I take over for a few minutes, Mr. Ingram?"

This is a good opportunity to watch an experienced teacher at work, I think, so I take my place at the back of the room. The head continues the lesson from the point at which I had broken off.

"Observe that there are lots of rivers in Greece, children. What use are rivers, Morrison?"

"They provide water-power, sir."

"Correct. Plenty of hydro-electric power. Give me another use for rivers, Simpson."

"For transportation, sir."

"Right. For transporting goods. Hydro-electric power and transportation. Don't forget those two facts, children. And what does hydro-electric power suggest to you, Johnson?"

"Industry, sir."

"Yes, electricity for industry." And so on.

And having got my nicely prepared lesson into a tangle the head beams at me and says, "Carry on, Mr. Ingram," and departs. Ah, well, how many students have had that sort of thing happen to them on school practice? I suppose that a teacher who has worked his way up to become headmaster, so that most of his time is devoted to administrative matters, relishes the opportunity of taking a class again, and the presence of students in his school gives him that opportunity. Once a teacher, always a teacher — so I have been told.

The bell rings for the mid-afternoon break, and my class streaks off to the playground. Students and staff can be seen making for the staff-room, where cups of tea are waiting for them, but there is no time for me to drink tea today, for I have a problem to solve. When the class returns from play the geography lesson will be resumed, and to make it more interesting and instructive I propose to show a filmstrip illustrating life in Greece. Then the class will be told to write an essay about what they have heard and seen.

The difficulty is that it is not possible to show filmstrips in the classroom, because there is no way of darkening the windows, and the only spare room where a projector can be operated is in a semi-basement, now empty. The film-strip projector and screen must be prepared before the class arrives, and the ten-minute break is just long enough for me to do this. But at that moment the head calls me — confound him! — and is apparently prepared to go on talking for the next ten minutes. It is not good policy for a student to stop a head from talking, but if that film-strip projector is not ready when the break ends, then my class will be left idle, and I shall be in trouble.

Relying on the kindliness which practically all working teachers show towards students in their school, I stop a passing teacher and explain my dilemma, and ask him to put the projector in position for me. He promises to do this, so I can listen to the head with an easier mind, and the minute he lets me go I dash back to my room, collect the class, and the geography lesson is continued in the basement. It is stuffy and crowded in there, but all schools seem to be overcrowded these days. The girls emit the usual giggles, and the boys provide entertainment by holding up their fingers in front of the projector so that curious shadows are thrown on the screen, but otherwise the lesson proceeds without incident.

"See the women working on the roads," I explain. "Observe how the unmarried women wear their dowry round their necks in the form of a necklace of gold coins."

"Please, sir, what does dowry mean?" comes a voice from the darkness.

"It's the money a girl has to have saved up before her boyfriend will start courting," sagely observes one young miss of fourteen.

This part of the lesson over, we return to the classroom, and for the next forty minutes they are all busy writing essays about life in Greece. Towards the end of the period the head strolls in again.

"Nearly finished, eh?" he says. "I'll mark some of these papers for you, to see what sort of work they are doing. Hello! This sounds interesting!"

With a piece of chalk he writes extracts from various essays on the blackboard:

"In Greece girls have corns on their chests."

"In Greece women work harder than men. This is different from England where the men work harder than the women."

Now, where on earth did the children learn such statements? Not from my teaching, surely!

The bell rings, indicating that it is four

o'clock and another day at Bogglethorpe school is ended.

It is the following day, after play-time.

The bell rings, and the crowds of children who have been swarming round us, engaged in all sorts of juvenile activities, begin to form into long lines ready to march indoors to their classroom.

As I make my way back to my room I suddenly realise that the next lesson is art and craft, and that not only have I no lesson prepared, but I have not the slightest idea what I am going to do. To complicate matters there is the problem of "projects". In the good old days of education a system known as "chalk-and talk" prevailed, with the teacher standing by the blackboard writing part of the lesson and expounding at length about various aspects, while the class sat still and listened, or copied the notes down in their exercise-books.

That was the old-fashioned method, but nowadays a newer method has developed, in which children are no longer expected to sit quietly in their seats copying down notes, but are permitted, encouraged rather, to take an active part in the lesson by splitting into groups and indulging in some form of co-operative activity. They build models, design plans and posters, conduct field-studies, these activities being planned to combine such subjects as geography, history, art, arithmetic, and literature into one entity. It is believed that children learn better this way than by studying the various subjects in isolation.

Now, many students believed that there is a lot to be said for the old system of teaching by more formal methods, but on school practice our scheme of lessons is dictated not by our own beliefs or desires, but by what may be demanded of us by the college authorities. It was known that various college supervisors perambulating about the schools were keen protagonists of this "activity" or "project" method of teaching; therefore it behoved each and every student to have at least one project up his sleeve, ready to be put into action should it be demanded of him. I had no project, nor any idea which appeared capable of developing into a project. Therefore I was worried.

Outside the classroom three boys button-hole me, and one says, "It's art and craft now, sir. Please, you know you were telling us about visiting a lumber camp out in Canada. Can we make a model of a lumber camp, sir?"

The suggestion sounds dubious to me, for it does not seem to have the makings of an art and craft lesson in it. Which only goes to show how wrong a student can be, owing to his lack of experience.

"Do let us make a model lumber camp, sir," chorus the other boys. "We can get some clay from the craft-room, and make model trees and cabins and everything."

George, the class-teacher, comes hurrying along just then, so I put the proposition to him.

"A good idea," says he. "You'll need some base-boards, some wood, matchboxes, paint, and cardboard. Send two boys to the craft-room to get them."

When I enter the classroom the girls have gone to needlework, and the boys are left eagerly discussing what they plan to do. I am surprised at the change which has come over them. From being a crowd of ungainly louts who cannot sit still in their seats and who appear to be utterly bored with some of my most carefully prepared lessons, so that I feel that a good hiding would do them all no harm, they have been transformed into a crowd of keen-eyed youngsters eager to get to work. Their jackets are off, and since the girls are out of the way and there is more room to move about, they push some of the desks together, and on these place two large oblong pieces of wood which have been brought from the craft-room. These are to be used as the bases upon which the model lumber camps are going to be constructed. For we are going to make two models, the boys having split themselves up into two teams, each anxious to do better than the other.

While I draw a plan of a lumber camp on the blackboard some of the boys smear the two base-boards with clay, moulding the rounded outlines of hills and river-banks. Some of the boys request permission to go out to the playing-field to collect small pieces of shrubbery to serve as model trees, and though I am a bit doubtful of the wisdom of letting the class go off by itself during lesson-time, I agree. Meanwhile some of the other boys have started on models of their own; two are making a dry dock, and one a copy of Sydney Harbour Bridge. There is not a boy in the room who is idle; it is a revelation to me.

Other boys collect match-sticks and proceed to glue them to empty match-boxes, producing credible imitations of log cabins. The boys who went in search of shrubbery now return with bunches of dried twigs, which they proceed to convert into miniature trees. A model forest gradually makes its appearance on the green clay landscape, which begins to bear some resemblance to a part of the Canadian forest. The boys work quietly without being admonished, and when one of them starts to act the fool he is speedily told by his mates to shut up or get out. I need not worry about discipline, for a group of children will discipline themselves if they are doing a task which interests them, without any need for grown-ups to interfere. So much I had learned on a previous school practice.

The bell rings for dinner, but the boys work on, unwilling to leave their models unfinished, and only when I promise that the work will be completed as soon as the time-table permits do they depart. It happens that we have a period to spare that afternoon, and are able to resume model-making. I am constantly being asked to provide information about trees and timber and methods of working, or to give an opinion about the appearance of the model landscape and the buildings and equipment erected upon it. It dawns upon me that in a way the boys are learning quite a lot about Canada. I realise something else — that quite unwittingly I have developed a "project".

To cut the story short, the next day the boys eagerly continue their model-making. George looks in, surveys the work critically, and says, "Good! I'll tell the head to come and see it," and presently the headmaster walks in, surveys the boys working diligently at their self-appointed tasks, walks round looking at the models displayed on top of the desks, and without a word walks out. Like an old hen concerned for the welfare of her chicks, I wonder what he thought of it all. Actually the episode has sealed my fate, for in the report about me which goes back to the college is the statement: "Mr. Ingram appears to have a special gift for handling backward children." This is complimentary, but is not exactly what I desired.

And the next day? Why, the boys' interest in model-making has completely vanished as suddenly as it arose, and they can think of nothing better to do than pelt each other with lumps of clay.

On the point of starting a lesson one morning I observe that one of the boys is crying bitterly.

"What are you blubbering for?" I ask.

"Please, sir, it's my uncle — he's committed suicide. Cut his throat with a razor, sir."

Hastily I pull him to one side, so that the class cannot hear all the gory details. George nods to me, takes the boy by the arm, and leads him outside, while I order the class to take out their arithmetic books and start working out the problems on the blackboard. While they are doing this I take the opportunity of correcting some exercises in English which did not get done the day before. "Use the following words in sentences . . ." As my eyes scan the papers in front of me I am also watching the three boys from whom most of the trouble in the class originates.

Hello, what's this? "I am a doctor: I like to examine ladies' bodies." That is Keith Norwood's work. "My mother is expecting again." Which of the girls wrote that? How children reveal themselves in their work.

A hand shoots up, and a boy asks me to explain the workings of one of the problems on the board. I leave the English corrections and take the opportunity of pointing out various mistakes in arithmetic. Some of the boys offer to work out the problems on the blackboard for the benefit of the rest of the class, so I hand over pieces of chalk and tell them to get on with it. The class and I get some amusement out of watching them go wrong, and other boys are just volunteering to make a better job of it when we suddenly realise that there is somebody else in the room, watching us. It is Mr. Brewin, the lecturer who is to observe me taking lessons, and already he has his notebook in his hand.

I am jumpy this morning. Students are always jumpy when they anticipate some-body coming to examine them and calculate what sort of teachers they will make. For all students and all teachers will know that the day on which you put on a really good show, when the lessons all go smoothly and the class is all that it should be, then that is the day when no examiner or supervisor bothers to come near you; while if it is the sort of day when everything goes wrong, when the class threatens to get out of hand and your lessons do not go as well as they ought to, then that is the day when headmasters and inspectors and examiners all decide to come along and see what you are doing.

It is lesson-preparation which decides the student's fate. The experienced classteacher of some years' standing can pick up a book and with his practical knowledge of teaching behind him can conduct a lesson with no further preparation. Not so the student. Not only must he have a fairly full synopsis of that lesson written down on paper for the examiner to study and comment upon, but he is expected to put on a show. He must have maps and posters and photographs ready at a moment's notice to display upon the walls or blackboard, and in the preparation of those maps and photographs and illustrations he has probably sweated blood and burnt the midnight oil. The snag is, you see, that when the bell rings he must immediately switch from one subject to another, from arithmetic to geography, and in the space of a minute or two there simply is not time to remove the material put on the blackboards to impress one examiner and substitute for it material relating to another subject; because the moment he turns his back on the class it is going to start being a nuisance, and that is the moment also when examiners and supervisors usually decide to enter the classroom. This may be one reason why many students are prematurely bald.

Luckily for me I have anticipated Mr. Brewin's arrival and have pinned some illustrative material for the next lesson on the back of the reversible blackboard, so that when the bell rings indicating that it is time to change over to the history lesson I have only to reverse the board. Mr. Brewin, tall and thin and with wavy hair curling round his forehead, has already discovered the empty chair placed ready at the back of the room for him, and is now waiting expectantly for me to continue.

The arithmetic lesson concludes without mishap, the bell rings, and I tell the children to put their exercise-books away and take out their atlases. The history lesson deals with Sir Francis Drake's voyage round the world, and as we have already dealt with part of this in a previous lesson I follow the good old question-and-answer technique to discover how much they have remembered.

But how to convey to children some idea of the problems and difficulties confronting voyagers starting out on a journey four centuries ago? A short discussion shows that they have a fair idea of the type of sailing vessel in use in those days (I suppose one must thank historical films for this), so I take them on an imaginary tour of the docks where such a vessel is being fitted out for a voyage to the Pacific. What sort of stores and equipment would such a ship require? "Cannon and gunpowder," promptly replies one young realist. Why? "Because of pirates, sir." What else would be needed? "Sails and and canvas." How will the captain navigate the ship — by radar? The class looks at me pityingly. "Radar wasn't invented four hundred years ago." What did they use then? "Compass, sir, and the stars by night." What sort of food would they take with them? There were no refrigerators or tinned foods in those days. The class has to consider this question for some time. "Ship's biscuit, sir, full of weevils." What else? Much wrinklings of brows and scratching of heads. "Meat packed into barrels, sir, and kegs of rum."

Question-time over, we trace Drake's route on a map pinned to the blackboard, and then I get them to find the various places in their own atlases. The boys are rather good at this sort of exercise, but the girls think less of it. Some of the boys express willingness to show the girls what I am talking about, and as this is not my first school practice and I have discarded the impression that every time the boys offer to do something they are trying to take advantage of me, I let them do some teaching themselves.

I then read from a book borrowed from the public library how Drake, having brought the *Golden Hind* through the Straits of Magellan, sailed along the South

American coast in search of a Spanish treasure-ship which he had heard about. This goes down well with the class, especially the account of how the English sea-dogs routed the Spaniards and captured the ship. There is just time for a short discussion, and then the bell rings and the class disappears outside. I see Mr. Brewin beckoning to me.

"Quite a good lesson, Mr. Ingram," he says. "I like the way you handled your questioning. I'm glad to see you had your illustrations displayed ready. Adequate preparation, that is the secret. I have no serious criticism to make. Good-morning."

I do not need him to tell me that it was a good lesson, for one can tell whether a lesson is going well or not, but it is gratifying to have one's opinion confirmed. My school-practice notebook is lying open on my desk at the page containing the synopsis of the lesson I have just given. Mr. Brewin has read it through and written a brief comment. He will visit me again, to observe other lessons, and so will the head and perhaps other examiners, but that lies in the future. At the moment I am jubilant, and my thoughts go back to earlier school practices, when examiners were critical and nothing I did seemed right.

A few days later it is all over. We are standing in the headmaster's office, waiting for him to comment upon our performance. His words are brief and to the point:

"I have called you in here to say good-bye. I will not pretend you have not made a lot of mistakes — you have; even though I have not corrected you publicly. I have made a note of them. On the whole, though, I should say you have put up a pretty good show. As you know, the last two days of any school practice are pretty hectic, and usually I walk along outside the class-rooms wondering what trouble the student's are going to get into next. I am glad to tell you that this school practice I have not had the feeling that I was sitting on a volcano waiting for it to bubble over. So on that point you are to be congratulated. Good-afternoon!"

13

TRAINING-COLLEGE DAYS — AND AFTER

SOCIETIES of many kinds are a feature of college life. They cover every aspect of human activity — there is a Historical Society and a Geographical Society, a Science Society, a Music Club, Art Club, Chess Club, and ever so many more. Oddly enough there is one society which does not feature on the list of college organisations, and the avoidance of membership of which is every student's ambition. I refer to the Campanologists' Society. As this statement may strike the reader as rather curious, and as my elevation to membership of this society was typical, a brief description of my experiences may be of interest.

Lectures in educational psychology were given by the Principal of the college, Dr. Wing, and began promptly at nine o'clock in the morning. One morning I delayed my departure from the hostel for some minutes in order to attend to more pressing business, and when I started off alone for college I had the uneasy feeling that I had not left myself enough time to reach the lecture hall before Dr. Wing began. It seemed hardly likely that he would postpone the start of his lecture until I condescended to put in an appearance; in plain English, I was going to be late.

Sure enough, late I was, as I quickly discovered when, walking into the lecture hall, I discovered Dr. Wing already addressing the students. A broad grin spread over a couple of hundred faces when I appeared in the doorway; I was soon to discover the reason.

"Profound apologies, sir," I began.

"That's all right," said Dr. Wing, without anger. "Just sign this."

I took the paper and pencil he offered me and signed my name.

"You are now a member of our Campanologists' Society," Dr. Wing remarked pleasantly. "See Mr. Smith. He will explain."

I knew that the word campanologist had something to do with bell-ringing, but what connection this had with my being late was something I could not fathom; I slunk along to a seat, and the lecture proceeded. Afterwards I sought out Smith, who was another first-year student.

"What's it all about?" I asked.

"It means you have to do some bell-ringing," said he, grinning. "I'll put your name down for Fridays."

I had been at college long enough to realise that throughout the day, at fifty-minute intervals, electric bells shrilled loudly along the corridors warning staff and students that another lecture was about to begin. But what caused these bells to ring at such regular intervals was something I had never bothered to investigate. Now I discovered that it was due to human agency — to wit, a student, who posted himself or herself beside the bell-push every fifty minutes and, watch in hand, sent the alarm ringing throughout the college. These students did not per-form this service out of sheer altriusm, as one might have imagined, but because they could not get out of the task. In other words, they had arrived late at Dr.

Wing's lectures, and this was the way in which they expiated their crime.

For the next few Fridays most of my time seemed to be spent in dashing about, watch in hand, in an endeavour to be at the bell-push at the right moment to indicate the termination or commencement of a lecture period. Sometimes I was a bit early and various lecturers found their discourse cut off short by the sudden ringing of the bell, and sometimes I was late and students impatiently watching clocks in different lecture-rooms had to endure five minutes more of culture than they desired.

Having thus become a member of the Campanologists' Society, I immediately developed an ambition to get out of it. That, however, was also the ambition of every other member of the Society, and it was not easy. Had we had our way the Society would have ceased to exist, a state of affairs which would have caused jubilation among us members. Just as members of a normal society felt impelled to join together, so members of this society felt impelled to disassociate themselves from one another at the earliest opportunity. Dr. Wing, however, was determined that the college should not be left without some stalwarts to keep the bell ringing, and kept an observant eye on us to see that we did not fail in our duty.

"Just about time for a spot of bell-ringing, eh, Mr. Ingram," he would remark pleasantly. "You had not forgotten, had you?"

"How do I get out of this job?" I demanded bitterly. "It's getting me down."

He smiled. "That is simple. Just get me a few more bell-ringers, and I shall not require your services any longer."

Profiting by this hint, I stationed myself just inside the door of the lecture-room one morning at nine o'clock, and as soon as Dr. Wing strode in and began to lecture I waited grimly for any luckless late-comers. There was bound to be someone, and that someone could take my place at the bell-push. The first late-comer was a timid, first-year girl, who jumped when I pounced on her.

"No excuses now," I said, severely. "Just sign here, please."

While she was writing her name on the paper I collected a couple more late-comers, though, to my chagrin, a third, more wary than the others, escaped my clutches.

"What's it all about?" the two demanded.

"Just a spot of bell-ringing for you," I replied sweetly. "Sign the dotted line, please."

I could afford to be cheerful now, for I was no longer a member of the Campanologists' Society.

Another duty which students had to undertake in rotation was the locking up of the college and hostel. A calendar hung in the hall of the men's hostel with each man's name indicated beside the date when his turn of duty was due. At ten o'clock that night he would have to walk down to the college, see that all the lights were switched off and windows shut, lock all the doors, then return to the hostel, ascertain which students were in their rooms and which ones had a late pass to be out, then sign a report and present it to the Principal.

The wise student, when his turn of duty comes round, will solicit the aid of one or two of his friends, preferably the biggest and strongest. Equipping themselves with an electric torch and raincoats — for it always rains the night *you* are on duty! — they sally forth. While those students who are not burdened with the cares of the world indulge themselves in riotous living about the common-room fire, the duty student plods dutifully through the rain down to the college, which looms up out of the dark, desolate and cheerless. Inside this forlorn building, which is apparently uninhabited, the duty student's first task is to sound the bell, an action which should indicate to any persons who may be on the premises that it is time for them to clear out. Actually it does nothing of the kind, for, having perambulated each room and corridor in turn, switching off lights which have not been switched off and closing windows which have been left open, he discovers various groups of people here and there. No; they are not keen, studious types putting in a bit of overtime in the library. A few will be card-players, but in the main they will be courting couples.

Look into the large common-room — how quiet it seems! — and spaced out at intervals will be seen youths and maidens holding hands. Where else can they go on a wet winter's night? This procedure of getting rid of card-players and courting couples is known as "winkling out", and here the wisdom of bringing a friend or two with you becomes evident. The process resembles that required to persuade a mollusc to emerge reluctantly from its shell; similarly, card-players and courting couples may require persuasion. The card-players may try high-handed tactics, blustering at being interrupted, but the courting couples try wheedling. "Have a heart, pal; you were young yourself once," they plead.

The duty student, his thoughts on the warm fire and cup of tea waiting for him back at the hostel, turns a deaf ear to the claims of romance, and as the clock strikes ten he turns them all out into the rain. With his hand on the lock of the door he pauses — better glance in the library to see if anybody *is* studying there; it *has* been known to happen, long, long ago — but the library is deserted; so with a feeling of well-being he shuts the college door and locks it. The courting couples are now huddled in the porch, or under the trees, or on the steps, as forlorn as displaced persons who have been refused a visa to enter the United States. They look at the duty student reproachfully, but he is hard-hearted and passes on.

Arrived back at the hostel, he flings off his raincoat and scrutinises the list laid out on the table in the front hall. The list contains the name of every student in the hostel, and every student has to sign it each night before going to bed. If the student's signature is not on the list by 10.45, then it is presumed that he had obtained a door-key from the Principal, so that he can come in late. If he has not borrowed a key, then he has the choice of flinging gravel against the window of a friend's room, until that worthy awakes and comes down to let him in, or of ringing the night-bell and waiting for the Principal to come and unlock the door. The Principal will not be pleased to see him.

The duty student seats himself on the table by the list and waits for 10.45. As the momentous hour approaches students come flocking into the hostel, and hurry to sign their names. The duty student continues to wait. He knows that Parker has developed to a fine art the practice of timing his arrival to the very, very last second, that Colam and Cooper will be five minutes late, and that sundry other individuals will rely on his good nature not to lock the door before eleven. He rings the bell, then scrutinising the list, discovers that several names are not yet accounted for. Are they still out, or have they forgotten to sign the list?

Up one corridor and down another he goes, calling out, "Anybody here seen Jones? Who knows where Robinson is? Where the heck is Smith?" Nobody has seen Smith all evening, and the duty student is just about to conclude that he is out when it occurs to him to look inside the man's room. The room is in darkness, but the outlines of a human form can be seen on the bed, snoring lustily. Smith, it seems, came in unobserved, and decided to go to bed early.

The duty student curses him for being forgetful and goes in search of the next missing name on the list, Robinson, and eventually tracks this individual down in one of the bathrooms. Jones is still unaccounted for, and as none of his friends have any idea where he may be, the duty man anathematises him. For certain irresponsible students have developed the practice, when arriving back at the hostel late, of entering by way of the fire-escape, instead of by the front door.

Now, in the neighbourhood of any college, hospital, or similar institution there always live persons who appear to have nothing else to do with their time except watch what students are doing and report to the Principal any actions of which they personally disapprove. Some, and they are not necessarily the governors of the institution, appear to consider it their duty to act as moral watch-dogs, and no Principal likes to be aroused from his bed by a telephone call informing him that some of his students have just been seen entering their hostel by means of the fire-escape or staggering up the road obviously under the influence of alcohol. Consequently fire-escapes as a means of entry are definitely taboo, so the duty student must try and get everybody inside by the legitimate means of entry.

The duty student, if he is lucky, will

find by the time he has completed his rounds that Mr. Jones has taken the opportunity of slinking in unobserved. The night-list is now complete, and with a sigh of relief the duty student can sign it, thrust it through the letter-box in the Principal's front door, and go to bed. What happens tomorrow night will be somebody else's affair.

So the academic year grinds round. Lectures on the history of education, the philosophy of education, on health education, child development, on psychology, English, maths, religious knowledge — the lot; essays to write; weekly evidence of books read to summarise; then school practice; then lectures again; then more school practice; then more lectures, and pieces of teaching apparatus to produce; then examinations. Whoever invented that classic definition, "Students do not mature by studying, they survive by hurrying", certainly had the training colleges in mind.

Then suddenly it is all over; one's two years at college are at an end, and all this activity, physical and mental, has blended into the fabric of one's being, so that we can understand a remark made by the Vice-Principal: "Whatever you were like before you came here, if you are the same sort of person when you leave, then there is something wrong with the course here." After two years spent in this fashion the student is bound to be a very different person.

As described in the previous pages, spending two years at college may appear to have presented few difficulties; actually, it was far from easy. Getting a place at the training college was one matter; getting sufficient money to maintain my wife and daughter for two years was another. The Emergency Training Scheme, which provided allowances for students' dependants, was finished in 1952; no one could tell me how a married student was to provide for his family. I wrote to the man on top, Sir Stafford Cripps, asking how it was to be done. I did not know Sir Stafford personally, but from what I had read about him he appeared to be an understanding kind of man.

The encouraging letter I received in reply came, not from Sir Stafford, who was ill, but from Lady Cripps; she said she would approach the Ministry of Education on my behalf. Some time after this I received a friendly letter from a Ministry official stating that under the Disabled Persons (Employment) Act my wife would receive an allowance to maintain her and Anne while I was studying at college. This was gratifying, but the Civil Service takes time to act. In the meanwhile, worried that I would be unable to start college in September because of lack of funds, I prepared the synopses of two books and submitted them to publishers. One was accepted, and now it would have to be written.

Written it was, in my scanty spare time. In the evenings after lectures I would sit down at my typewriter and spend the next two or three hours completing the book; sometimes it would be midnight before I got my day's stint of writing finished. Evenings, weekends, holidays, were devoted to getting that book written and retyped; but at least I had the prospect of some money coming in to pay my own expenses while at college.

The West Riding refused me the grant

customarily given to students to pay their personal expenses, on the grounds that I was already receiving a grant from the Ministry; this conveniently ignored the fact that the grant was for the maintenance of my wife and child, and not for my own use. So I received nothing. Students who grumble about the smallness of their grant may consider how they would manage without a grant at all. Until I completed the writing of my book and had some money coming in I had to swallow my pride and apply to charitable organisations for help.

What of my wife during these two years? For her life was a hard struggle. She had already had the problem of keeping our home going during the six months I was in hospital. So difficult was it for a sick person to get into hospital that I had had to wait three months or more for a bed — actually, Joyce had had to go to the hospital and practically weep on the surgeon's shoulder before I could get admitted at all — and when I came out again it was another three months or so before I was capable of doing anything strenuous. At times our income was only

my National Health insurance payments —
less than four pounds a week. For over a
year, then, it was her good management
and stout heart which kept us going.

Now I was to be away for a further two
years, and again it would fall upon her to
keep our home going and look after Anne.
Again she never faltered. She was, indeed,
a grand-hearted lass, and the finest wife a
man like me could have. Though throughout my life I had been unlucky in any
number of things — health, social background, upbringing — I had certainly been
lucky in my choice of a wife. There was
nobody in the world like her, I believed.
It was up to me to get back home at every
opportunity, at weekends and holidays,
in order to help her. Only by working
together as a team, each trying to cheer the
other up when down-hearted, could we survive to a better future.

And the end of it all?

After the lectures, the school practice,
the final examinations, that cherished
piece of paper from the Ministry of
Education, stating: "The Minister is
pleased to inform you that, having com-

pleted to his satisfaction an approved course of training, you are entitled to be regarded as a qualified teacher."

The next time I faced a class of children in a school it would be as a real teacher, not a student.

The great day had arrived — my first day as a real teacher at a secondary modern school. I arrived at school early to have time to study the time-table and to get my classroom organised. The school, an old wooden, one-storeyed structure, was deserted, so I sat on a brick garden-wall and waited for some other members of staff to appear. A young man with the look of training college about him joined me; I hardly needed to be told that he was another new member of staff. We sat there in silence, wondering how we should cope with the several hundred boys who would soon be streaming in through the gateways.

A quarter of an hour before school was due to begin several members of staff appeared, called out a cheery "Good-morning" to us, and disappeared inside the staff-room. The headmaster arrived, handed each of us a complicated-looking document occupying three sheets of fools-cap-size paper, and said, "Here is the time-table — it is a seven-day one. Mr. Ingram, you have Room Number Two. We will hold assembly in five minutes."

We followed a line of marching boys into the assembly hall, which also served as dining-room and gymnasium. No chance to study the time-table now, I thought, so I stuffed it into my pocket. Prayers over, I hurried along the corridor seeking Room Number Two. A crowd of thirty or forty boys was waiting outside. I turned the door-handle, but the door did not open.

"Please, sir, it's locked," a boy explained.

"Please, sir, the deputy head has the key," volunteered another boy.

I waylaid the deputy head as he hurried past.

"I will lend you my key this time, Mr. Ingram," he said. "But in the future you will have to get one of your own."

Unreasonable as this appeared to me, there was no time to argue, with a crowd of boys waiting. They shuffled inside to their desks. Some sat down, and some remained standing.

"Sit down, sit down!" I said.

"Please, sir, we haven't any chairs to sit on."

"Then go and get some," I ordered.

"Please, sir, there aren't any. The school is short of chairs."

"Very well, you will have to stand then," I said. "Get out your pencils and exercise-books."

While they looked inside their desks for the required articles I hurriedly wrote some questions on the blackboard relating to general knowledge. "Never be caught without a lesson," a friend, an experienced teacher, had advised. "Get the children working as quickly as possible, and then you will have some time to take stock of the situation." After I had told the class to write down answers to the questions I noticed that a number of boys were still standing around shuffling.

"Got your books and pencils, boys?" I asked.

They looked at me stolidly, and then one said, "We ain't got no pencils, sir."

Choosing the likeliest-looking boy to be monitor, I sent him to the classroom adjoining mine to borrow some pencils.

These were given out, but still some of the boys stood there idly.

"What's wrong now?" I demanded.

"Ain't got no exercise-books to write in, sir. The headmaster only gives us a new book when we takes the old book along for him to examine."

"Then go to the headmaster and tell him Mr. Ingram needs some exercise-books before he can start his lesson."

The boy departed quickly, and came back just as quickly.

"Please, sir, the headmaster says you can't have any exercise-books — 'cos the new exercise-books haven't come yet."

"And what are we supposed to write on then?"

"On paper, sir — if you can find some paper."

Paper was found, and eventually they were all able to start work. The headmaster walked in with several books in his hand.

"Is your register marked, Mr. Ingram, and your dinner money collected?"

"I am afraid not, sir," was my reply. "I have not had much time because I have been coping with a shortage of chairs and exercise-books."

"Then I will show you how I like my books kept," the head said. "After that you should be capable of doing the job yourself."

Not until four o'clock and the end of the school day did the opportunity arise to study the time-table and discover which lessons I was supposed to be taking. As I passed the headmaster's office he called me inside.

"I suppose you understand how the time-table operates? Monday of the first week is Day One, Tuesday is Day Two, and so on, and the following Monday is Day Six and Tuesday is Day Seven, so Wednesday becomes Day One again, and so on with each successive day. You will soon get the hang of it."

"Now, about the lessons you are to take," he went on. "You are taking history throughout the school — that will be eight forms — also biology, with four forms. Geography is your subject, you say, so I am giving you two forms. And you are to take first-year maths also — one form."

I made a quick calculation.

"That is fifteen forms, sir. Isn't that rather a lot?"

"That is what is expected of the teacher who takes on this post," the headmaster said.

Fifteen forms! Thinking it over at home that evening, the thought came to me that this was not fair treatment for a new teacher. But not until I had started at my second school and heard experienced teachers complaining when the number of forms they were expected to take exceeded twelve did I fully realise how unfair it was. Well, it would not do to have an argument during my first week at my first school, so I should have to try to cope with the situation as best I could. Maybe the headmaster would prove less unbending when one got to know him better.

By the end of my first week as a teacher I knew why experienced friends of mine had been careful to find out all they could about a school and its headmaster before they accepted a teaching post there. Life seemed to be one mad rush, with me always struggling to get lessons finished before the bell rang, and always with some job left undone. How different it was from what I had expected. I was frequently in trouble; my register marked wrongly, dinner money not tallying with the number in my book, boys up to mischief when I turned my back on them. Every job had to be done in precise order and at speed. This was no place for an inexperienced teacher, much less a disabled one. What galled me was that some mistakes for which I was blamed sometimes related to matters which the local educational authority no longer required of its teaching staffs, thus every Friday afternoon we had to work out percentages of attendance, though the head himself admitted that the practice had been abandoned five years previously.

The headmaster used to patrol the whole school at intervals throughout the day. He carried a large sheet of plywood strapped to his arm, and pasted on this were the pages of the seven-day time-table. He would stop outside your classroom door, look at the column in the time-table to see what lesson you should be taking at that moment, check the time by his watch, then come striding into your room to make sure that you were actually taking that particular lesson. He would walk up to your desk to see that your lesson-notes were prepared, and then study the blackboard to see that the lesson material was written out correctly. At this point he might walk out of the room again, or he might walk about among the desks to see how the boys were getting on with the lesson. I got used to this procedure, and it did not bother me.

To take fifteen forms of thirty or more boys each meant that every seven days I had several hundred exercise-books to mark. The head was a stickler for having books marked, for he would not issue a new exercise-book to a boy unless all the work in the full book had been marked and corrected. Marking several hundred books at regular intervals became a burden which blighted my whole existence. I tried to get some marking done in play-time, or during the dinner-hour, but inevitably I had to take great piles of books home to mark in the evenings. But the number of books to be marked kept mounting, and try as I might I got behind with the job.

Eventually I found myself sitting up until midnight at weekends marking books; it was evident that if I continued to do this my health would suffer. The preparation of lessons in history for the whole school, also in biology and geography, took a lot of time. I tried to explain these difficulties to the headmaster, but he was unsympathetic.

"Mr. Ingram, I do not understand you," he declared. "You are paid a good wage to do this job, and if you do not feel competent enough to do it, then please do not come complaining to me."

"I feel that I am not being fairly treated," I said. "Don't you think that looking after fifteen classes is asking a lot of an inexperienced teacher?"

"We all have to learn," was his reply. "It will come with experience. I will come into your classroom when I have some spare time and show you how to take one or two lessons."

And with that I had to be content.

At first I struggled to cope with all the difficulties for fear of losing my job, as I had a wife and small daughter dependent upon me, but as I became more tired and despondent the feeling grew upon me that if I did not get away from that school soon I would not be in a fit state to get another job anywhere. But there was the bogey of the probationary year to haunt me. New teachers spend their first year on probation, and are dependent upon obtaining a good report from their headmaster, who if not satisfied can recommend that the period of probation be extended.* The head's powers over a new teacher are considerable, for if he does not give him a fair chance the teacher concerned may have a bad reputation accorded him, which will follow him (or her) throughout his school career in that area.

There was nothing for it but to give in my notice at half-term, and hope that I could secure a job somewhere else.

Life at my next school was much pleasanter. The time-table was reasonable; the children were pleasant boys and girls; the headmaster was much easier to get on with. I found myself liking life as a teacher. So smoothly did things go that a year went

* A lady teacher at my present school tells me that at her previous school the headmaster refused to give five new teachers a good report at the end of their probationary year.

by almost without my being aware of it. All these things made me realise how unlucky I had been in the choice of my first school.

A year after that I decided to change over from teaching older children in a secondary modern school to teaching younger children in a primary school. I wanted experience of both types of teaching before applying for the post of teacher at a school for physically handicapped children. The West Riding Education Department was very helpful, and transferred me to a school with just the right kind of headmaster, one who was prepared to go to any amount of trouble to give his new teachers the training and the opportunities they needed. The months I spent at that school were very happy ones, and I learned a great deal.

"Thank you for all the help you gave me, Mr. Heslop of Flushdyke School."

I was to teach at two secondary modern schools and two primary schools before I got the kind of job I wanted, teaching physically handicapped children. It was several years before I felt that at long last I was a *teacher*; that I was not just somebody standing in front of a group of children. And it was some time after that before I realised that a teacher is one who never stops learning himself, and that we go on learning all our lives.

14

THE MIDNIGHT-OIL UNIVERSITY

TO go to university, to study for a degree in geography, historical geography for preference — how that old will-o'-the-wisp continued to lure me on! Even at a school for physically handicapped children, I reflected, a university degree would be of value, for disabled children needed contact with better educated persons just as much as grammar-school children. Ever since my abortive attempt to study at the Institute of Archaeology I had cherished the hope that some day it might be possible to prove that I had the type of brain which would benefit by a university education.

As an errand-boy in Manchester in the 1930's I had typed out the reading-list for the geography course issued by Manchester University, and during the intervening twenty years had managed to read most of the books and visit many of the places described in them. But for the past few years, since my marriage, the struggle to keep going had left little time to think of such matters. Earning my living, in competition with fit people; getting somewhere for Joyce and myself to live; undergoing operations in hospital; going to training college; these things had presented me with so many problems that there had been no room in my mind for anything else.

Classes organised by the Workers' Educational Association had been one way in which knowledge of a subject could be acquired. During the years I had learned something of a variety of subjects — astronomy, local history, art and painting, English literature, international affairs — by attending classes organised by the WEA. At such classes I had met friendly people with interests similar to my own, and lecturers who were educated and helpful. The WEA had helped to open windows on new worlds, but now I wanted to go further than its organisation could take me. Still I wanted to go to university, but the more I considered the problem the greater it became. The WEA lecturer obtained for me details of scholarships available to older students such as myself, and it might have been possible to get to Oxford or Cambridge, but that would have meant separation from my family, and this I was not prepared to do. Joyce and I had been separated by force of circumstances too much already.

How can a married man with a wife and child to support manage to go to university for several years unless he has private means? It could not be done, I was told, for although there were Government grants for mature students, one was disqualified from receiving one of these if the Government had already paid for your training as a teacher. There appeared to be only one chance of a person in my position obtaining a degree, I discovered, and that was by studying for the examinations of the University of London as an external student. It was possible to prepare for these examinations anywhere in Great Britain by means of correspondence courses, or by attending evening classes at a college of technology. Before going to Sheffield Teachers' Training College I had attempted to obtain a place at Leeds University, but Professor Williamson of the

Department of Geography there had quickly disillusioned me on that point; I had no chance at all.

Teachers have one advantage over other workers: they have a fair amount of spare time, in the evenings, at weekends, and holidays. Suppose one decided to devote this time to the attainment of one particular objective — obtaining a university degree? Suppose also that one is prepared to concentrate upon this objective for a certain length of time — say, seven years? A university degree in exchange for seven years' spare-time work appeared a not unreasonable proposition. After all, one might spend seven years watching television programmes, and have less to show for it. One would need some money, also, to pay for correspondence courses, textbooks, lecture fees, instruction in field-geography. I thought it might be done.

While at training college I had discussed the problem with Professor Bryan, of Leicester University, our external examiner.

"Try for the Diploma in Geography of London University first," he advised. "Get that, and you have a specialist qualification to start with. Then try for university entrance. You will need two GCE subjects at 'A' level. Get these, and then try for a degree in geography. I know it can be done because I have a crippled student who is doing it, and I wish you every success."

Acting upon his advice, I studied for the examination for the Diploma in Geography by means of correspondence courses, and passed. The examination consisted of five papers, and some evidence of field-work in geography. As long as I live I will remember the Examination Halls of London University, of hundreds of students all milling about the entrance, waiting for the attendants to remove the barriers so that they could go charging inside to locate their seats and get started as quickly as possible. The mob of students swept me forward like a leaf borne away by flood-waters, and almost before I knew it I was deposited in a large room filled with hundreds of desks, with a row of invigilators in academic dress seated along the side. The number on my admission ticket was 10,909, but could I find the desk bearing that number? No! I wandered helplessly around, found myself back among the desks labelled eight hundred, then among the twelve hundreds, while all about me the scratching of hundreds of fountain-pens warned me that the other students were already at work. At last I found the desk bearing my name and number, whereupon another problem presented itself, one which I had not thought of. An examination has to be *sat*, just that, and sitting down for any length of time was sheer torture. I endured the first hour or two, but after that life was misery. And there were two and a half days of it. But I passed.

The next hurdle was university entrance. A person educated in Canada could not submit the required number of General Certificates in Education required by the university, nor was the fact that I had passed the necessary examinations to become a qualified teacher at training college accepted by the university authorities as sufficient evidence. They told me I should be required to sit a special examination for mature students. Taken altogether, my prospects of becoming a university graduate did not appear very promising.

I had to start all over again by studying to obtain the various GCE passes. This took two years, because when the time came to sit the examination I was taken ill and had to wait until the following year. I passed. With university entrance thus secured, the way was now clear to prepare for Part One of the examination for the degree of Bachelor of Science in Economics. I chose this degree because it was a good all-round one, comprising various social sciences — geography, history, economics, government, politics. The degree of BA was not possible, because I had forgotten my Latin and my knowledge of foreign languages was sketchy; the degree of BSc was out of the question, because my knowledge of science was limited. But I thought I knew something of geography and history and economics.

Even so, the syllabus for this degree nearly made my hair stand on end. The examination was in two parts, so that one had to pass in thirteen papers, spend a stipulated number of days undergoing geographical field-studies, and submit notebooks containing one's practical work to the examiners. Whether or not it was possible to accomplish all this was something I did not know.

The thing to do, I decided, was not to worry about the future, but plod on with one's studies and see how far one got. Seven years was a long time. Even if one never completed the courses, never got a degree, one's mind would surely have been improved by contact with the writings of the world's great thinkers. What was it Stephen Leacock, the Canadian humorist and economist, had written: that all that was necessary to get a university education was a good chair and plenty of books. Now was the time to put this theory to the test and discover if it was true.

Pass that batch of correspondence lessons, will you, and let's get started!

The student body whose ranks I had joined, the men and women striving to master a subject by means of lessons dispatched to them by post from an educational institution many miles away — what sort of people were they? Teachers, parsons, clerks, housewives, mechanics, schoolboys, young, old, dull, clever — with little in common except the inability to attend a recognised educational centre.

People who wanted to learn something and who had no means of gaining the knowledge except by correspondence courses. People who were prepared to make the effort to acquire such knowledge in the comfort (or otherwise), of their own homes or lodgings, in their spare time in the evenings, at weekends, during holidays. "The submerged academic tenth, about which little is known and in which there appears to be little or no interest," to quote Dr. Stephen Cotgrove, senior lecturer in sociology at the London Polytechnic. And yet they constituted one of the largest groups of students in the country — over 150,000 according to one estimate — equal to the combined total of all the students in all the universities and colleges of advanced technology. Here was a huge body of students who had little contact with the academic world, except through the printed word. These students never saw the colleges from which their instruction was derived; their lecturers and tutors remained faceless and anonymous.

Much later, in a Sunday newspaper, I read the following summing up of this situation:

There are more people in Britain studying for London external degrees than there are undergraduates at Oxford and Cambridge put together. They form a large, amorphous periphery to the academic world — people from all walks of life, of all ages, of high aspirations but widely varying ability. They are examined — but given no tuition — by London University, the only British university that can award external degrees. And only a small proportion of those who enrol as degree candidates ever finish up with letters after their name.

The heartbreak rate among external students is high; in many subjects as many as half give up their studies before even taking the examination. And in some subjects, the failure rate is as high as 70 per cent, after months of ploughing through correspondence courses or attending drab night-schools. . . . Surprisingly little research has been published into the motives and special problems of external students, who they are, and why so many fail to achieve their ambitions. . . . Paradoxically, the failure rate tends to be highest in the subjects that are most appropriate for home study — arts, economics, and so on — which are essentially "reading" degrees. In subjects like engineering, which often require specialised equipment and training, results are better.*

At the other end of the scale, it was pointed out, some of the most brilliant successes were gained by external students; the highest marks in the university in both German and Philosophy were gained by external students, and a housewife and a prep-school teacher both took excellent firsts in English Literature.

The weekly lessons provided by the correspondence school with which I had enrolled varied in quality, but on the whole were very good. Each lesson consisted of several pages of notes based on the portions of the textbooks being studied, a weekly test, and model answers to the previous week's test. The answers to the weekly test were sent to one's personal tutor to be corrected, and were returned to you

* "Education; The Midnight-oil University" — *The Sunday Times*, October 13, 1963.

some time later with his comments. Some tutors skimped their corrections, but, speaking generally, the staff of the correspondence school did appear to take an interest in the student's work. Some tutors proved to be the authors of the textbooks one was studying. Many were quite friendly, scribbling personal notes of encouragement and advice at the end of their corrections.

Yet this was not enough, as I was presently to discover.

"Will you be typing again this evening, Jim?"

Joyce has asked this same question almost every night now for four years. I consider my answer carefully. I don't feel like studying this evening; at school I have been on yard-duty, and it's been a wet day and the children have been full of mischief. I am tired. Also I know Joyce gets tired of the sound of my typewriter tapping out lessons and answers to weekly tests. But it is no good feeling tired after a day's work when you are preparing for a tough examination.

"Yes, I'll be typing as usual," I reply.

"But I have some school-books to mark first."

Joyce looks disappointed, but does not protest. This eternal studying leaves little time for family life, for the more time spent in idle conversation, then the later you are in tackling your correspondence lessons. Some subjects are so difficult that it may be eight or nine o'clock in the evening before you feel you have got your teeth into the topic under review. Once you have got started, the temptation to go on till midnight or beyond is great, but this must be resisted, for this means you will feel half-dead next morning. A school is no place for anyone feeling like that.

You pick up the first of the test papers and study the questions to see what sense can be made of them. Here is something from the Principles of Economics paper:

How will the quantity of a commodity bought by a consumer change in the following cases?
(a) The commodity's price is raised by an indirect tax.
(b) An increased proportion of the con-

sumer's income has to be paid in income tax.

(Tastes and prices of all other goods should be assumed constant.)

You stare at this a second time and then again, but still your brain refuses to make any sense of it. Your daughter Anne, playing on the hearthrug in front of the fire, trips over something, falls, and starts to howl.

"Can't you shut that kid up?" you ask. "This stuff is difficult enough without having to put up with kids screeching."

"She hurt herself when she fell down," Joyce explains.

"Well, it's time she was in bed then she wouldn't be falling down and hurting herself," you reply crossly.

You stare at the Economics paper, but all the questions seem incomprehensible, so you fling it down. Maybe one of the other test papers will prove easier. You pick up the Elements of Government, and start to consider one of the questions: " 'First among Equals.' How far is this a true and adequate description of the Prime Minister's position in the twentieth century?" The way you feel, this question makes as much sense as the previous one. You stare at it, conscious that you have a headache. What does "First among equals" mean? Who is equal? Another howl from your daughter jerks your mind back to more immediate problems.

"Why is that kid howling again?" you ask. "Isn't she in bed yet?"

"She *is* in bed," comes Joyce's voice from upstairs. "But the wind is blowing half a gale against the windows, and the noise upset her."

"Well, keep her quiet somehow," you exclaim.

You fling the Elements of Government paper down on top of the Principles of Economics, and, more hopefully, reach for the paper dealing with Historical Geography. After all, you like geography so much that you can read the subject even when very tired. Now here is a question: " 'The geography of Roman Britain differs as markedly from that of the preceding prehistoric period as it does from that of the succeeding Dark Ages.' Examine critically the truth of this statement." Your mind begins to dictate an answer.

For a moment you are no longer in that cosy living-room, surrounded by books and lesson-papers; you are out in the open air, an amateur archaeologist once more, helping to excavate the remains of a Roman villa in east Yorkshire. As in a dream, you see the geography of Roman Britain spread out before you — forts, villas, towns, roads, industries — for much of the subject-matter of the question is part of your being, based on knowledge gained by personal experience. You have *tramped* the Roman roads, *excavated* Roman settlements, *handled* Roman tools and weapons. You do not have to scan lines of print to answer this question; you have *lived* it all. With a piece of paper inserted in the typewriter you begin to write an essay on the geography of Roman Britain.

Some time later you realise that all is quiet. Anne must be asleep. Joyce sits beside you, silent. She waits until you look up before speaking.

"How is it going?"

"Not so bad," you say. "Quite good, in fact. Here, just listen to this."

She listens, while you read out what you have written, and then she smiles.

"Do you remember the time we helped to dig those Roman pottery kilns at Norton? We hoped to meet somebody who would tell us where we could find a house to rent. But we never did."

You smile at the thought, feeling more relaxed now.

"I remember. What a struggle we have had to keep going, ever since we got married! I'll bet if lots of other couples had half the setbacks we've encountered it would just about break their hearts."

"Well, if we have got a nice home together it's all due to our own efforts," Joyce remarks. "We do not have to thank anybody."

You take her hand in yours.

"It is all due to you," you tell her. "You are the best wife in the world. I cannot imagine life without you. You are the only woman in the world I could have married."

For once, it seems, my wife cannot think of anything to say.

Four years passed by, and now it was 1958. One thing after another went wrong with me. Again I found myself in hospital, undergoing the most unpleasant surgical operation of all — to cure a gnawing pain suspected to be cancer of the rectum. This was one of the blackest periods of my life.

Pain! I thought I'd experienced enough pain and discomfort, enough hospitals and operations, for one man's lifetime. Imagine being in such pain that it is not possible to get in a comfortable position, however you try — either sitting or standing, lying down or walking. Life is absolute misery. This was worse than being confined to bed, in plaster, for months; worse than lying in bed for days with my eyes bandaged. The discomfort went on for months, sometimes breaking out into such savage bouts of pain that it was hardly possible for me to keep going.

Each time the pain got too bad I went back to hospital again, to undergo the ordeal known as a sigmoidoscopic examination. The sigmoidoscope is a tube with an electric light at its tip, which gently expands the sides of the rectum and allows the doctor to see the area where most cancers are found. The spells of pain lasted for more than four years, until they gradually became less and finally died away.

I was told there was nothing to worry about.

While I was fighting this gnawing pain in my backside other things went wrong with me. My leg gave me trouble, so that walking became difficult. I slipped on an icy road and twisted a finger in my right hand; by the time the doctor had decided that it ought to be examined in hospital I had lost the use of it. My eyes started giving me trouble, so that I made mistakes when marking the class register, but at this school no allowance was made for the fact that one might be in pain and disabled. Do the job or get out, seemed to be the attitude of staff and headmaster. The headmaster refused to allow teachers with only a few years' teaching experience to cane or otherwise punish disobedient children, yet would not deal with them himself; then he declared that we did not know how to maintain discipline.

I was developing a distaste for teaching in junior and in secondary modern schools, and began considering a move to another part of England where I should be near a school for physically handicapped children. Perhaps if we could make a fresh start somewhere else we could shake off the feeling that life held nothing but misfortune and despair for us. Puzzled by the rejection of an application for a teaching post at a school nearer our home, I was astounded to receive back with my application form a copy of a confidential report about myself; this had been scribbled down by some unknown person in the education department and had apparently been returned to me in error. Its contents damned any chance I had of getting another teaching post in that district, for not only was I "too clever", but I "would never make a teacher" and also I was "physically unattractive". My unknown enemy certainly hated me, and was using every unfair means to hurt me.

The shock of this discovery was like a blow on the chin, but although the National Union of Teachers acted promptly, they were unable to find out who was using his (or her) official position to hurt me.

All these troubles, coupled with the pain which at frequent intervals gnawed at my backside, took the heart out of me. I felt baffled, frustrated, just about beaten. It seemed that nothing could go right with me, that I was under a hoodoo. Surely one man could not have such continuous bad luck, so many misfortunes? It was unreal. It was uncanny. *The News Chronicle* published a column in which the Rev. Wilfred Garlick, of St. George's Church, Stockport, Cheshire, gave advice on spiritual matters to readers. In reply to a letter which I sent describing my sequence of misfortunes, Canon Garlick replied:

I must admit that you seem to attract to yourself the most remarkable chain of ill-fortune, but I am not inclined to attribute this either to God or the Devil, as such. Rather do I feel that in the randomness of things there will be times when we seem to enjoy more luck than usual and times when we seem to be in misfortune above average, but in all, there is no need to postulate anything but the ordinary, inscrutable working of events which are so far above us in their scope that those who tend to put an agnostic interpretation on them can well be forgiven.

I think they are wrong, and I think you will be wrong if you do not see in the course of time — and I hope a short time —

that things have probably worked for the ultimate good. After all, you have pitted yourself against life and won so much, both physically and spiritually, that the fact that you take an occasional beating is to say no more than that you are attempting a big job. Perhaps to put it another way, "Whom the Lord loveth he chasteneth, and scourgeth every son whom he receiveth." Indeed, I would commend to you the philosophy of Hebrews 11 and 12, and their OT counterparts. I think that all you need to break the "hoodoo" is to persist, and then it is likely you will run into much fairer weather.

Mind you, I think a bit of your trouble may be due to your own character. Not always are the most intelligent people the best disciplinarians, nor do they suffer fools gladly, and some people in authority are just that. You appear to have had your share of bureaucratic uppishness and schoolmasterly double-dealing, and there is plenty available. Of course, unusual people arouse hostility.

In the meantime reflect that as you are trying to climb higher than your natural attributes of health indicate, and you have started without some of the advantages that other people have, perhaps it is not a hoodoo which afflicts you, but merely that you have more to overcome than most people, and indeed have already done better and will do better again.

Self-pity was something I hoped I rarely suffered from, but when I wrote to Canon Garlick I was really feeling sorry for myself. The mood passed, and I was already planning for the future when his stimulating and encouraging reply came; it helped to put new heart into me.

Unusual people arouse hostility. A biologist once told me that if you take a small fish such as a minnow away from its companions, and put it by itself in a tank for a while, and then return it to the place from which you took it, the other fishes will immediately turn on it and drive it away. Your little fish may look exactly the same and be performing the same pattern of movements as the other fish, but they will no longer accept it as one of themselves. I had not realised how such an attitude existed among human beings also, towards those who for one reason or another — illness, disability, social background — were different. Disabled people, ambitious people, people who were prepared to work harder or take bigger risks to get what they wanted, were very likely to arouse hostility. Disabled people, no matter how hard they might try to be like the people round them, were bound to be different.

Somewhere in England, I felt, was a school where I would be able to teach the kind of children who interested me, a niche in the teaching profession for a teacher who was himself disabled — if I could find the right school. Thus I could embark upon the career where my disability would be an advantage instead of a disadvantage.

Now, about studying for a university degree by means of correspondence courses — alas, my progress was so slow that it caused me to despair of ever achieving my ambition by this method. To sit down with a pile of textbooks, evening after evening, after a tiring day's work, became more and more difficult as the years went by. One could stare at lesson-notes for hours and yet fail to grasp their meaning.

The point was reached when one's brain refused to function. One had the feeling that it was foolish to continue, a feeling which became overwhelming as the years went by. One lost touch with friends and family.

What was to be done?

The only solution was, somehow, to spend a year or so in full-time study, in personal contact with tutors and fellow-students, preferably at a university. So seven years after trying for a place as a student at Leeds University I was trying for a place there once again. This time instead of Professor Williamson it was Professor Dickinson of the Geography Department who confronted me across a desk. The results were the same as my previous interview; there seemed no hope of a middle-aged man going there to study. University places were for the young, for people who had headmasters pushing them.

I was compelled to realise that I should never go to university in this lifetime.

Professor Dickinson advised me that I should continue to study for a degree by means of correspondence courses. He declared that I stood a better chance of achieving my goal that way. Experience had taught me otherwise. There were times when one felt completely baffled by statements in text-books, and problems which a college lecturer could have cleared up in a few minutes' conversation continued to perplex one for days. One needed more than books. The human contact with teachers, the ability to ask questions and receive individual answers, was lacking. One recalled the pathetic remark made by a correspondence student who was able to attend a vacation course in economics at Cambridge University: "It's the first time I've ever talked to a real economist. Never even *seen* one before."

Attendance at a university was not possible, but there was a way of obtaining tuition in degree subjects which was open to external students of the University of London. This was by attending lectures at one of the Colleges of Advanced Technology (CAT for short), which were being established in various cities of Great Britain. The ten CAT's were the top-level technical colleges, and recognised as institutions of university standard. At these various colleges students could work for a degree in subjects ranging from zoology to music. Nowadays technical colleges have their sports clubs and students' societies and a strong corporate spirit. One had a much better chance of studying for a degree at one of the CAT's than at one of the provincial universities.

After discussing the difficulties with my wife I resigned from my job as teacher in a primary school, and enrolled as a student at the Institute of Technology in Bradford; I could be attending lectures there while waiting for the post of teacher in a school for physically handicapped children to materialise. Attendance at the college meant a twenty-mile journey each way, to and from the Yorkshire mining village in which we lived. The college buildings towered up atop a steep hill which it was always a struggle for me to climb. I had no money to buy meals at the canteen, so took sandwiches and a flask of tea and ate these in the common-room, in company with a number of coloured students whose financial position appeared similar to mine.

Lectures for the degree of BSc (Economics) took place, not in the imposing main building of the college, but in a dilapidated old house called The Vicarage, which was linked to the rest of the college by a covered alleyway. The Vicarage was a rambling, gloomy old building, full of dingy little rooms and twisting staircases. Yet the lecturers were first-class, the atmosphere constructive and helpful, so that one hardly noticed the dingy surroundings. My progress became much more rapid; I realised it had been a wise move to come here for instruction.

Government, politics, economic theory, applied economics, economic history, economic geography — I found myself absorbing these subjects as a cat laps up cream. Such subjects were the very basis of our civilised way of life, so that studying for the degree of Bachelor of Science in Economics was well worthwhile in itself, apart from any other advantages which might accrue from the possession of it. I liked to study for the sheer joy of learning, liked the feeling of gaining mastery of a subject. Most of my fellow-students wanted to obtain a degree for a specific purpose — a better job, a bigger salary. What mattered most to them were the letters after their names, not the learning.

Part One of the examination comprised eight papers, of which seven had to be passed on the same occasion; a student was allowed to be weak in only one paper. Otherwise he had to sit all eight papers again. I heard of one candidate, now middle-aged, who had taken the same law examination fifteen times! Most gratifying was the progress I found myself making in the subject which baffled me completely at times — modern economic theory. Much modern theory seemed to run counter to common-sense, certainly contrary to the habits of thrift and self-denial which had been taught me by my mother as a child. It took me a long time to realise the great value of hire-purchase debts to the well-being of a modern economic system, for example. It was thanks to the remarkable gift for making this abstruse subject understandable, possessed by John Hall, the senior lecturer in economics, that I eventually grasped enough theory to pass Part One of the examination.

My fellow-students, I quickly discovered, were a friendly, helpful crowd. Mostly they were older men, with families to maintain. Some were part-time students, with jobs which enabled them to attend lectures between periods of duty. Coloured students from Nigeria, Ghana, Iraq, Pakistan, and British Guiana described economic and social conditions in their respective countries. We learned how the newer countries of Asia and Africa were providing the younger, educated coloured people with a wide variety of problems.

As to how Joyce and Anne and I lived during that year when I was studying instead of earning my living, all I can say is — we lived. It was a hard struggle. It was thanks to my wife's efforts, to her cheerfulness and co-operation and good management, that we kept going. No financial help was available from any Government source, no encouragement from anyone; we had to make do with what money we had saved up, plus various sums granted us by charitable organisations. Students could not live on the "dole" while preparing for an examination, I was told; a Court of Appeal upheld this decision.

There my studies for a degree had to end for the time being. One day in the advertisement column of the *Times Educational Supplement* appeared details of a new residential school for physically handicapped children in Cheshire which needed teachers. I applied for a post there, went for an interview, got the job. At last I could embark upon the work which I had been stimulated to undertake by reading Albert Schweitzer's words nine years before:

"If you have been delivered from bodily anguish, you must not think you are free. From that moment on, you feel bound to help to bring others to deliverance."

Just as some time previously everything had seemed to go wrong with us, so that we felt we were under a hoodoo, now in that same mysterious fashion everything seemed to go right for us. The teaching post at the new school seemed to have been made for me, and when Joyce and I sought to obtain a mortgage to buy a house a mile away we secured both mortgage and house without difficulty. I still regard this happening as a miracle, as if some unseen power was guiding our movements. So we exchanged the Yorkshire pit-village in which we had lived for eleven years for a housing estate in Cheshire. In place of slag-heaps and coke-ovens were streets of semi-detached houses and bungalows, and green lawns and flower-gardens. For the first time in her married life Joyce had a decent house and a clean atmosphere to live in.

As Canon Garlick had suggested in his letter, things *had* worked out for the ultimate good.

The struggle proved worthwhile. I passed Part One and could proceed to Part Two.

15

LIFE BEGINS AT FIFTY

ONE August day in 1961 I sat on a block of dried mud and with notebook in front of me sketched the defences of the oldest town in the world. Before me was a deep trench, and at the bottom could be seen part of a stone wall and bulging circular tower. Stone tower and wall appealed to my imagination, for they were part of the defences of ancient Jericho. According to archaeologists, they were nine thousand years old. Men had been living a civilised life here, in walled Jericho, in the Jordan Valley, when my skin-clad ancestors had been gaining a precarious livelihood by hunting and fishing.

All about me was a vast, sun-baked mound of dried mud, towering above the green oasis which concealed the modern town of Jericho, a mile or two away. This great mound, or *tell*, was the accumulated remains of a number of ancient Jerichos, each of which had in turn occupied this site, and then crumbled into ruin. Remains of houses and streets, walls and towers, were visible at the bottom of the trench. Town after town had occupied this site, fifteen or sixteen of them one above the other, but now all had disappeared into the limbo of forgotten things, and only the great mound was left, scarred here and there by pits and trenches, memorials to seven seasons' work by archaeologists.

Students of the University of London who were studying geography had to present to the examiners notebooks containing details of geographical studies which they had undertaken in the open air, as evidence that they had performed the required amount of field-work. This was an essential part of the examination, and it had seemed to me that a couple of outstanding note-books might improve one's chances of passing should one be weak in certain written papers. One notebook of mine was filled with maps and notes collected during a course organised by the University at Preston Montford field-centre near Shrewsbury; then, seeking other aspects of field-geography to explore, the idea came to me that it would be a fine thing to go to Jordan and Israel and investigate the Jordan Valley. Archaeology and geography were my two loves, and these could be profitably combined by studying the historical geography of the Jordan Valley.

The Jordan Valley gripped my imagination. A great rift in the earth's surface, two hundred miles long, hemmed in by towering mountain walls, getting deeper and deeper as it approached the Dead Sea, where it became the lowest place on earth, a sheer quarter of a mile below sea-level. Geographically and historically there was nothing else like this spectacular rift-valley on our planet. Where else could you find such a river as the Jordan, flowing sinuously along through the tangled thickets of the *zor*, or jungle: where else could you find such an ancient city site as Jericho; or where else find the ruined monastery of Qumran and the caves where the Dead Sea Scrolls were discovered? Three traverses across the Jordan Valley would supply enough material to satisfy the most exacting of examiners.

"Hello, you must be a keen student of

the past to be out in this heat sketching old ruins."

The Bishop of Crediton was looking at my handiwork. Joyce and I were on pilgrimage to the Holy Land, and the Bishop was the leader of our party. When we had stopped to view the mound of Jericho I had taken the opportunity to collect some material for my notebook, just as I would take the opportunity to study the ruins of ancient Qumran when we reached the Dead Sea. A pilgrimage to the sacred sites of Palestine inevitably compelled a study of sites connected with the archaeology of the Bible.

"I expected to see the remains of the walls which Joshua brought down with his trumpets," I said.

"These walls are older," the Bishop remarked. "Much older."

"Seven thousand years before Christ," said I, peering into the trench again, and marvelling.

"So Dr. Kenyon informs us," he replied. "She and her colleagues worked here long enough — seven years, was it not?"

The archaeological excavations which we were investigating had been conducted during the years 1952–58 by Dr. Kathleen Kenyon, whose lectures on archaeology I had attended in London so many years before. The name Jericho for most people conjures up a picture of the Israelites under Joshua marching round the town, and the collapse of its walls at the sound of their trumpets. But Jericho was already a very old town at the time of Joshua, and excavation has traced its origins back into the New Stone Age, and shown that it is the earliest town in the world so far discovered.

"The blocks of stone in that wall are quite big," I remarked. "Some of them must be five feet across. If they were brought from the quarry half a mile away, then the whole undertaking indicates a well-organised community."

"It would appear to indicate some form of orderly government," the Bishop agreed. "And also considerable technical skill on the part of the builders."

He took a handkerchief out of his pocket and mopped his brow.

"How hot it is — it is getting too hot for me here, I fear! If you have finished your sketch it is time for us to be moving on. We want to reach the Dead Sea before midday." I took a final look at the great mound into which Dr. Kenyon's team had burrowed for seven seasons, peeling away the layers of occupation, like skins off an onion. The archaeologists had gone now, and only the silent mound with its trenches and pits was left.

"It is a pity about Joshua," I remarked. "I should like to have seen the walls which the trumpets brought down."

"All gone," said the Bishop. "Gone long ago. And it is time we were gone also."

Later we came back along the road from Jericho, by car, and entered Jerusalem by St. Stephen's Gate. We passed into the Old City on foot. Before we passed through the gateway we looked back at the now-familiar scene — the deep valley of Kedron, the Mount of Olives, the Garden of Gethsemane. And before us stood the walls of Jerusalem all golden in the sun. We passed through the gate. Ahead of us was a long street lined with old buildings, the Via Dolorosa, the Way of the Cross. The street was empty; perhaps imagination made one people it with unseen crowds of times gone by.

In the basement under the Convent of

Ecce Homo we were shown a wide expanse of paving-stones, grooved to stop horses' hooves slipping, and displaying the outlines of gaming-boards scratched on the stone with sword-points. This place is quite literally the *Pavement*, where, according to tradition, Christ was brought before Pilate, and where Roman soldiers off duty sat around gaming. The pavement was then in the Praetorium, though it is below street-level now, and from here Christ began that last journey which was to end at Calvary.

We follow in His steps.

The narrow street, arched and buttressed, leads us on. Stations of the Cross, each marking an episode in that last journey, are passed, until the journey's end is reached — where now the Church of the Holy Sepulchre stands. The Bishop leads the way inside; we, the pilgrims, follow. Somehow one is not conscious of entering the church or of being in a church; one is still continuing in one's mind that last tragic journey of Christ, and the fact that there is now a roof over one's head and walls around is of minor significance. The impression is of being still out in the open, under a dark sky, looking towards a hill crowned with three crosses.

True, you will not see the hill now as it was when Christ died there, for Byzantine engineers centuries ago cut away the surplus rock from round the mound of Calvary — Golgotha, as it was known — leaving the hill isolated so that they could build a great church round it. The little hill is still there, but embodied inside the church; the wonder of it is concealed behind the façade of a rather ornate, dingy Greek chapel. But if you can forget the dinginess, and see it in your imagination as it was when He was crucified there, then with a shock the realisation comes that the New Testament is not just a pretty story: Christ was a real person; he lived, he suffered, he died. You are standing on holy ground for THIS IS CALVARY, WHERE CHRIST DIED TO REDEEM MANKIND.

We follow on the last few yards of the journey to the Holy Sepulchre itself. The Holy Sepulchre also had been left as an isolated block of rock by the cutting away of the stony hillside surrounding it. The tomb of Christ lies within the mass of rock, enclosed within the walls of the church.

Well-worn steps lead down into the tomb; before you is the spot where the body of Christ was laid, the tomb from which He rose again on that first Easter morning. This is the goal of all pilgrims, the place to which for over nineteen hundred years millions of people of many different races, tongues, and colours have come.

Here, if anywhere, one can say as thousands of believers before us:

"Into Thy hands we give ourselves, O Lord, for life or death."

"Please, sir — sorry to disturb you, sir, but is this object one of those stone axes which the Stone Age people used, sir? You told us about them in that lesson on archaeology, sir."

I looked up from the pile of exercise-books which I was trying to mark, and found several excited boys of Class Four grouped round my desk. There was Hugh, a spastic, tall and gawky, with arms and legs which did not seem to belong to him, and his pal Tony, a deformed boy with one shoulder higher than the other, and Bill of the bellowing voice in his wheelchair. It was Friday afternoon at our School for

Physically Handicapped Children, when the time-table allowed the children "Free Choice", so that they could spend an hour or so doing anything they chose. Some children were sitting at their desks reading or writing or drawing. Others were watching a television programme. Hugh and his cronies regarded such activities as much too unexciting, and had chosen to dig the garden in the hope of uncovering buried treasure.

A grubby-looking stone implement was thrust under by nose, and a chorus of youthful voices asked me to tell them what it was used for. I explained that similar objects could be seen in Manchester Museum.

"You are quite right, Hugh. It does look like a prehistoric stone axe, though it would have a wooden handle fixed to it originally of course. Where did you find it?"

"While we were digging a new piece of ground for the garden, sir. It was mixed up with some clay and bits of flint."

"You dug up things like this when you were a boy out in Canada, didn't you, sir?" asked Tony.

448

It is always instructive for a teacher to discover how much of a lesson which he has given is remembered by the children. That lesson on archaeology had filled in an odd half-hour one afternoon, yet the children seemed to have retained a clear impression of the excavation of a prehistoric Indian village which I had witnessed as a boy in Ontario.

"Well, we did find stone weapons something like this," I admitted. "But the Indians used stone tools in Canada in the seventeenth century. This axe-head will be much older than the things we found out in Canada."

"Maybe the school is built on top of a Stone Age settlement, sir," Hugh suggested hopefully.

"It is possible," was my reply. "Go on digging, boys, and see if you can find some more stone implements. We could start a school museum with a few more finds like this."

"That would be smashing, sir," Tony exclaimed. "A museum of our own! When can we start?"

"Maybe we can find some spears or arrow-heads for our museum," Bill shouts excitedly. "Come on, lads, let's get cracking."

His wheel-chair spun round as he charged outside, nearly knocking Tony's crutches from under his armpits. Tony staggered, clutched at the door-handle for support, and Hugh good-naturedly proffered a steadying hand. Then they were gone, uttering shouts resembling war-cries, and I was left to contemplate the remainder of Class Four. Several boys and girls looked up to see what the commotion was about, then resumed their own occupations. Though it was nearly five years since I came to work there, after experiences in primary and secondary modern schools, I could still marvel at the good-humour and courage of the crippled children I taught.

These are the children who confront me across several rows of desks — children who at the moment are happy, excited, interested, so that the room buzzes with their private conversations, and the person familiar with their appearance tends to forget that they display between them almost the whole range of crippling diseases known to mankind. Poliomyelitis, cerebral palsy in its various forms, spina bifida, muscular dystrophy, congenital deformities — they are all here in front of me, but the experienced teacher learns to think of them just as children, ordinary children. They have the normal fit child's capacity for getting into mischief, for being helpful, the normal child's enthusiams, emotions, ideals. Only the sight of the wheel-chairs, the crutches, the callipers, enable the visitor to distinguish a group of such children from the children in an ordinary school. The striking factor about being a teacher of such a class is the wonderful way in which such handicapped children face up to the realities of life.

The picture on the television-screen faded away, and I saw John switch off the set with a gesture of annoyance. John is crippled by polio, though not badly enough to need crutches, but he limps as he walks towards me. He is nearly sixteen, and soon will be leaving school.

"Not much of a programme, eh, John?" I remarked.

"It was one of those 'Going to Work' programmes, sir," he replied. "All about leaving school and getting a job — as a postman, or a joiner, or a forester."

"What was wrong with it?" I asked.

"There wasn't much wrong with it, sir. Those programmes must be quite useful — if you are physically fit. It is just that none of them are much good to people like us. We're disabled. What chance have we got of getting jobs like that?"

"We'll be lucky to get any kind of job," put in Mary.

Mary is a tall, dark-haired handsome girl of fifteen, with little visible trace of the deformity which brought her to our school.

"Girls can get married," John remarked.

"It takes two people to make a marriage," Mary said, with wisdom older than her years. "Men don't marry crippled girls. Fit people dislike having anything to do with anybody who is disabled."

"Sir is married, and he's got a smashing daughter," said John.

"It's easier for a man than for a woman," Mary replied. "Anyway, I'm going to work in an office."

What will happen to them in the future is a favourite topic of conversation among physically handicapped children. Fit children can take the future for granted, more or less, confident that they will get some sort of job, live a normal, useful life, probably marry and have a family. Not so the physically handicapped children. They know that they will be lucky to have the opportunity to be trained for a job where the difficulties are not too great for them to cope with. They have no illusions concerning the fact that for them life will be a long, hard struggle. Not for them the things which the fit take for granted. Many of them will spend their lives in institutions or hospitals, undergoing operations.

"That's right, sir," put in Richard, another polio case. "What chance have we got of going in for the kind of job which interests us? I'd like to be a vet. But you need a grammar-school education for that."

"You'd have to pass the GCE exam," Mary added.

What can one say in reply to such statements? It is true that in Britain the educational ladder is geared to a grammar-school type of education, and that children who are physically handicapped may find it difficult, if not almost impossible, to get the higher education necessary to obtain jobs to which they may be suited. Children at our School leave at the age of sixteen, selected ones going to a residential training centre, where they are prepared for various types of employment. There are few grammar schools for the disabled in England.

Several other boys and girls stopped what they were doing to join in the discussion.

"I'd like to be a teacher and work with crippled children," declared Kay, a spastic.

"You haven't a chance, girl," said Linda, a clever, dark-haired Welsh girl, who will spend all her life in a wheel-chair.

"That's not true," John protested. "Sir is crippled too, same as us. He has been in hospital lots of times and had lots of operations. But he managed to get to a training college and become a teacher."

I wear thick-lensed spectacles, and because my right hip is solid I walk stiffly as they do.

"That's right, sir is one of us," Richard agreed. "But it has not stopped him from becoming our deputy-headmaster."

"Why did you come to teach at a special school, sir?" asked Linda.

It is one of their favourite questions. The children always find it difficult to understand why any person who has become a qualified teacher should want to come to a special school in preference to teaching fit children at an ordinary school.

"Yes, why did you, sir?" Mary put in.

"Maybe it is the best place for a teacher like me — a disabled person." I replied. "Nobody really knows what it is like to be handicapped unless they were born that way. I feel that I can do more useful work here than somewhere else."

Conscious that the children's eyes were all looking at me questioningly, I went on hurriedly: "I wanted to do lots of exciting things when I was your age — to get a better education — to be an explorer and travel across foreign lands — to be an archaeologist and dig up the remains of past civilisations. And I have managed to do many of the things I wanted to do, although I was born handicapped. But of course it has not been easy. Now, I feel that by working at this school I can help other young people who are disabled as I was to make something worthwhile out of their lives. That about sums it up, I suppose."

As I talked I reflected how shut off from

the ordinary world of fit people is the world of the disabled. What other children save these would have thought to discuss such problems? The general public is familiar with the pattern of education in Britain — public school, grammar school, secondary modern and primary school, but how little is known of the struggles of handicapped children to get an education!

"Please, sir, will you tell us some more about your experiences in foreign countries some time?" Richard asked. "How you walked across Morocco and Lapland and other countries. And about your adventures on ships and looking for gold and digging up old ruins."

"And about how you became a teacher and got married and came to work at our School," Mary put in.

"It would take a whole book to tell you of all the things which happened to me before I came to teach here," I replied.

"Then write it all down in a book, sir," Richard suggested. "Then you can read it to us, and other people can read it, too — handicapped people. Maybe it will help them."

"Perhaps I will put it all into a book one

day," I replied. "But I hardly know where to begin."

"Begin when you were fourteen years old, sir, and going to a special school for children with bad eyesight," Mary suggested. "Tell how you wanted to go to university to study geography, and go on from there until — "

" — Until now," Richard interrupted.

"All right, I will do as you suggest," was my reply. "But I have another job to finish first."

Hugh, Tony, and Bill suddenly reappeared, charging into the room clutching various mud-covered objects.

"Pl-please, sir, we've dug up some more prehistoric implements, sir," Bill bellowed. "Spearheads by the look of them."

"We will parcel them up and send them to Dr. Owens at Manchester Museum. Maybe one of his staff can identify them for us," I told him.

"I'd like to go to university and learn to be an archaeologist," Hugh said. "Can a disabled person do that, do you think, sir?"

"Well, it is not easy," was my cautious reply. "You have to pass some examinations first."

The bell rang for play-time, and the children's interest in worldly affairs evaporated. I watched them dash off into the playground. The sunlight streamed in through the classroom windows, beyond which was a wide vista of green Cheshire countryside. The suggestion that I write a book about my experiences as a disabled person was worth considering; it *might* help and encourage other disabled people.

Ten miles northward was Manchester, my birthplace, from which I had started out years ago on the long road which had brought me to this School. My thoughts went back to the days when I also had been a crippled child experiencing the same doubts and problems which troubled the children here. Most of my life had been spent fighting disability, often in pain, poor, alone. It had taken me years of struggling to get the things I wanted from life — a better education, the kind of job which suited me, recognition as a writer and traveller, a home and family of my own. From Manchester to Canada the road had led me, then to the Arctic, Africa, Europe, and beyond. Now the wheel had turned full circle, and here I was settled down not far from my birthplace. It had been a long, hard journey, but perhaps good had come out of it all.

But before the writing of a book there was that other job to be finished first — sitting Part Two of the final examination for the degree of Bachelor of Science (Economics).

There was a knock at the door, and a voice said, "May I come in?" and John Thompson, our headmaster, entered.

"Hugh and Tony seem excited," he remarked.

"The children have been talking about the kinds of jobs they would like to get when they leave school," I explained.

John's face clouded. "And I suppose the discussion ended as such discussions usually end — with the realisation that only a few lucky ones will obtain the kind of education and opportunities which they need?" he declared.

"Many of our children have lost so much education because of time spent in hospital that they simply cannot compete with children who have been to grammar school," I said bitterly. "If we could only keep our most promising young people here longer and give them the type of education they need."

"If we could only expand this school into one big comprehensive training centre for all the physically handicapped young people in north-western England," John went on. "A grammar school and technical school combined, so that young people could stay here until they were twenty, or even older."

This is our dream. Our school expanded into one big establishment of fine new buildings — classrooms, workshops, bungalows for young workers who were chair-bound, a big physiotherapy centre with a swimming-pool; one community in which physically handicapped people could feel they had a part to play in life. As it was, we were having to send our most promising young people, when they were sixteen years old, to the Queen Elizabeth Training College near Leatherhead, in Surrey. When they came back again to north-west England they were liable to remain unemployed because they could not obtain work.

"Give us £250,000, and we can do it," I said, chuckling. "If such a training centre does not exist in this part of England, then it is time one was established."

"£250,000 — what's that?" John asked. "Suppose all the people in this country who like their beer were to forgo a pint once a year, and give the money to help our physically handicapped children. How much would the cost of those pints add up to?"

"Quite a lot, I imagine," was my reply. "How do we set about raising the money?"

"When you have figured out an answer to that question just let me know," was the headmaster's response.

Well, how do you raise £250,000? How do you?

In 1962, at the age of fifty, I sat Part Two of the final examination for the degree of Bachelor of Science, in Economics. I quite enjoyed that examination. Much of my experience of life during the past twenty-five years was worked into the fabric of answers to questions — facts about geography, about travel, history, archaeology, economics, science, most of which had been acquired at first-hand. Nothing I had experienced was wasted. The notebooks of field-geography, which I presented to the examiners were my especial pride, and I often wonder what they thought of them. Some time later I was told that I had passed; it was one of the proudest moments of my life, and I looked forward to the day when I should be presented to the Chancellor of the University as the newest graduate.

The nebulous dream of that fifteen-year-old boy, in Canada long ago, had become reality thirty-five years later, the dream to be a graduate of a great university. True, it was "a degree by the back door" (to quote a phrase used by a writer in the *Sunday Times* when describing degrees gained by external students), but it was good enough for me. I had done what I set out to do.

How much did it cost? About £150, which includes fees for correspondence courses, books, maps, postage, tuition at the various colleges, examinations; when we moved to Cheshire I attended evening classes for the degree course at the College of Commerce, Manchester. And there was the loss of a year's salary as a teacher. Also, it would be ungenerous to omit mention of the assistance given me by such organisations as the West Riding County Library and Cheshire County Library, in loaning me the many expensive textbooks needed; without their ready co-operation the costs of one's studies would be greatly increased. My thanks go out to them. Manchester's Reference Library also deserves praise, as those students who frequent its big circular reading-room will agree. So many people — lecturers, students, strangers, in the lecture-room, in libraries, in the country-side when taking part in courses in field-geography — gave me a helping hand and contributed to my success.

In the end one difficulty arose which nearly prevented my *sitting* the examinations. Operations to cure arthritis had left my right hip stiff, so that sitting down in a chair for any length of time was an ordeal; I had to stand up every few minutes to alleviate the discomfort. Cramp in my fingers made writing by hand for more than a few minutes very painful; normally I used a typewriter. Under these conditions it would not be physically possible for me to sit through a whole series of examination papers each lasting three hours. I would not be able to sit down or to write, so would have little chance of gaining sufficient marks in each paper to pass.

Confronted with this dilemma, I wrote to the Superintendent of examinations, explaining how handicapped I was. He replied saying that I would be allowed to use my typewriter to answer the questions, in a room by myself where I should be able to get up and walk about whenever I began to feel uncomfortable. For this I should have to have special invigilation — a person sitting near me and watching me at work — and this would cost me an additional fee. This special invigilation added to the cost of taking the examination, but it was worth it, for without these special facilities it would not have been possible for me to take the examination with any chance of passing.

A question I am often asked is: "Was it worth it?"

My reply is very definitely: "Yes."

Yes, for a number of reasons. First of all, there has been the sheer joy of learning, of finding new fields of knowledge to explore. The study of such a range of subjects — economics, history, geography, government, politics, philosophy — has vastly improved my knowledge of and my interest in the modern world in which I live and must make my living. Now I can pick up a book or newspaper and understand a fair amount of what it contains. There was the joy also of knowing that my belief in my own powers was justified, and that, had I been given the opportunity when I was younger, I could have done as well as any other student.

And I had achieved much more than a degree: *I had lived my life*. There had been the fun of seeking experiences in far-off lands, of tramping and meeting people, the satisfaction of overcoming difficulties, the joy of getting married, of having a family, of earning my living, of finding my place in life. All this had been an achievement also.

It is not given to all of us to make a great contribution to the world's advancement. We cannot all cross the Antarctic with Dr. Fuchs, or emulate Albert Schweitzer's achievements in the African jungle, or uncover past civilisations with Sir Mortimer Wheeler. For we are the people who were born in the world's back streets, who had little chance of acquiring an education or of obtaining the money or the leisure to achieve great ends. The gates of opportunity were closed to us; it took most of our time and energy to earn a living. And yet in our humble way we have perhaps been of some service to humanity, if only by example.

This book is my own small contribution.

Perhaps a quotation copied from an article in a weekly magazine sums it up. At that time I was in hospital, in plaster, in pain after an operation. This is what I wrote:

We must leave ourselves to God, content only to do an honest job with the life He has given us for a while, living kindly, patiently, honestly, as simply as possible, and trying to see that when the time comes for us to leave the little bit of world which has known us, it will be the better, and not the worse, for our having been there.

If one can do this, in spite of difficulties and failures and handicaps, then one has not lived in vain.

I walked along the strip of red carpet to make my bow to the Chancellor of the University of London.

Five thousand pairs of eyes stared at me, and it was so still inside the vast circle of the Albert Hall that one could almost — to use that most hackneyed of clichés — have heard a pin drop. I felt hot and uncomfortable, and the black silk gown which proclaimed me to be a new graduate did not seem to hang properly. I envied the apparent air of self-possession displayed by the long line of graduates waiting behind me, and wished it had not fallen to me to be the first of them to be presented to the Chancellor. Also I was wondering what Joyce, seated down there amid several thousand spectators in the central part of the hall, thought of my appearance.

The Dean of the Faculty of Economics called out a name — *Ingram* — my name! — and I moved forward along the strip of red carpet — alone.

The Chancellor of the University of London — Her Majesty, Queen Elizabeth the Queen Mother — looked at me and smiled encouragingly. She sat there on her high-backed chair, with her Lady-in-Waiting and Gentleman-in-Waiting seated behind her. Seated behind and above them, tier upon tier, was a gorgeously hued company, all scarlet and black and gold, it seemed to me — members of the liveried companies of London, masters, doctors, and deans of the University, flanked by a group of crimson-coated bandsmen of the Welsh Guards. The Queen Mother wore her black-and-gold academic gown, and on her head was a mortar-board with a gold tassel dangling from it; when she moved her head the tassel fell forward over her eyes, and had to be pushed firmly back into place. She had to do this fairly often, but showed no sign of annoyance.

It is said that a drowning man sees his past life flash before his eyes, and in a way that is what happened to me.

For a moment of time I was no longer in the Albert Hall, but was somewhere else, far away. I was tramping the Great Arctic Highway to the Polar Sea, a hungry, ragged, pathetic figure. I was walking across Morocco to the Saharan outposts. Instead of that red carpet it was a ship's deck I was standing on, on the *Herzogin Cecilie* that great, white, towering windship. I seemed to see again the men with whom I had journeyed — goldminers, seamen, Berber tribesmen, Lapp reindeer herders, men of the French Foreign Legion — that brave, gay, laughing, reckless company.

I said to myself, "Is this *me*, standing here among this mob? Well, well!"

What experiences I had undergone in the cause of getting that university degree! And now this ceremony was the public recognition of it all. I wished my mother had lived long enough to have seen me there, but she, alas, was dead, and my father too had been dead for many years. Well, well!

So I bowed to the Queen Mother and passed on — Jim Ingram, graduate. Passed on to a new life, conscious that there were still lands left to explore, jobs to accomplish. With Tennyson's *Ulysses* I could exclaim:

. . . for my purpose holds,
To sail beyond the sunset, and the baths
Of all the western stars, until I die.

Why stop at a bachelor's degree. Why not a master's degree? Why not *Dr.* Ingram!

THE FIGHT GOES ON. IT NEVER ENDS.

WHAT HAPPENED AFTER THAT

In 1966, after another three years of spare-time study Jim Ingram passed the examinations for a Master's Degree, as an external student of London University. His thesis was an archaeological study of Lundy Island, in the Bristol Channel. That same year, with his wife Joyce, he went to the USSR to study historical geography. One of the most memorable experiences of the journey was a flight over the glacier-clad Caucasus Mountains. Later, almost completely crippled by osteo-arthritis, he was compelled to give up his job of deputy headmaster, and retire prematurely. At the age of sixty he became a student at Manchester University, studying the archaeology of Roman Britain. On another archaeological journey he and his wife went to Malta to study prehistoric temples. Increasing pain compelled him to spend more and more time in bed. Doctors said the only cure was to have his knee joints replaced by artificial ones, but before undergoing that operation Ingram planned a journey to Egypt, Israel and Turkey to investigate recent archaeological discoveries.

This book is published under the auspices of the
ULVERSCROFT FOUNDATION,
a registered charity, whose primary object is to assist those who experience difficulty in reading print of normal size.

In response to approaches from the medical world, the Foundation is also helping to purchase the latest, most sophisticated medical equipment desperately needed by major eye hospitals for the diagnosis and treatment of eye diseases.

If you would like to know more about the
ULVERSCROFT FOUNDATION,
and how you can help to further its work, please write for details to:

THE ULVERSCROFT FOUNDATION
The Green
Bradgate Road
Anstey
Leicestershire

We hope this Large Print edition gives you the pleasure and enjoyment we ourselves experienced in its publication.

There are now 1,000 titles available in this ULVERSCROFT Large Print Series. Ask to see a Selection at your nearest library.

The Publisher will be delighted to send you, free of charge, upon request a complete and up-to-date list of all titles available.

Ulverscroft Large Print Books Ltd.
The Green, Bradgate Road
Anstey, Leicester
England